"I was encouraged as I read each story and strengthened in my confidence that the gospel is truly sufficient for all who seek rest in a weary world. This book is brutally honest about sin and suffering and wonderfully hopeful as they point us to our true Savior."

—TIMOTHY S. LANE, Executive Director,
The Christian Counseling and Educational Foundation,
Glenside, PA

"The authors have written a book that will, like few others, encourage, comfort, instruct, challenge, and perhaps even occasionally enrage the body of Christ. It deserves to be read, weighed, and deeply considered."

—GARY THOMAS, author, *Sacred Marriage; The Beautiful Fight*

"The stories portrayed in the chapters of this book are all too real, but more importantly, the pastoral responses offer riveting applications of the cross for true and lasting transformation."

—BRUCE A. WARE, Professor of Christian Theology,
Southern Seminary

"A key reason for my confidence in this book is its brilliant presentation of the historic theology of the cross and how it defends reprehensible attacks against it."

—GREGG R. ALLISON, Associate Professor of Christian
Theology, The Southern Baptist Theological Seminary

"Practical and powerful. It applies the sufficiency of Jesus to the real-life challenges we face in the church each and every day. If you work with hurting people, you need *Death by Love*."

—DAN JARRELL, Teaching Pastor, ChangePoint Church,
Anchorage, Alaska

"I can't remember the last time a book about theology made me this emotional. I got angry and uplifted and stunned and encouraged in almost every chapter! This may be the first time you ever found theology outrageous and logical, challenging and comforting, but never boring."

—RENÈ SCHLAEPFER, Senior Pastor, Twin Lakes Church,
Santa Cruz, California

"For anyone who thinks that theology is dry, boring, and disconnected to real life, read this book. Mark Driscoll and Gerry Breshears not only demonstrate the relevance of theology to life, but also convincingly show how it has the most compelling and satisfying answers to life's tough issues."
> —CLINTON E. ARNOLD, Professor and Chairman,
> Department of New Testament, Talbot School of Theology,
> Biola University

"Another incredible book by Mark Driscoll and Gerry Breshears! I can't think of anything more important in our world today than protecting the truth about Jesus' brutal death on the cross. At times this book will be painful for you to read, but it won't leave you where it finds you. It will leave you more in love with the God who died for you. It will leave you more resolved to devote your one and only life to his cause, and it will leave you loving the people you are called to lead. I highly recommend this book—for students, professors, Christ followers, or those seeking the truth about Jesus. It will challenge the way you think and subsequently change the way you live."
> —JOHN BISHOP, Senior Pastor, Living Hope Church, Vancouver,
> Washington; Founder, ONLY GOD network

# DEATH BY LOVE

# DEATH BY LOVE

## LETTERS FROM THE CROSS

MARK DRISCOLL & GERRY BRESHEARS

CROSSWAY BOOKS
WHEATON, ILLINOIS

*Death by Love: Letters from the Cross*



Published by Crossway Books
a publishing ministry of Good News Publishers
1300 Crescent Street
Wheaton, Illinois 60187



Illustration by: Christopher Koelle at Portland Studios

Cover Illustration and Design by: Christopher Koelle and Matt Mantooth at Portland Studios

First printing 2008



All emphases in Scripture quotations have been added by the authors.

PDF ISBN: 978-1-4335-0423-5

Mobipocket ISBN: 978-1-4335-0424-3

**Library of Congress Cataloging-in-Publication Data**

Driscoll, Mark, 1970–
Death by love : letters from the cross / Mark Driscoll and Gerry Breshears.
p. cm. (Re:Lit)
Includes bibliographical references.
ISBN 978-1-4335-0129-6 (hc)
1. Suffering—Religious aspects—Christianity. 2. Jesus Christ—Crucifixion. 3. Theology of the cross. I. Breshears, Gerry, 1947– . II. Title. III. Series.
BV4909.D75 2008
232'.3—dc22 2008008947

LB 18 17 16 15 14 13 12 11 10 09
15 14 13 12 11 10 9 8 7 6 5 4 3 2

# Contents

# Preface

**Because no one is born into this world with a theology,** each generation must rediscover the truths of Scripture for itself. In doing so it must labor to connect the unchanging answers of God's Word with the ever-changing questions of its culture. Sometimes this project is successfully undertaken, and the result is a glorious resurgence of a faithful and fruitful Christian church. Sometimes this project is unsuccessfully undertaken, and the tragic result is false teaching that renders the church impotent to see the power of the gospel unleashed because she either has a false Jesus or is embarrassed by the real one.

Today, the church finds herself in yet another of these epic opportunities as emerging pastors and churches strive to make up their mind on nearly every belief that has been previously considered Christian. Perhaps chief among them is the doctrine of the atonement or, simply, the accomplishments of Jesus' death on the cross.

Some are emotionally reluctant to embrace the cross because it is a symbol of violence and shame. Others harbor mental resistance to the cross because, throughout the history of the church, various theological explanations have been given to explain what it accomplished, leading to confusion as to whether or not any are in fact true or even helpful. Yet, because it is the crux of both the Christian faith and human history, the implications of the cross cannot be avoided and require thoughtful consideration.

We write this book not with the intention of pleasing all of the scholars who may find here various points about which to quibble. Rather, our hope is to make otherwise complicated truths understandable to regular folks so that their love for and worship of Jesus would increase as they pick up their cross to follow him. Additionally, we write in hopes of serving fellow pastors and other Christian leaders who bear the responsibility of teaching and leading people. We are heartbroken that the cross of Jesus Christ is under attack by some and dismissed by others. This book is our attempt to respond in a way that helps to ensure that the cross remains at the crux of all that it means to think and live like Jesus.

Before we begin, it is important that we establish four central truths regarding the cross. We will introduce them briefly so that we can focus on the Scriptures throughout the rest of the book without getting sidetracked.

First, the cross is a multi-faceted jewel. Throughout church history much ink has been spilled as various theologians and Christian traditions have debated the effects of Jesus' death. In this book we are essentially arguing for all of the perspectives that are nourished by biblical roots in an effort to teach the totality of what Scripture says without obscuring any faithful view of the cross. One theologian has called the cross the great jewel of the Christian faith, and like every great jewel it has many precious facets that are each worthy of examining for their brilliance and beauty. Therefore, you will be well served to see each side of this jewel shining together for the glory of God in complimentary and not contradictory fashion. Most poor teaching about the cross results from someone's denying one of these facets, ignoring one of these facets, or overemphasizing one of these facets at the expense of the others, often due to an overreaction to someone else's overreaction. Such narrow and reactionary theology has tragically caused the beauty of the cross to become obscured by the various warring teams that have risen up to argue for their systematic theology rather than bowing down in humble worship of the crucified Jesus.

Second, the cross is not a pagan jewel. Tragically, some have argued that the crucifixion of Jesus is little more than the makeover of ancient pagan concepts borrowed from other religions. It is then argued that since the Bible itself adapts pagan thinking, we should do the same and reinterpret the work of Jesus on the cross through such modern-day paganism as goddess worship, atheistic therapy, postmodernism, secular feminism, and Marxism. This in turn leads to a wholesale departure from any understanding of the cross that has previously been accepted as faithfully Christian.

The seed for such theological weeds is simply an evolutionary view of truth that sees the Bible in general, and the Old Testament in particular, as archaic, primitive, and embarrassing to modern people who are grossed out by all of the talk about blood and too sophisticated for talk about sin and punishment. Both the Old and New Testaments clearly declare that our understanding of the cross is the result of God's revelation to us and not human speculation borrowed from paganism. In the great Old Testament chapter on atonement offerings, Leviticus 17, God says, "I have given it for you . . . to make atonement" in verse 11. Paul, like Moses, is emphatic that the gospel message of Jesus' death for our sins is not something he made up or borrowed from pagan culture but instead is the result of divine revelation from God alone (1 Cor. 15:3–4; Gal. 1:11–12, 15–17). Therefore, the only way to faithfully interpret the New Testament metaphors regarding the atonement is to understand their origination as not coming from pagan culture but rather coming from the revelation of the Old Testament.

The gospel message comes from God to the culture but does not emanate in any way from the culture, though it must be effectively communicated to all cultures. Because of this, the truth of the gospel of Scripture is binding on all peoples, times, and places. Any gospel that emanates from or accommodates pagan culture is a false gospel with demonic inspiration (2 Cor. 11:3–4; Gal. 1:6–9). Echoing Paul on this point, D. A. Carson says, "No truth which human beings may articulate can ever be articulated in a culture-transcending way—but that does not mean that the truth thus articulated does not transcend culture."[1]

Third, the jewel doesn't stand alone but is mounted in the setting of Jesus' work in history. Curiously, varying Christian traditions each have particular appreciation for and emphasis on various sides of the great jewel of our faith. Jesus' work began with his incarnation as Immanuel, God with us. The Eastern church helps us see the importance of God's coming to bring divine life, energy, and power back to sinful humanity. Subsequently, the full humanity of Jesus is stressed without denying his divinity. Jesus lived a life that was not just a preparation for the cross but also an example of how we, as Jesus followers, should and can live, which the Anabaptist church helps us see.

Jesus made God's character dramatically real through his faithful obedience, sinless living, and unfailing love. His cross brings divine propitiation and forgiveness and is the basis of our justification, as the Reformed church helps us realize. His resurrection is the power of divine life breaking out in addition to being proof that the Father was satisfied with his payment on the cross. Jesus' resurrection is the basis of our regeneration and new life, in addition to the guarantee of our future resurrection. The pietistic church emphasizes this. Jesus' exaltation as anointed king culminates his victory over Satan and demons. Although appearing as a humble Galilean peasant while on the earth, Jesus is now the glorious Son of God who will defeat all enemies at his return, as the ancient church believed in the midst of its polytheistic and pagan culture.

Fourth, the cross does not reject the love of God but rather reveals it like nothing else. Some will protest that a loving God could not possibly pour out his wrath on Jesus. Yet this is precisely what Scripture says: "Yet it was the will of the Lord to crush him; he has put him to grief" (Isa. 53:10).

Others will protest that a loving God would never sanction the bloody, unjust murder of Jesus. Scripture plainly states, however, that it is at the cross of Jesus that the love of God for us is most clearly seen. Jesus himself said precisely this: "This is my commandment, that you love one another as I have loved you. Greater love has no one than this, that someone lay down his life for his friends" (John 15:12–13).

Other Scriptures echo the words of Jesus—his death on the cross is the place where love is most clearly seen in all creation. If we translated John 3:16 exactly from the Greek, it would say, "For God loved the world in this way: he gave his only Son, that whoever believes in him should not perish." It tells us how God expressed his great love for the world. Romans 5:8 says, "But God shows his love for us in that while we were still sinners, Christ died for us." Finally, 1 John 4:9–10 says, "In this the love of God was made manifest among us, that God sent his only Son into the world, so that we might live through him. In this is love, not that we have loved God but that he loved us and sent his Son to be the propitiation for our sins." Clearly, Jesus' bloody death on the cross is about love. The depth of our sin and the depth of God's love cannot be fully known apart from Jesus' cross.

This book aspires to faithfully and passionately articulate the truth about Jesus' cross. Therefore, as you read this book you may be surprised to discover that we in no way seek to be theologically innovative, because theological innovation is inevitably the road to heresy. Instead, this book is an attempt at faithfulness to the timeless truths of Scripture that have served the church well since the first promise of Jesus' suffering was pronounced by God to our first parents in the garden. We hope to present the timeless truths of the cross in a timely manner that is biblically faithful, culturally relevant, and personally helpful. Our objective is to think God's thoughts after him as revealed in Scripture, and if at any point we fail in this, we ask God's forgiveness and your kindness.

As you read each chapter, a simple logic should emerge. Each begins with the introduction of someone I have worked with in my role as one of the pastors at Mars Hill Church. I then proceed to write a personal letter to him or her explaining one side of the great jewel of the cross so that the person and work of Jesus are made intensely practical for that person's life (Sources for quotations used in these letters are documented in the "Helpful Information" section at the end of the chapter.) In doing so I am following in the example of many books of our Bible that were essentially letters written from a Christian leader to someone he loved; for example, Luke and Acts were written to Theophilus by Luke; the letters to Timothy and Titus were penned by their mentor Paul; Philemon was written to Philemon, Archipus, and the godly woman Apphia by Paul; 2 and 3 John were written to an elder, a godly woman and her family, and Gaius by John. Personally, this was a very painful book to pen and, although I am not a man who cries often, much of this book was written through my tears.

Our approach is an effort to show that there is no such thing as Christian community or Christian ministry apart from a rigorous theology of the cross that is practically applied to the lives of real people. Subsequently, unlike my public preaching, my tone will be deeply pastoral and more like the private meetings I have with people whom Jesus has entrusted to my pastoral care. By way of warning, this book takes the pain of human sin very seriously and, consequently, it may be brutally harsh to read at some points (perhaps in part because we have been inundated with fluffy Christian books about victorious living).

Each chapter includes a portrait of God, because to remain true all theology must begin and remain God-centered. Each chapter then proceeds to examine a biblical aspect of sin and a correlating effect of Jesus' death as the solution to the sin problem as dictated by God. As you read, we would like you to note that we consider both the death and resurrection of Jesus as intimately related truths that are, in fact, a singular event. Thus, when we speak of Jesus' death or cross, do assume that we are including Jesus' resurrection and empty tomb, because apart from his ongoing life the cross is without any power.

In each chapter of this book we have sought to teach the very practical and pastoral implications and applications of the work of Jesus on the cross. We also know there are additional theological questions that many of our readers will have about specific issues raised in each chapter. Therefore, we have sought to answer a variety of such questions to be of further service to those who are kind enough to read this book. Because of his expertise as a seasoned theologian, my friend Gerry Breshears is responsible for these answers, and I trust you will benefit from his humble and biblical insight, as I have.

Lastly, our prayer is that this book will be intensely practical in nature, pastoral in tone, theological in depth, biblical in content, and worshipful in consequence.

*Mark Driscoll*

# Acknowledgments

**Resurgence Literature (Re:Lit) is a ministry of Resurgence** (www.theresurgence.com). There you will find a growing repository of free theological resources along with information on forthcoming conferences we host. The elders of Mars Hill Church (www.marshillchurch. org) have generously agreed to fund Resurgence along with the Acts 29 Church Planting Network (www.acts29network.org) so that our culture can be filled with a resurgence of timeless Christian truth that is expressed and embodied in timely cultural ways.

Free audio downloads of the roughly sixteen hours of sermons that comprise the basic outline for this book are available at www. marshillchurch.org. While preaching this series, originally called "Christ on the Cross," in Seattle, which is among the least churched cities in America with more dogs than evangelicals, I saw our attendance grow by as many as eight hundred mainly young, single, college-educated, twenty-something hipsters in a single week. I yelled myself hoarse for well over an hour at each of our Sunday church services about the depth of sin, the wrath of God, and the propitiation of Jesus and am happy to report that the gospel of Jesus Christ remains the power of God.

This book is a collaborative project between friends. As a young pastor, I desired to be as competent a Bible preacher as possible. This led to a close friendship with my professor Gerry Breshears, whose biblical insights have been invaluable to my understanding of the person and work of Jesus as revealed in Scripture. In this book you will hear my voice, since I crafted the words onto pages, but many of the concepts were shaped and formed by my good friend who gave me helpful input when I sent the chapters to him. You will also hear Gerry's voice in the Answers to Common Questions at the end of each chapter, where his professorial insights will help deepen your understanding of the person and work of Jesus. Our hope is that this book will be readable, practical, and biblical so that everyone from seminary professors and pastors to non-Christians would benefit from our work. We are tremendously grateful to our friends at Crossway Books who have kindly agreed to publish this book as the second in the Re-Lit series and have been nothing short of amazing to work with.

*Mark Driscoll*

# We Killed God: Jesus Is Our Substitutionary Atonement

*All we like sheep have gone astray; we have turned—every one—to his own way; and the LORD has laid on [Jesus] the iniquity of us all.*

ISAIAH 53:6

**Jesus was born in a small town to a poor,** unmarried teen mother roughly two thousand years ago. He was adopted by Joseph, a simple carpenter, and spent the first thirty years of his life in obscurity, swinging a hammer with his dad.

Around the age of thirty, Jesus began a public ministry that included preaching the truth, healing the sick, feeding the hungry, and befriending crooked sinners who were despised by religious types. Jesus' ministry spanned only three short years before he was put to death for declaring himself to be God. He died by shameful crucifixion like tens of thousands of people had before him.

In the pages of Scripture, which exist to reveal him, we discover that while Jesus loved children, fed the hungry, befriended the marginalized, healed the sick, encouraged the downhearted, and rebuked the religiously self-righteous, the light of Scripture shines most clearly on the final week of his life and his work of atonement through the cross and empty tomb. In total, the four Gospels, which faithfully record his life, devote roughly one-third of their content to the climactic final week of Jesus' life leading up to the cross. While only two Gospels mention Jesus' birth, and each speaks sparsely of his resurrection, all four Gospels give great attention to the final week leading up to Jesus' cross. In fact, John's Gospel devotes roughly half of its content to that week.

Perhaps most peculiar is the fact that the symbol for Jesus, which has become the most famous symbol in all of history, is the cross. While the early church embraced several symbols, including the fish and the loaf, the cross has always symbolized the believer's connection with the death of Jesus. The church father Tertullian (155–230) tells us of the early practice of believers making the sign of the cross over their bodies with their hand and adorning their necks and homes with crosses to celebrate the brutal death of Jesus. In our day, this would be akin to a junkie's needle or a pervert's used condom becoming the world's most beloved symbol and adorning homes, churches, and bodies.

The ancient Jewish historian Josephus called crucifixion "the most wretched of deaths."[1] The ancient Roman philosopher Cicero asked that decent Roman citizens not even speak of the cross because it was too disgraceful a subject for the ears of decent people.[2] The Jews also considered crucifixion the most horrific mode of death, as Deuteronomy 21:22–23 says: "If a man has committed a crime punishable by death and he is put to death, and you hang him on a tree, his body shall not remain all night on the tree, but you shall bury him the same day, for a hanged man is cursed by God."

Crucifixion was likely invented by the Persians around 500 BC and continued until it was outlawed by the first Christian Roman emperor Constantine around AD 300. Although crucifixion was created by the Persians, it was perfected by the Romans, who reserved it as the most painful mode of execution for the most despised people, such as slaves, poor people, and Roman citizens guilty of the worst high treason.

Throughout history, crucifixion has remained perhaps the most horrid form of execution. Under the leadership of Adolf Hitler, German soldiers crucified Jews at Dachau by running bayonets and knives through their legs, shoulders, throats, and testicles. Under the leadership of Pol Pot, the Khmer Rouge performed crucifixions in Cambodia. Today, crucifixion continues in Sudan and online with the multiplayer video game *Roma Victor*.

The pain of crucifixion is so horrendous that a word was invented to explain it—*excruciating*—which literally means "from the cross." The pain of crucifixion is due in part to the fact that it is a prolonged and agonizing death by asphyxiation. Crucified people could hang on the cross for days, passing in and out of consciousness as their lungs struggled to breathe, while laboring under the weight of their body. It was not uncommon for those being crucified to slump on the cross in an effort to empty their lungs of air and thereby hasten their death.

None of this was done in dignified privacy but rather in open, public places. It would be like nailing a bloodied, naked man above the front entrance to your local mall. Crowds would gather around the victims to mock them as they sweated in the sun, bled, and became incontinent from the pain that could last many days. Once dead, the victim was not given a decent burial but rather left on the cross for vultures to pick apart from above while dogs chewed on the bones that fell to the ground, even occasionally taking a hand or foot home as a chew toy, according to ancient reports.[3] Whatever remained of the victim would eventually be thrown in the garbage and taken to the dump unless his family buried it.

Not only was crucifixion excruciatingly painful and publicly shameful, it was also commonly practiced. Tens of thousands of people were crucified in the ancient world. For example, when Spartacus died in battle, six thousand of his followers were crucified in one day. They were lined up along a road that stretched for one hundred and twenty miles, not unlike the shoulder of a modern freeway.

As a general rule, it was men who were crucified. Occasionally a man was crucified at eye level so that passersby could look him directly in the eye as he died and cuss him out and spit on him in mockery. In the rare event of a woman's crucifixion, she was made to face the cross. Not even such a barbarous culture was willing to watch the face of a woman in such excruciating agony.

On the day Jesus was crucified, two men were hung with him, one on each side. Some years later, when the leader of Jesus' disciples, Peter, was to be crucified, he reportedly did not consider himself worthy of dying like Jesus and therefore requested that he be hung upside down. His request was granted, and he hung upside down until he closed his eyes in death and opened them to gaze upon his scarred Savior and heard, "Well done, good and faithful servant."

Among the scandals of the cross is the fact that Christians call it their *gospel*, or good news, and celebrate it every year on Good Friday. It is the means by which God has chosen to forgive our sins. Indeed, not everyone considers the cross of Jesus such good news. For example, speaking of Jesus' crucifixion, the Hindu Gandhi said, "His death on the cross was a great example to the world, but that there was anything like a mysterious or miraculous virtue in it, my heart could not accept."

## GOOD NEWS

The question begs to be answered, how can Christians celebrate the crucifixion of Jesus as good news, indeed, the best news they have ever heard? To answer this question we must move from the historical fact of Jesus' death to the theological meaning of that fact.

The most succinct summary of the gospel in Scripture provides insight into this theological meaning: "That Christ died *for* our sins in accordance with the Scriptures, that he was buried, that he was raised on the third day in accordance with the Scriptures" (1 Cor. 15:3b–4). In this packed section of Scripture, Paul appoints the death, burial, and resurrection of Jesus as the most important event in all of history and the verification of the truthfulness of all Scripture. He then explains why this is good news with the simple word *for*, showing that Jesus died "for our sins." The word *for* (*huper* in Greek) can mean either "for the benefit of" or "because of." Think for a moment: Jesus did not die "for the benefit of" our sins. He did not help them at all! Rather, he died "because of" our sins. So it was *our* sins, but *his* death.

From the beginning of sacred Scripture (Gen. 2:17) to the end (Rev. 21:8), the penalty for sin is death. Therefore, if we sin, we should die. But it is Jesus, the sinless one, who dies in our place "for our sins." The good news of the gospel is that Jesus died to take to himself the penalty for our sin. In theological terms, this means that Jesus' death was substitutionary, or vicarious, and in our place solely for our benefit and without benefit for himself. Therefore, we find the cross of Jesus to be the crux of good news, because it was there that Jesus atoned for our sin according to the promises of Scripture.

Among the central events in the Old Testament was the act of atonement, including the annual celebration of the Day of Atonement (Yom Kippur) according to the regulations of the book of Leviticus.

The Day of Atonement was the most important day of the year. It was intended to deal with the sin problem between humanity and God. Of the many prophetic elements on this special day, one stands out. On that day, two healthy goats without defect were chosen; they were therefore fit to represent sinless perfection, perhaps in spite of the protests of animal rights activists.

The first goat was a sin offering. The high priest slaughtered this innocent goat, which acted as a substitute for the sinners who rightly deserved a violently bloody death for their many sins. He then sprinkled some of its blood on the mercy seat on top of the Ark of the Covenant inside the Most Holy Place. The goat was no longer innocent when it took the guilt of sin; it was a sin offering for the people (Lev. 16:15). Subsequently, its blood represented life given as payment for sin. The dwelling place of God was thus cleansed of the defilement that resulted from all of the transgressions and sins of the people of Israel, and God's just and holy wrath was satisfied. Theologically, we call this the doctrine of *propitiation*, whereby God's wrath is propitiated, or taken from us, because of Jesus so that we are no longer under God's wrath.

Then the high priest, acting as the representative and mediator between the sinful people and their holy God, would take the second goat and lay his hands on the animal while confessing the sins of the people. This goat, called the scapegoat, would then be sent away to run free into the wilderness away from the sinners, symbolically taking their sins with it. Theologically, we call this the doctrine of *expiation*, whereby our sin is expiated, or taken away, so that we are made clean.

In summary, all of this foreshadowed the coming of Jesus Christ, our High Priest who mediates between unholy people and our holy God, the sinless substitute who died a bloody death in our place for our sins, and the scapegoat who takes our sins away to be remembered by God no more. Subsequently, only by rightly understanding the function of the two goats is the atonement fully appreciated. Although there were two goats, there was only one slaughter. The first goat was slaughtered for the propitiation of sin. The second goat was not slaughtered but rather sent away with sin, showing the cleansing expiation from sin. Both of these great themes, propitiation and expiation, will be further explored in separate chapters in this book.

These great images of the priest, slaughter, and scapegoat are all given by God to help us more fully comprehend Jesus' work for us on the cross. Theologically, this is called *atonement* (at-one-ment); Jesus our

God became a man to restore a relationship between God and humanity. This is also what is meant throughout the English Standard Version of the Bible when the word *atone* and its related variations, such as *atoned* and *atonement*, appear nearly one hundred times.

Theologically, the concept of Jesus' dying in our place to pay our penalty for our sins has been expressed in theological shorthand as *penal substitution*. While the church has always affirmed this aspect of atonement, it was highlighted in the Reformation and in the theologies of John Calvin and Martin Luther.

This aspect of the atonement is under the most vehement attack today by people who do not believe that people are as sinful as they truly are, that God is as holy as he truly is, or that God has chosen an appropriate penalty for sin (death). Curiously, such critics are also commonly known to be the most vocal of hypocrites, simultaneously demanding justice on the earth for the poor, oppressed, and abused, while denying God the same kind of justice that is due him by those people that he created to glorify him with sinless obedience. Nonetheless, Scripture repeatedly and clearly declares that Jesus died as our substitute paying our penalty "for" our sins, as the following examples illustrate:

> He was wounded *for* our transgressions; he was crushed *for* our iniquities; upon him was the chastisement that brought us peace, and with his stripes we are healed. (Isa. 53:5)

> He poured out his soul to death and was numbered with the transgressors; yet he bore the sin of many, and makes intercession *for* the transgressors. (Isa. 53:12)

> [He] was delivered up *for* our trespasses. (Rom. 4:25)

> But God shows his love for us in that while we were still sinners, Christ died *for* us. (Rom. 5:8)

> Christ died *for* our sins. (1 Cor. 15:3)

> Christ redeemed us from the curse of the law by becoming a curse *for* us. (Gal. 3:13)

For Christ also suffered once *for* sins, the righteous for the unrighteous, that he might bring us to God. (1 Pet. 3:18)

He is the propitiation *for* our sins, and not *for* ours only but also *for* the sins of the whole world. (1 John 2:2)

Indeed, the human problem is sin, the divine motivation is holy love, and the death and resurrection of the God-man Jesus is the solution. Consequently, the death of Jesus is the most important event in the history of the world and the crux of how a relationship with God is made possible. Because of this, Christianity is not based upon ideas or philosophies, but rather upon the one man Jesus Christ and the one event of his death by crucifixion. Therefore, we must now examine the final days of Jesus' life leading up to his crucifixion to more fully comprehend that event.

## THE SUBSTITUTIONARY DEATH OF JESUS

In the days leading up to his death, Jesus was a young man of perhaps thirty-three. He was in good health due to his job as a carpenter and his constant walking of many miles as an itinerant minister. Jesus began speaking openly of his impending death, including at the Passover meal he ate with his friends as their Last Supper. There, he broke with fifteen centuries of protocol. In so doing, he showed that the Passover meal, which God's people had been eating annually, found its ultimate fulfillment in him. The Passover memorialized the night in Egypt when in faith God's people covered the doorposts of their home with blood so that death would not come to the firstborn son in their home but would rather pass over them (Exodus 6–12). Jesus, the firstborn Son of God, likewise had come to die and cover us with his blood so that God's just wrath would literally pass over us sinners as the essence of the new covenant (Luke 22:19–21).

During the Last Supper, Satan entered one of Jesus' disciples, Judas, who had been stealing money from Jesus' ministry fund for some time and had agreed to hand him over to the authorities to be crucified. After Judas left the meal to lead the soldiers to Jesus, Jesus went to the garden of Gethsemane, where he spent a sleepless night in an agony of prayer. Meanwhile, his disciples failed to intercede for him in prayer and instead kept falling asleep. At this point, Jesus was fully aware of his impending crucifixion and was so distressed that, as the Bible records, he sweated drops of blood, a physical condition that doctors say is rare because it requires an elevated level of stress that few people ever experience. It is also possible, if not likely, that this refers to sweat pouring from him as blood does from an open wound. Either way, only in the most horrifying experiences of life are such things possible, and this is the central point of the biblical account as Jesus faced the cross.

After Jesus' exhausting, sleepless night of distress, Judas arrived with the soldiers and betrayed Jesus with a kiss. Jesus was then arrested. He was made to walk a few miles to a series of false trials where contradicting false witnesses were brought forward to offer false testimony. Despite the absence of any evidence supporting the false charges, Jesus was sentenced to be murdered. He was eventually blindfolded as a mob of cowardly men beat him mercilessly. He was then stripped naked in great shame, and the Bible just says that they had him scourged.

Scourging itself was such a painful event that many people died from it without even making it to their cross. Jesus' hands would have been chained above his head to expose his back and legs to an executioner's whip called a cat-o'-nine-tails. The whip was a series of long leather straps. At the end of some of the straps were heavy balls of metal intended to tenderize the body of a victim, like a chef tenderizes a steak by beating it. Some of the straps had hooks made of either metal or bone that would have sunk deeply into the shoulders, back, buttocks, and legs of the victim. Once the hooks had sunk deeply into the tenderized flesh, the executioner would rip the skin, muscle, tendons, and even bones off the victim as he shouted in agony, shook violently, and bled heavily. Hundreds of years prior, the prophet Isaiah predicted the results of Jesus' scourging: "Many were astonished at you—his appearance was so marred, beyond human semblance, and his form beyond that of the children of mankind" (Isa. 52:14).

Jesus then had a crown of lengthy thorns pressed into his head as onlookers who had previously hailed him with shouts of "Hosanna!" mocked him as the "King of the Jews" (Matt. 27:29). Blood began to flow down Jesus' face from the thorns, causing his hair and beard to be a bloodied and matted mess. Later, if Jesus could have seen clearly through the blood and sweat that burned his eyes, he would have witnessed soldiers rolling dice to see who would win the prize of his robe.

Jesus' bare back and shoulders, though bloodied and traumatized, were then forced to carry his roughly hewn wooden crossbar of perhaps one hundred pounds to his place of crucifixion. The cross was likely already covered in the blood of other men. Timber was so expensive that crosses were recycled; therefore, Jesus' blood mixed with the layers of blood, sweat, and tears of countless other men who had walked that same path before him.

Despite his young age and good health, Jesus was so physically devastated from his sleepless night, miles of walking, severe beating, and scourging that he was unable to carry his cross alone. A man named Simon of Cyrene was appointed to carry Jesus' cross. Upon arriving at his place of crucifixion, they pulled Jesus' beard out—an act of ultimate disrespect in ancient cultures—spat on him, and mocked him in front of his family and friends.

Jesus the carpenter, who had driven many nails into wood with his own hands, then had five- to seven-inch, rough, metal spikes driven into the most sensitive nerve centers on the human body, through his hands and feet. Jesus was nailed to his wooden cross. His body twitched involuntarily as he screamed in sheer agony.

Jesus was then lifted up, and his cross dropped into a prepared hole, causing his body to shake violently on the spikes. In further mockery, a sign was posted above Jesus that said, "Jesus of Nazareth, the King of the Jews" (John 19:19). A painting later discovered from a second-century Roman graffito further shows the disrespect of Jesus at his crucifixion. The painting depicts the head of a jackass on Jesus' body being crucified, with a man standing alongside of it with his arms raised. The caption reads, "Alexamenos worships his god."

At this point during a crucifixion, the victims labored to breath as their body went into shock. Naked and embarrassed, the victims would often use their remaining strength to seek revenge on the crowd of mockers who had gathered to jeer them. They would curse at their tormentors while urinating and spitting on them. Some victims would become so overwhelmed with pain that they would become incontinent, and a pool of sweat, blood, urine, and feces would gather at the base of their cross.

Jesus' crucifixion was a hideously grotesque scene. Hundreds of years in advance, the prophet Isaiah saw it this way: "He was despised and rejected by men; a man of sorrows, and acquainted with grief; and as one from whom men hide their faces he was despised, and we esteemed him not. Surely he has borne our griefs and carried our sorrows; yet we esteemed him stricken, smitten by God, and afflicted" (Isa. 53:3–4).

In addition to the horrifying spectacle of the crucified Jesus, Isaiah also saw his silent response: "He was oppressed, and he was afflicted, yet he opened not his mouth; like a lamb that is led to the slaughter, and like a sheep that before its shearers is silent, so he opened not his mouth" (Isa. 53:7).

Rather than reviling his mockers or declaring his innocence, Jesus chose to die with his masculine dignity intact. He spoke seven last words from the cross. These words provide great insight into the final thoughts of Jesus and his purpose for dying.

First, Jesus said, "Father, forgive them, for they know not what they do" (Luke 23:34). Jesus' first word is a word of forgiveness for the very people who are murdering him. He knew that in a moment he would die to atone for their sins, including the sins they were presently committing against him. In this we see the utter selflessness of Jesus and his unbroken devotion to saving even the worst of sinners through the cross.

Second, Jesus said to one of the thieves being crucified at his side, "Truly, I say to you, today you will be with me in Paradise" (Luke 23:43). Jesus' second word is a word of salvation. Jesus was about to die to atone for that man's sins and open heaven as a gift for him to enjoy as the pattern for all who would come to trust in Jesus for salvation.

Third, Jesus said to his mother, Mary, and his best friend, John, "Woman, behold, your son! . . . Behold, your mother!" (John 19:26–27). As Jesus looked down from his cross, he saw his loving and godly mother, Mary, who was undoubtedly distressed at the sight of her eldest son. Worried for his mother, Jesus' third word appoints his closest friend, John, to look after his mom and care for her like a son and a pastor in his place. Again we see the absolute selflessness of Jesus—his first three words are devoted to his murderers, a thief, and his mother, without yet speaking of his own great needs.

Fourth, Jesus said, "I thirst" (John 19:28). Jesus' fourth word confirms that he humbly suffered as a human being and experienced all of the same physical pain and hardship as anyone in his place would have suffered. Jesus did not do anything to take a divine shortcut or ease his very real physical anguish. Shockingly, the God who created water desperately needed a cup to quench his own thirst and was denied that simple pleasure.

Fifth, remaining a Bible teacher to the end, Jesus quotes Psalm 22:1, saying, "My God, my God, why have you forsaken me?" (Matt. 27:46). At this moment, Jesus died spiritually; the eternal communion he shared with God the Father and God the Spirit as the one Trinitarian God in three persons was broken as their backs were metaphorically turned on Jesus. It was in this moment that our sin was laid on the sinless Jesus (Isa. 53:6), and three hours of darkness came upon the earth, giving the ominous impression that the dominion of darkness had in fact conquered Jesus.

Speaking of this darkest moment in all of time, 2 Corinthians 5:21 says, "For our sake he [God] made him to be sin who knew no sin." The great Protestant Reformer Martin Luther rightly declares that at that moment Jesus became the most grotesque, ugly, and hideous thing in the history of all creation. In what Luther calls "the great exchange," the sinless Jesus so thoroughly took our place that he became the worst of what we are—rapists, thieves, perverts, addicts, liars, gluttons, gossips, murderers, adulterers, fornicators, homosexuals, and idolaters. Importantly, Jesus' work on the cross was not just a bookkeeping transaction in the divine economy. Jesus actually took to himself our sin with all its horror and shame (Heb. 12:2–3).

Also speaking of what transpired at the moment of Jesus' fifth word, Galatians 3:13 quotes Deuteronomy 21:23, saying, "Christ redeemed us from the curse of the law by becoming a curse for us—for it is written, 'Cursed is everyone who is hanged on a tree.'" As our sin was laid upon Jesus and he became the most heinous of beings, Jesus Christ was literally cursed by God on the cross. He came under the judgment of God the Father and God the Spirit as nothing less than the ugliness of damnable evil. Again we see the substitutionary reality: it was our sin and our condemnation, but it was Jesus, the sinless one, who took our place and in so doing took our sin and condemnation so that we could live a new life with a new nature by a new power free from sin and condemnation.

Sixth, Jesus said in a loud voice of triumph, "It is finished" (John 19:30). At this moment, the atonement for sin was made, and the holiness, righteousness, justice, and wrath of God were satisfied in the crucifixion of Jesus Christ. Sadly, some have taught, based on a later revision in the Apostles' Creed, that Jesus did not fully secure our salvation on the cross but rather suffered in hell for three days prior to his resurrection as further atonement. As we have seen, however, Jesus said he was going to paradise on that day and that his work was finished, which negates three days in hell to conclude his work. The Scriptures merely say that Jesus went to the tomb but never declare that he went to hell (Matt. 27:59–60; Mark 15:46; Luke 23:52–55; John 19:41–42).

Seventh, Jesus said, "Father, into your hands I commit my spirit!" (Luke 23:46). Jesus reserved his final breath from the cross to shout his triumphant victory to the world by confirming that he had been restored to God the Father after atoning for human sin. Though we cannot prove it, we do wonder if he was smiling at the conclusion of his mission while gazing heavenward and longing for his rightful return to glory.

The Bible then simply records that Jesus breathed his last and died. Oddly, Islam officially teaches that Jesus did not die on the cross but merely swooned and passed out. If Jesus had not died, that would in and of itself be a miracle, especially in light of the fact that the soldiers were not yet finished ravaging his body.

Jesus hung on the cross for at least six hours—from the third hour to the ninth hour, when the darkness ended (Mark 15:25, 33). How long thereafter that he breathed his last and died is not clear in Scripture. What is clear is the fact that if a victim remained alive on the cross for too long so that it interfered with another event such as a major holiday, it was customary to break the victim's legs, thereby disabling him from pushing himself up on his cross to fill his lungs with air and thereby prolong his life. However, in accordance with the promise of Scripture, Jesus died quickly enough that his legs were not broken (Ps. 34:20; John 19:36). Furthermore, to ensure Jesus was dead, a professional executioner ran a spear through his side, which punctured his heart sac, and water and blood flowed from his side. Jesus died with both a literal and metaphorical broken heart.

For many years, the most sacred place on earth had been the temple, where the presence of God dwelled behind a thick curtain. Only one person a year, the high priest, was allowed to pass by that curtain and enter the presence of God on one day, the Day of Atonement. At the death of Jesus, however, the temple curtain was torn from top to bottom, signifying that God had opened his presence to the world through the cross of Jesus.

Though it was daytime, darkness came as Jesus was prepared for burial. Because Jesus died in poverty, there was not even a burial site prepared for him. A wealthy man named Joseph of Arimathea generously gave his own tomb as a gift to house the body of Jesus, in fulfillment of the promise Isaiah had made hundreds of years earlier, that Jesus would be laid with the rich in his burial (Isa. 53:9).

Three days after his death, Jesus rose with the sun on Sunday morning, triumphing over Satan, sin, and death, just as he had repeatedly promised (Matt. 12:38–40; Mark 8:31; John 2:18–22). Jesus then escaped from his roughly one hundred pounds of burial wrappings and spices, rolled back the large stone covering the entrance to his tomb, walked past the guards on duty, and walked into town on the feet that still bore the scars of his crucifixion.

Over the following forty days, Jesus appeared to crowds upward of five hundred people, proving that he was God who had come to fulfill the promise given to our first parents, that a boot would stomp on the head of the Serpent and liberate those who were held captive in sin and death (1 Cor. 15:1–11). Among those who witnessed Jesus' resurrection and were convinced of his deity were Thomas the doubter, who needed to touch Jesus' scars before he would believe, and Jesus' own mother and brothers, James and Jude, who began worshiping him as their God. His two brothers became Christian pastors and wrote books of the New Testament bearing their names.

Following Jesus' ascension back into heaven, the early church, numbering only one hundred twenty people, gathered informally for a time of prayer, seeking what God would have them to do and awaiting the empowerment of God the Holy Spirit that Jesus had promised. The first pages of Acts record that on the Jewish holiday of Pentecost, which commemorated God's giving the Law to Moses, God the Holy Spirit came with supernatural power, and three thousand people converted to Jesus in a single day.

The flame of Pentecost has continued to burn brightly ever since; today, a few billion people worship Jesus as their only God because they, like Paul, have realized that Jesus died for them personally (Gal. 2:20). They gather together each Sunday, rather than the traditional Jewish

Sabbath day (Saturday), because Sunday was the day of Jesus' resurrection; they gather as the church that was purchased by Jesus at the cross (Eph. 5:25). In these churches, the faithful preachers of the gospel, like Paul, preach nothing but the cross and the crucifixion of Jesus Christ (1 Cor. 2:2). In these churches, the faithful servants of the gospel are not ashamed of the cross (Rom. 1:16) but rather boast in the cross (Gal. 6:14), though they are deemed by many to be nothing but fools for Christ (1 Cor. 3:18). Their greatest fear is that they would live as hypocrites and enemies of the cross (Phil. 3:18). In sum, the Christian church lives as a witness to the work of Jesus on the cross for sinners.

In conclusion, it is tempting to look upon the crucified Jesus with condescending pity and feel sorry for his brutal suffering. Yet, out of respect for Jesus' dignity we must resist that temptation, because Jesus did not die as yet another helpless victim. Rather, with the cross on the horizon of his life, Jesus said that no one would take his life from him in defeat, but rather he would give it and take it up again in victory (John 10:18). Furthermore, Hebrews 12:2 encourages us to "[look] to Jesus, the founder and perfecter of our faith, who for the joy that was set before him endured the cross, despising the shame, and is seated at the right hand of the throne of God." In dignity and triumph, Jesus endured the cross because of the joy that awaited him on the other side of his resurrection, where the Father is glorified in heaven and sinful people have been atoned for on the earth. Today Jesus sits upon his throne in heaven, smiling as he rules over all creation and prepares for the day of his final coming to establish his eternal throne upon the earth. This triumphantly joyous Jesus is not served by our pity but by our praise.

Having established that the substitutionary atonement made possible by Jesus' death on the cross is the great jewel of our faith, we will turn to examine twelve glorious sides of that jewel that together shine forth the glory of God. In an effort to make these points personally relevant to you, each of the remaining chapters will be written in the form of a letter to individuals who are very dear to me, their pastor. Some have sinned greatly and others have been sinned against greatly. Some are young and some are old. Some are male and some are female. Some are Christians and some are not. What they each need is what every person desperately needs—a proper biblical understanding of and personal faith in what Jesus has accomplished for them on the cross.

# Answers to Common Questions about Substitutionary Atonement

*What does "substitution" mean?*

"Substitution" refers to a person or thing acting or serving in place of another. Biblically, the concept of substitution was first practiced not by God but by human beings. When our first parents chose to disobey God and believe the lies of our Enemy, they chose to substitute themselves for God in an effort to become their own gods. Subsequently, to save sinners God had to reverse that tragic substitution and did so by becoming a human being and dying in our place to atone for our sins.

In his marvelous book, *The Cross of Christ*, John Stott insightfully explains this fact:

> The concept of substitution may be said, then, to lie at the heart of both sin and salvation. For the essence of sin is man substituting himself for God, while the essence of salvation is God substituting himself for man. Man asserts himself against God and puts himself where only God deserves to be; God sacrifices himself for man and puts himself where only man deserves to be. Man claims prerogatives which belong to God alone; God accepts penalties which belong to man alone.[4]

Therefore, the concept of substitution beautifully shows forth the love and mercy of God, who is willing to endure the worst for us and give the best to us—namely, himself as our only God and Savior.

*Does not substitutionary atonement portray God as angry and vengeful?*

Inevitably, substitution does mean that God is punishing human beings according to their sins. This concept is increasingly unpopular, as it has been overshadowed by accepting people as they are, forgiving what they do, and forgetting the evil they have done and the pain they have caused.

Interesting, however, is the proclivity of people to reverse their position when the proverbial shoe is on the other foot. What I mean is this: when I sin against someone, I want them to accept me, forgive me, and let me off the hook, because that is what sinners want. As long as we view the cross only from the perspective of sinners, this is all we will see. However, when we or someone we love is sinned against, we cry out for justice because that is what victims want. For example, a father who learned that his young daughter had been sexually abused by his brother told me he "wanted blood." This, precisely, is the perspective of God, who has never sinned against anyone but is continually sinned against by everyone and is truly the greatest victim in all of history. While he is not to be pitied, such injustice must be acknowledged.

Some will protest that such a desire for blood and justice is primitive. But what is the appropriate response to someone who deliberately sins, shows no remorse or repentance, and maintains ongoing devotion to doing evil? The hard truth is that our sin hurts God and hurts the people that God made and loves. Like anyone who truly loves, God takes it personally when harm is done, precisely because he is loving, not because he is unloving.

Sadly, what to do with sinners has led to a political tug-of-war between the right and left. The right generally prefers retribution, which punishes sinners with such things as prison time and capital punishment but usually bypasses rehabilitation and diminishes community responsibility for correction. The left generally prefers rehabilitation, which seeks to improve sinners with such things as therapy and medication but usually bypasses punishment and diminishes personal responsibility for sin. You can see more of this in C. S. Lewis's great essay on the humanitarian theory of punishment.[5]

At the cross we see that God deals with sinners through both retribution and rehabilitation. God made us for glory, not sin. Through Jesus' death on the cross, God honors the dignity of our personhood—we are more than animals incapable of good. By dying for us in our place and suffering our rightful punishment, Jesus also satisfies the retributive justice necessary for God the victim. Through Jesus' death, God has secured for us who believe in Jesus the benefit of a new nature empowered by the Holy Spirit that is not only capable of being reformed but eternally guaranteed to be sinless, thereby satisfying the rehabilitative needs of us sinners.

In conclusion, sin affects both God and the sinner, and only through the cross are God and sinners simultaneously served.

*Does the Bible really speak of substitution, of the Messiah's taking the punishment for my sin in my place?*

While this question has already been answered in the chapter, it deserves stressing yet again, because it is vitally important and vehemently opposed.

The Bible says that Jesus died for all, including dying my death for me personally. We've already seen substitution in 1 Corinthians 15:3–4, where "Christ died for our sins" has to mean that he died *because of* our sins. Similarly, we saw that Jesus took our curse in our place in Galatians 3:13. These are not isolated passages.

For example, 2 Corinthians 5:14–15 says, "For the love of Christ controls us, because we have concluded this: that one has died for all, therefore all have died; and he died for all, that those who live might no longer live for themselves but for him who for their sake died and was raised." Paul's phrase "one has died for all" includes the fact that Jesus died for our benefit. But that does not exhaust the meaning of this text. It also says that Jesus' death is our death, even though we weren't even born yet. The only way Jesus' death can be my death is if he took the penalty of my sin to himself, and in his death he took my place and suffered the death I deserve.

John gives us another clear teaching about substitution. The Jewish leaders were worried that Jesus was going to bring trouble on the people of Israel by claiming to be the Messiah. John 11:48–51 says:

> "If we let him go on like this, everyone will believe in him, and the Romans will come and take away both our place and our nation." But one of them, Caiaphas, who was high priest that year, said to them, "You know nothing at all. Nor do you understand that it is better for you that one man should die for the people, not that the whole nation should perish." He did not say this of his own accord, but being high priest that year he prophesied that Jesus would die for the nation.

Caiaphas wanted Jesus dead so that the people of Israel would not have to die. John's point is that this substitution is actually an unwitting prophecy of the substitution of Jesus taking our penalty in our place.

Also consider Hebrews 9:26–10:12, which makes the same point. There, the author says that Christ has appeared once for all to put away sin by the sacrifice of himself. He was offered once to bear the sins of many. We have been sanctified through the offering of the body of Jesus Christ once for all. After Christ had offered for all time a single sacrifice for sins, he sat down at the right hand of God.

Jesus' death is not a tragedy perpetuated by oppressive Roman soldiers but a self-initiated sacrifice, an offering he came to make. In that offering, he, though sinless, bore or carried our sins. Through his sacrifice, guilty sinners are sanctified or cleansed of sin, defilement, and shame.

God says through his divinely inspired Scriptures that somehow Jesus' death was my death and your death. We were helpless, spiritually dead, and separated from God. Yet, when Jesus died on the cross, his death was somehow ours so that we don't have to be separated from God anymore. We no longer have to be lost in a maze of self-centeredness, living for ourselves. Because Jesus' death was our death, we can live like, with, and for Jesus, spiritually alive and connected to the living God.

# CHAPTER ONE

# "Demons Are Tormenting Me": Jesus Is Katie's *Christus Victor*

*And you, who were dead in your trespasses and the uncircumcision of your flesh, God made alive together with him, having forgiven us all our trespasses, by canceling the record of debt that stood against us with its legal demands. This he set aside, nailing it to the cross. He disarmed the rulers and authorities and put them to open shame, by triumphing over them in him.*

COLOSSIANS 2:13-15

**Katie is my friend, and I am her pastor.** Katie was raised in what was supposed to be a Christian home, complete with a dad, mom, siblings, and semi-regular church attendance. Outwardly, their seemingly happy dispositions masked painful sin and darkness. Although successful in business and a leader in the church, her dad was a coward who avoided most of his homeward responsibilities by ignoring the well-being of his kids and getting drunk all the time.

From an early age, Katie began experiencing various forms of demonic oppression. She would hear from spirits that her father was negligent toward her because she was stupid, ugly, and not worthy of protection. She also suffered from horrendous nightmares and many physical pains following her molestation at age six at the hands of a male relative.

During her teen years, Katie was a dangerous combination of gullible, needy, and rebellious. Partly due to the lack of affection from her father, she craved male approval and touch. Because her father did not teach her about boys, she quickly trusted the first young men who showed any interest in her. By the age of thirteen she was sexually active and, although it is painful to admit, in many ways traded the use of her body for the approval and companionship of young men. None of those young men ever truly cared about her, invested in her, or looked out for her.

In high school she was the quintessential party girl. She was regularly found drinking heavily, laughing loudly, and playing the role of the class slut under a list of boys so lengthy that to this day she cannot remember them all.

Over time, the sins she was committing and the sins that were being committed against her conspired to infect much of her soul. The flicker of passion that remained was for her father. Deep down she desperately wanted her father to cherish her, protect her, and rescue her.

At times she actually snuck boys into her bedroom to have sex with them while her father was home. Despite the noises coming from her bedroom, her father never once opened the door to check on his little girl. She wanted her father to know of her secret life but lacked the courage and relationship to confess it to him. She wished he would simply ask her how she was doing, speak to one of her boyfriends, or walk into her room late at night to discover that her sexual moaning was in fact a confused cry for help from a little girl's heart trapped in a ravished woman's body.

Tragically, her father never pursued or protected her. On one occasion he did knock on her door while she was having sex with a boyfriend but did not enter the room or do anything to show concern for his daughter. To make matters worse, rather than instructing and protecting, her father chose instead to mock her in front of the rest of the family for her parade of loser boyfriends, which only increased her shame and sense of worthlessness, since some of the boys who were the butt of her father's jokes were actually her rapists.

Some years later, Jesus did save her and draw her to himself. She found in Jesus the kind of love, forgiveness, and help that she had always needed. She stopped her party-girl ways and became a woman who deeply loved God and lived a life of repentant holiness by the power of the Holy Spirit. She married a very godly man who loves her, and God gave them beautiful children whom they are raising together as very godly parents. Together they are serving many people in active ministry. They have lived in complete faithfulness to one another as a loving Christian couple for many years.

Nonetheless, she describes feeling tormented. She struggles deeply with debilitating depression brought on by demonic lies. She is often haunted by the vain regrets of the sins of her past. She has endured a very long list of surgeries for innumerable physical problems and has undergone the removal of many body parts.

I have prayed for Katie for many years as she has suffered greatly while also growing in her love and appreciation for Jesus through her sanctifying afflictions. She has so blamed herself for all of the troubles in her life that she has been unwilling to also see the sins committed against her and the fact that behind it all is her great Enemy seeking to destroy her. However, she has recently concluded that perhaps her troubles include a spiritual warfare component that she has been over-looking. For this revelation I rejoice, and the letter that follows is my loving attempt to help my friend Katie come to experience more fully the victory of Jesus Christ over Satan, demons, sin, and death.

◎　◎　◎　◎　◎

## Dear Katie,

I want to begin my letter by restating the deep love that my wife and I have for you and your family. We praise God for your friendship and often thank God that our paths have crossed so that we can enjoy you and your family.

In recent weeks some of our mutual friends have contacted us, saying that they are concerned for your well-being. They report that your out-look on life has become very dark, fatalistic, and in many ways hopeless, though at the same time you have a strong faith in Jesus as your Savior. Your husband also reported the same thing to me when we met. As an encouragement, I was thrilled to see how deeply he cares for you, and I praise God that he is exactly the kind of defending, protecting, and providing man that you have needed since you were a little girl. Your strong love for him touches his godly heart deeply.

As we have spoken over the years, you have mentioned on a few occa-sions how, in the midst of the pain of your life as a young woman, you desperately wanted your father to step in to save and defend you as his treasure. As the daddy of two daughters I adore, I can assure you that God creates daddies for just such tasks, and that any daddy who fails in his duty is in grievous sin, especially if he claims to be a Christian daddy. I am deeply sorry, and the thought of you being in your bedroom naked with a boy while your father knocks on the door without stepping in to liberate you haunts me when I pray for you.

However, I do believe that in such formative moments of your life, a pattern was established that needs to be broken. You have seen yourself as a sinfully wicked and dirty woman who is worthless and who deserves being violated and taken advantage of. Subsequently, you have become a passive victim waiting for someone—your father, husband, friends—to rescue you.

While your father did not fight for you, your husband will, as will your friends, along with me as your pastor. But, Katie, it is time for you to learn how Jesus has fought for you, and he is now calling you to fight with him for your own life and the life of your children. Because you belong to Jesus, you have all authority to rebuke and reject these evil influences in your life.

Without minimizing any of the many sins you have committed, or the many sins that have been committed against you, I also need you to understand the spiritual war that you are a part of. According to the Bible, angels are spirit beings created by God to serve his purposes. However, one angel became proud, which is the root of much sin, and preferred to be his own god rather than worship and obey the real God (Isa. 14:11–23; Ezek. 28:12). We now know him by various names such as Satan, the Dragon, the Serpent, the Enemy, the Devil, the Tempter, the Murderer, the Father of Lies, the Adversary, the Accuser, the Destroyer, and the Evil One. Tragically, one-third of the angels sided with Satan to declare war on God.

Their rebellion culminated in a great battle against God and his holy angels. Satan and his demons lost and were kicked out of heaven without the possibility of ever being forgiven or reconciled into a right relationship with God (2 Pet. 2:4). Practically, this means that only judgment and torment await Satan and demons.

Before we continue, I must also stress that Satan and demons are in no way equal to God. Unlike God, they are created beings with finite limits. They are not all-present, all-knowing, or all-powerful like God. They are, however, very real and very powerful. They have been observing human behavior since the beginning of history and are keenly aware of how people live, and they have been continually perfecting their tactics on how to destroy us.

Without seeming unsympathetic, I do want you to see some ways in which this is encouraging. First, the fact that you are facing such great spiritual warfare is because you are serving Jesus faithfully.

Second, the warfare you are experiencing has been ongoing since you were a little girl and likely goes back even further into previous generations of your family. But God intends to bring it to an end before it continues in the lives of your children and grandchildren.

Third, although this battle has raged in your life for many years, God has recently opened your eyes to see it because you are at the point in your walk with Jesus that, for the first time, you are able to join Jesus in his battle for your life.

Fourth, God intends to work in your life as he did in the life of Joseph as recorded in Genesis 50:20. There we learn that even evil that is intended to destroy us is used by our sovereign God for good and the saving of many lives. No enemy can stop God's ultimate intent to do good.

Katie, the lessons you learn about Jesus' victory over Satan and the ways to live practically in light of his conquest will enable your ministry to help even more hurting people experience the full freedom and joy of their liberation.

Continuing on with the story of Scripture, the great war in heaven then moved to the new battlefield of earth. Here, Satan attacked our first parents, your father Adam and mother Eve. Satan lied to Eve and tempted her to sin, just as he did you. Adam, whom God appointed to love and care for Eve, failed to protect her, just like your father. Worse, he knowingly joined her in sin.

Both Adam and Eve chose lies over truth, pride over humility, folly over wisdom, death over life, and Satan over God. Subsequently, each of us descendants of our first parents is conceived with a sinful nature marked by a disposition to follow in their tragic footsteps. Furthermore, as a sinner you have experienced the same painful consequences as your mother Eve. Because of the sins you committed and the sins that were committed against you, you were alienated from God and hid from him in shame. The demons took advantage of this evil situation to torment you.

The battle for your soul has been very real, and you were held for many years like a captive in war, being tortured and brainwashed until Jesus came to rescue you. I know that you will find it difficult to accept the language, but Scripture clearly says that there is a very real war between Jesus and the angels and Satan and the demons. Sinners, including you, are taken as captives in war (Col. 1:13; 2 Tim. 2:25–26). Jesus himself confirmed this fact in Luke 4:18 when, at the beginning of his earthly ministry, he said he had come to set captives free. Jesus said this because there is no way that Satan would release you from his captivity and no way that you could liberate yourself. Therefore, Jesus came as your triumphant warrior and liberator.

The first promise of Jesus as your victor over Satan came to your first parents. In Genesis 3:15, God preached the first good news, or gospel, of Jesus to your mother Eve, who, like you, was a broken, shame-filled, guilty sinner. God promised Eve, and her daughters like you, that Jesus would be born of a woman and would grow to be a man who would battle with Satan and stomp his head, defeat him, and liberate people from their captivity to Satan, sin, death, and hell.

Years later Jesus was born to his mother, Mary, as promised. Satan's attack on Jesus commenced when Jesus was only a boy. King Herod, who was a descendant of a demonically influenced family line of evil dictators, decreed that all firstborn sons be put to death in an effort to murder Jesus as an infant. Satan was, in fact, working behind this plot because he rightly knew that Jesus had come to conquer him and liberate his captives. But God warned Jesus' parents of the plot, and they fled to Egypt as refugees, so Jesus' life was spared.

As a young man, Jesus was again attacked by Satan, who offered him a much easier life than the one planned out for him by God the Father. God the Father sent Jesus to earth on the mission of living a sinless life and going to the cross to die for sinners. In contrast, Satan offered a kingdom without a cross and promised that Jesus could rule in glory and power without any opposition or crucifixion so long as he bowed down in honor to Satan. Satan set forth his proposal with a simple friendship offer of food, of breaking bread with Jesus, while Jesus was very hungry following forty days of fasting. Jesus wisely rejected this "gift." Like Jesus, it is very wise to be suspicious of spirits bearing gifts, even if they should appear to be good things. This is why discernment is so vital.

I tell you about this because from it you can learn a basic principle of how your Enemy works. The great Puritan Thomas Brooks wrote one of my favorite books on spiritual warfare, *Precious Remedies against Satan's Devices*. Brooks uses a wonderful illustration that explains why Jesus rejected Satan's simple offer of bread. Brooks says that our Enemy will bait our hook with anything that we find desirable. This means that he will gladly give us sex, money, power, pleasure, fame, fortune, and relationships. Satan's goal is for us to take the bait without seeing the hook, and once the hook is in our mouth he then reels us in to take us captive. His gifts are often very good things offered for sinful uses. He'll challenge us to examine the gift to ensure its quality. That is the essence of the trap. The gift may be good, but the giver is evil. In this way, Satan and demons are akin to a pedophile who seeks to entice children into trust with gifts of candy and toys, only to destroy them.

When we take the gifts that Satan and demons give, we are in essence biting down on the bait. As a result, the hook of sin is in our mouth, and Satan reels us in as his captive so that, as Jesus says in John 8:34, we become slaves to our sin. Satan baited your hook with the affection of boys, sex, and alcohol, as well as with good things like protection and comfort. Having taken the bait, you were reeled into a dark and sinister life of evil that inevitably leads to death. Apart from Jesus, you would have seen your life continue to descend into darkness until you found yourself with Satan in hell forever. Furthermore, Satan is still using his gifts to tempt you today. His plan never changes, only his tactics.

Thankfully, the Lord Jesus came to rescue you. Unlike you, he resisted Satan's temptations on every occurrence and lived the sinless life that you have not lived. Jesus then went to the cross to die the death you should have died. On the cross, Jesus died in your place for your sins. Practically, this means that every single sin you have committed or will ever commit was forgiven, and every sin that was committed or ever will be committed against you was cleansed in full without exception. As 1 John 1:9 says, "If we confess our sins, he is faithful and just to forgive us our sins and to cleanse us from all unrighteousness."

Leading up to the cross, Satan entered one of Jesus' own disciples, Judas Iscariot, and conspired with him to betray Jesus and hand him over to be crucified. Through the cross, Satan and his demons thought that they had finally defeated Jesus. If we picture the Lord Jesus hanging on the cross, bloodied and dying, it admittedly appears in every way that Jesus was hanging his head in defeat at the hands of Satan. On this point, the great Reformation pastor Martin Luther was fond of reflecting on Isaiah 45:15, which says of Jesus, "Truly, you are a God who hides [yourself], O God of Israel, the Savior." Luther's point in this verse is that on the cross Jesus hid his victory in defeat, hid his glory in shame, and hid our life in his death. Satan and the demons did not see this because they lacked the sight of faith and did not understand the humility of Jesus.

Nonetheless, on the cross Jesus bled and died for you, and by faith, as you look to the cross, you will see the great lengths he has gone to in the conquering of your Enemy and the liberating of your life. Consequently, Jesus' words, "It is finished," from the cross are his heralding of your liberation. Crucifying Jesus was the biggest mistake the Devil ever made. Had he understood what was happening, he would never have killed Jesus, as it says in 1 Corinthians 2:6–9:

> Yet among the mature we do impart wisdom, although it is not a wisdom of this age or of the rulers of this age, who are doomed to pass away. But we impart a secret and hidden wisdom of God, which God decreed before the ages for our glory. None of the rulers of this age understood this, for if they had, they would not have crucified the Lord of glory. But, as it is written, "What no eye has seen, nor ear heard, nor the heart of man imagined, what God has prepared for those who love him."

My favorite portion of Scripture on the victory of Jesus over Satan, sin, and death is Colossians 2:13–15:

> And you, who were dead in your trespasses and the uncircumcision of your flesh, God made alive together with him, having forgiven us all our trespasses, by canceling the record of debt that stood against us with its legal demands. This he set aside, nailing it to the cross. He disarmed the rulers and authorities and put them to open shame, by triumphing over them in him.

It would serve you well, Katie, to commit these verses to memory and spend the rest of your life asking God the Holy Spirit to teach them to you and give you the faith to believe them.

The imagery from Colossians is actually taken from the great battle victories celebrated in antiquity. As best I can, with admitted poetic license, I want to explain to you what this section of Colossians, along with some imagery from Revelation, means, so you will see that Jesus, unlike your father, has fought for you. I know this has been the desire of your heart deep down for many years; you have repeatedly said that you have always wanted a man to fight for you and are most attracted to your husband when he is strong, courageous, and willing to fight for your life and joy.

To every unbelieving eye, the Great Dragon was the crowned victor, standing over Jesus Christ in the ring of human history, spewing blasphemies, spitting upon his face, placing a crown of thorns upon his head in mockery, and pulling out Jesus' beard as he lay beaten and stripped naked on the dust of his own earth. Placing a knee on one limb at a time, the Great Dragon held in his hands a large hammer and spikes to nail Jesus' body to a Roman cross. With his army of demons and human servants cheering their king and his conquest, the Great Dragon laughed loudly while nailing a mocking banner above Jesus' head that read, "King of the Jews." The Great Dragon raised up the broken, beaten, and bloodied crucified Jesus for all to see, so that Jesus would be shamed by the people and spirits he had made who gathered to cover him with spit, curses, and jeering. Jesus breathed his last as the Dragon raised his head in pride to declare his ultimate victory as new King and Lord. Meanwhile, Jesus' body was laid in a tomb, and his followers left in utter silence, leaving a path muddied with tears behind them.

But . . .

Three days later, Jesus your Warrior King rose in victory over death. Seeing Jesus alive, the Great Dragon snatched you as his captive, drew his sword of law, covered with the blood of your sin, and thrust its razor-sharp point at your head, naming every sin you have committed along with the name of every boy who ever touched you. Smiling, Jesus stepped forward and declared that he already paid the penalty for your sins on the cross, canceled any right Satan had to hold you captive, and defeated your Enemy along with his servants and their works and effects in your life.

With fear in his eyes, the Great Dragon dropped his sword from your head and was overcome with dread as he understood the victory Jesus had won for you through his seeming defeat. Drawing his own sword of truth, Jesus landed a crushing blow on the head of the Great Dragon, shattering his helmet and bloodying his head. Jesus then stepped toward the Great Dragon and thrust the pommel of his sword against his mouth, shattering his teeth and sending them violently down his throat. Then, with a blow to his armor, Jesus doubled the Great Dragon over, leaving him gasping for air and unable to bellow his curses and blasphemies anymore. With a crushing elbow to the back of the head, Jesus dropped the Great Dragon into the very dust in which Jesus himself had lain three days prior, and the blood of the Great Dragon fell upon the dried blood of your Savior. Jesus stripped the Great Dragon of all his armor and clothing as his bowed head and bloodied mouth moaned in the agony of utter defeat.

Ashamed of your many years at the Dragon's side, you stood off to the side alone, gazing at the ground until Jesus came to you. Taking your chin in his hand, Jesus lifted your face, looked you in the eye, and told you that your sins were forgiven, your Enemy conquered, and your life liberated from captivity, and that God is now your Father, new life is your gift, and heaven is your home. As tears streamed down your face, Jesus asked you always to remember to see yourself as he does, not in light of what you have done or what has been done to you, but rather solely by what he has done for you as your victorious Warrior King.

At that moment, Katie, you felt freedom for the first time. At that moment, what Jesus had done for you was made known to you by God the Holy Spirit. At that moment, you stepped over the fallen Dragon and embraced Jesus with a passionate joy you had previously never known.

You were finally known.

You were finally loved.

You were finally safe.

You were finally free.

One day, Jesus will chain the Serpent to his chariot and force him to walk naked, bloodied, and bowed into his kingdom. Following behind Jesus will be all of his warrior-saints, from bloodied Abel to John the Baptizer and Paul, who met their death on the battlefield of human history. With them will be Athanasius, Augustine, Luther, Calvin, and their comrades from church history. And you, Katie, will be among them, smiling and laughing and dancing and singing because you too have been set free from captivity to your Enemy.

Following you in shameful defeat will be all of the demons and unrepentant evildoers who have ever sinned against you. Joining your enemies will be Cain, Pharaoh, Herod, Judas, and their aged generals Sin and Death. They will all be chained together at the wrists and shackled at the feet with their mouths gagged so they can no longer blaspheme God or name your sin.

This triumphant procession will follow a flower-laden street with Jesus' chariot at the head, and it will enter the Holy City, a kingdom filled with worshipers clothed in white shouting, "Hosanna! Blessed is he who comes in the name of the Lord! Blessed is the coming kingdom of our father David! Hosanna in the highest!"

A hush will fall as Jesus, stepping upon his throne, preaches that he alone is King and Lord and that when he was nailed to the cross, so were your sins, so that you could be liberated from your captivity to the Dragon, demons, sin, and death. Overcome, you and the rest of the liberated captives will stand motionless and silent for about half an hour, completely overwhelmed by the grace that has been poured out through the cross of Jesus Christ (Rev. 8:1).

Katie, you will struggle for the rest of this life to comprehend this reality, because it is a matter of faith rather than sight. We see the Devil's work everywhere in this world and will until Jesus returns to bring it all to an end. Until then, it is by faith that we see the authority of the kingdom of God that has invaded this world (Eph. 1:17–23).

We long for the final defeat of the Dragon with the return of Jesus. But the authority of the Devil and his demons in your life has already ended. Matthew 28:18 makes it very clear that Jesus has *all* authority now, which means that Satan has no authority over you as a Christian. We who are by grace citizens of Jesus' kingdom will never again have to obey the Dragon's orders, satisfy his desires, or live as his captives. Jesus has thoroughly freed you from all your obligations to and agreements with the Dragon by bringing you into his kingdom of light. As a result, you can now live in accordance with Colossians 1:10–14 and

> walk in a manner worthy of the Lord, fully pleasing to him, bearing fruit in every good work and increasing in the knowledge of God. May you be strengthened with all power, according to his

> glorious might, for all endurance and patience with joy, giving thanks to the Father, who has qualified you to share in the inheritance of the saints in light. He has delivered us from the domain of darkness and transferred us to the kingdom of his beloved Son, in whom we have redemption, the forgiveness of sins.

The Bible uses the word *grace* to explain the victory Jesus achieved for you on the cross, because there is no logical reason that God would love you and die in your place to liberate you from captivity to Satan, sin, and death other than his wonderful nature.

Furthermore, though defeated, Satan and demons are not yet fully destroyed until the final judgment at Jesus' white throne (Rev. 20:11–15). Subsequently, their work continues on the earth, which means you must be wise. As the Puritan William Gurnall once said, "Where God is on one side, you may be sure to find the devil on the other." Therefore, in an effort to help you be wise, I want to share with you some things from the Bible that have been of great help to me personally.

There are some truths regarding Satan that I need you to believe and to highlight in your Bible so that you can revisit them often. First, Satan and demons are your foes and not in any way friends (1 Pet. 5:8).

Second, Satan and demons are actively at war against you (Eph. 6:10–13).

Third, Satan and demons want you to die because Satan is a murderer; he wants to bring death to everything in your life, including your love, joy, marriage, and ministry (John 8:44).

Fourth, Satan and demons have no claim to you, because you have been delivered forever from Satan's kingdom of darkness to Jesus' kingdom of light (Col. 1:13).

Fifth, in Jesus there is for you personally protection from and authority over Satan and his demons (Luke 10:18–20).

Sixth, because you are in Jesus Christ positionally and all things are under his authority, you too can command Satan and demons to obey you by the authority delegated to you from Jesus (Eph. 1:18–2:8). Practically, this simply means that if in Jesus' name you command a demon to leave you alone, it must.

Despite the fact that he is a doomed, limping enemy, the old Dragon remains crafty, as Scripture says. To fool you, Satan will use various tactics that Scripture warns us about. I want to tell you about some of these tactics, Katie, because it is my assumption that Satan will most likely use them against you. On this point, 2 Corinthians 2:11 says that Satan cannot trick us if we become familiar with the tactics he uses against us.

Satan will lie to you because he is a liar. If you believe him, your life will be destroyed, because you will be trusting the person Jesus calls the "father of lies" (John 8:44b). Your response to lies must be reading your Bible and listening to Jesus, who throughout John's Gospel repeatedly says, "I tell you the truth." Furthermore, when you hear the lies, speak honestly about them with godly friends and your husband so that Jesus can speak truth into your life through them. Remember, you never have to persuade the Liar that he is wrong and you are right. Instead, be like Jesus, who, in Matthew 4:8–10, ignored the Liar's lies and remained devoted to the truth of Scripture.

Satan will come to you when you are weak and tempt you to sin just as he did Jesus, because he is the Tempter (Matt. 4:1–11). The goal of his temptation is to draw you near to him and away from Jesus in rebellion. Your response to sinful temptation must be to resist the Devil so that he will flee from you (James 4:7–8). When you do sin, you must keep short accounts with God by repenting of your sin to Jesus and anyone else you have sinned against.

Satan will come to you as your accuser (Rev. 12:10). Satan's accusations often come in the form of a second-person speaker. Some people who think they have psychological problems because they hear voices or have negative self-talk are in fact undergoing demonic opposition. For example, I would not be surprised if you often hear such things as "You are a slut," "You have no right to enjoy sex with your husband," "God could never forgive you," "You deserve what was done to you," and "You should just kill yourself to end your pain." In these seasons you must realize that Jesus would never say such things to you, and if you are hearing accusations in the second person, then a demon is whispering in your ear, hoping you will believe him over Jesus.

Satan will come to you, often during a season of God's grace being poured out, to rob you of joy by condemning you. He will remind you of past sins that Christ died for and that you have earnestly repented of. In doing so, he will attempt to get you to disbelieve in the sufficiency of Jesus' work on the cross for you. If you believe the Dragon, you will either doubt God's forgiveness or seek to do something in addition to

Jesus' work to merit your own forgiveness. Either way, you disbelieve in the finished work of Jesus on the cross for your sin, and you will be compelled toward either despair or religion but not toward Jesus. In these seasons, you will find an anchor for your soul by meditating on Romans 8:1, which says, "There is therefore now no condemnation for those who are in Christ Jesus."

Satan will use your sincere heart to heap upon you a very vague, general conviction that, if not recognized, will propel you into deep introspection as you frantically search for some sin. This is because Satan mimics God and perverts his work. God convicts you of specific sins so that, with his compassionate help, you can repent and move on to freedom and joy. Satan, however, will seek to defeat and discourage you through guilt that is so general that you never know exactly what to repent of and are thereby left in paralyzing bondage and despair. In John 8 we are told that Satan is basically an abusive parent and, like all abusive parents, his intent is not to correct you but to harm you, causing suffering and grief so that you feel destroyed without any clue as to what you have done or how to fix it.

Because so many sins of both omission and commission have been committed against you, Satan will also seek to gain ground in your life through bitterness (Eph. 4:17–32). The sad truth is that there is virtually no way that everyone who has ever sinned against you will come forward to repent and ask your forgiveness. If you wait for the people who have sinned against you to repent before you can forgive them, you will be prone to bitterness, which Hebrews 12:15 describes as a root that will feed other demonic weeds in your life.

Therefore, as God the Holy Spirit brings to mind the people who have sinned against you, you must forgive them. This does not mean minimizing or accepting what they have done, but rather entrusting them to God for his justice through Jesus' suffering on the cross or their deserved torment in hell. Your part in forgiveness is giving up your just right to hurt them for the hurt they did to you. God may also ask you to confront some of them in order to give them an opportunity to repent, and if they do not, you must trust Jesus to judge and sentence them justly on the day of final judgment.

Satan will seek to get your eyes off of Jesus. In *The Screwtape Letters*, C. S. Lewis writes, "There are two equal and opposite errors into which our race can fall about the devils. One is to disbelieve in their existence. The other is to believe, and to feel an excessive and unhealthy interest in them."

So, as my letter to you is nearing its conclusion, I would warn you that Satan has had much freedom with you because you functionally disbelieved in his existence and as a result overlooked his active work in your life. As you grow in your understanding of how Satan and demons work, however, my caution to you would be not to blame everything on them as Eve did, but rather continue to take responsibility for your own sin and entrust the punishment of those who sinned against you to the Lord.

Furthermore, because the root of Satan's work is pride, you must also continually speak, think, and act in humility, as God's grace to you requires. As Jesus said in Luke 10:20, "Do not rejoice in this, that the spirits are subject to you, but rejoice that your names are written in heaven."

Katie, there is much more that could be written on this subject. But I trust that God the Holy Spirit will continually reveal to you the victory of Jesus as you read, study, and meditate on Scripture. Scripture is the sword of truth and is only useful against the Liar if it is regularly pulled from its scabbard. In closing, I would give you the following four practical steps to continue walking in joy over Satan and demons.

First, Jesus is your shield. The psalms often speak of God as our shield; remaining under Jesus Christ is your only place of safety. Therefore, the key is to walk continually and closely with Jesus, and if you should stray from under his shield to return quickly in repentance.

Second, continue in fellowship with faithful Christians who love Jesus and who will speak with you as honest friends. You will be a blessing to them as you share the things that Jesus has taught you, and they will be a blessing to you by speaking loving truth into your life and praying for you. It is no coincidence that Jesus was most tempted by Satan when he was alone. If you become isolated from God's people, you are leaving yourself open to spiritual attack. Therefore, remain actively involved in Bible-based, lovingly honest, accountable relationships, because it is indeed not good to be alone.

Third, do not be unduly fearful of Satan or demons. Satan is called a serpent, and demons are like snakes. They are dangerous only if you pick one up or provoke one to bite. Jesus' perfect love and kingdom victory on the cross are sufficient for you to overcome excessive fear of Satan and demons.

Fourth, pray offensively for protection and wisdom before the demonic attacks come. Too often, Christians pray defensively only when trouble comes. To help teach you how to pray this way, the book of Psalms is filled with offensive prayers. Some of my favorites include Psalm 18, Psalm 27, Psalm 31, Psalm 35, and Psalm 83. I would also suggest that you follow Jesus' example in Matthew 4:1–10. When the Serpent attacked him, Jesus fought back by quoting Scripture that perfectly applied to the lies and temptations of the Enemy. Then, Jesus used his authority to command the Serpent to leave him. This is the same authority that Jesus has delegated to Christians so that we, too, can command Satan and demons to depart from us.

I implore you out of great love to live continually in light of the great, final defeat of Satan and demons and their servants, works, and effects at the white throne of Jesus (Revelation 20). Until that day, I pray Romans 16:20 for you, my dear sister: "The God of peace will soon crush Satan under your feet. The grace of our Lord Jesus Christ be with you."

# Answers to Common Questions about *Christus Victor*

### Can Christians be possessed by demons?

This is one of those questions that many people answer too quickly. The problem is that the word *possess* has several meanings. According to the Merriam-Webster dictionary it can mean three things. First, *possess* can mean "own" so that a Christian would essentially belong to Satan. Second, *possess* can mean "dominate" so that a Christian would be controlled by Satan. Third, *possess* can mean "influence" so that the life of a Christian would be marked by the influences of Satan. Obviously, what people mean when they use the word *possessed* matters very much when answering the question, "Can Christians be possessed by demons?"

In the first sense, the Devil never *owns* a Christian. We have been rescued from the dominion of darkness and transferred into the kingdom of the Son, Paul tells us in Colossians 1:13.

In the third sense, the Devil can *influence* a Christian. We are in warfare against the Enemy who seeks to steal and kill and destroy (John 10:10). Even Jesus was attacked by the Devil in this way according to Matthew 4:1–11 and Luke 4:1–13.

It is the second sense where there is a lot of debate among Christians. Can demons dominate a Christian? While some teach that through personal sin, generational sin, or even curses, demons can have authority to dominate believers, Scripture is clear that Christians are never under the ruling authority of darkness. The Devil can never take authority over a Christian. Others teach that if we pray and feast on God's Word we never need fear a demonic attack. But if Jesus can be attacked, how can we say we cannot?

We believe Christians may be deceived, accused, or tempted by Satan and may yield to those attacks (though they do not have to). If believers begin to respond wrongly to such things, they may give demons influence in their lives. Apparently an evil spirit can empower, energize, encourage, and exploit a believer's own sinful desires. Examples would include Peter (Matt. 16:22–23) and Ananias (Acts 5:3). As children of God, regenerated and indwelt by the Spirit, we are responsible to and empowered by God to resist Satan, and if we do resist, we need not suffer from his influence (Eph. 6:10–18; James 4:7; 1 Pet. 5:7–9; 1 John 4:1–4; 5:1–5, 18–19).

### What can I do if a demon attacks me?

It is vital to remember that Jesus has already disarmed the rulers and authorities and put them to open shame by triumphing over them at the cross (Col. 2:15). We don't have to do anything to win authority over a demon. That victory has already been won for us by Jesus. Our challenge is to believe and live in that authority.

Jesus is our example. When he was attacked by a demon, he refused to argue theology. Jesus didn't get into whether the Devil actually could have given him the kingdoms of this world, and he didn't ask for names or information but quoted Scripture and commanded the demon to get away (Matt. 4:1–11).

Below is a typical pattern of prayer to employ when dealing with demonically empowered desires. It is important to note that the specific wording is unimportant, because our power does not come from speaking a mantra but rather from Jesus and the truth:

1) "Lord Jesus Christ, I acknowledge that this [name the specific area of sin] may be empowered by demons and evil spirits. If it is, I want nothing to do with them."

2) "Lord Jesus Christ, I confess that you triumphed over these demons and evil spirits by the power of your shed blood that purchased forgiveness for all my sins, and by your death, burial, and resurrection that provided my new life in you."

3) "Lord Jesus Christ, I ask that you send any demons and evil spirits away from me. Demon, in the name and authority of Jesus, I command you to get away from me now."

4) "Lord Jesus Christ, I thank you for hearing and answering my prayer. Please fill me anew with your Holy Spirit so that I will be empowered to live in obedience to you and in freedom from sin and harassment."

### Can sins done against me defile me?

They can, as we've seen in Katie's story. But Jesus can cleanse that aspect of sin too. For example, Matthew 8 begins with Jesus healing a leper instantaneously by his power and ends with Jesus driving demons out of two men instantaneously by his power. The point is that whether we are physically or spiritually defiled, Jesus can cleanse us. In 1 John 1:9 we are told to confess or talk about our sin. Such sin can be either sin we have committed or sin committed against us. In either case, bringing the sin to Jesus and his people will result in forgiveness of any and all guilt and cleansing of any and all defilement. The removal of defilement is usually not immediate; it is more likely to be a process, but the outcome is sure because "we have an advocate with the Father, Jesus Christ the righteous. He is the propitiation for our sins, and not for ours only but also for the sins of the whole world" (1 John 2:1–2). This subject is also covered more fully in chapter 7 of this book.

*I have some questions about Satan and demons. What else can I read to learn more?*

For a theological summary, we recommend *Powers of Darkness: Principalities and Powers in Paul's Letters* by Clinton E. Arnold (Downers Grove, IL: InterVarsity, 1992). For a practical understanding, we recommend *Three Crucial Questions about Spiritual Warfare* by Clinton E. Arnold (Grand Rapids, MI: Baker, 1997); *Precious Remedies against Satan's Devices* by Thomas Brooks (Carlisle, PA: Banner of Truth, 1968); *The Screwtape Letters* by C. S. Lewis (New York: HarperCollins, 2001); and *Lord Foulgrin's Letters* and *The Ishbane Conspiracy* by Randy Alcorn (Sisters, OR: Multnomah, 2001; both titles).

There are many books and videos that teach that we need to know a demon's name in order to cast it out. But neither Jesus (Mark 1:23–27 is the first of many places where he did his work without appealing to a name) nor Paul (Acts 16:16–18) needed a demon's name to cast it out. Similarly, such teaching commonly argues that sin gives a demon the right to inhabit a Christian, so until we confess the sin, we cannot force the demon to leave. Because these teachings go against the Bible, however, such books must be read critically by constantly asking the question, "Where does the Bible say that?"

## HELPFUL INFORMATION

In the letter to Katie, reference was made to C. S. Lewis's book *The Screwtape Letters* (New York: HarperCollins, 2001), *ix*.

# CHAPTER TWO

# "Lust Is My God": Jesus Is Thomas's Redemption

*Waiting for our blessed hope, the appearing of the glory of our great God and Savior Jesus Christ, who gave himself for us to redeem us from all lawlessness and to purify for himself a people for his own possession who are zealous for good works.*

TITUS 2:13-14

**He seems like a pretty good guy** in his early forties when you first meet him. He looks you in the eye, flashes a broad smile, and has mastered the corporate art of firm handshakes and meaningless chitchat. His beautiful wife sweetly stands at his side, tenderly embracing his arm and holding his hand, their fingers interlocked. His young children are the kind of adorably cute and well-behaved blessings from God that couples pray for.

Tragically, it is all an illusion, like a river with a calm appearance but with a deadly undertow. Thomas would tell you he's a Christian and would be able to answer correctly the basic questions about Christianity. Furthermore, he would tell you that he believes Jesus is God, and that if you do not repent of sin and trust in Jesus, you will die and go to hell. He is so charming, confident, smart, and successful that he has actually been approached and asked to consider helping to lead various ministries.

However, he won't tell you that he has never been faithful to any women in his life, including his most recent wife. In fact, he has trouble remembering exactly the number of people he has committed adultery with or the number of times he has been unfaithful to his wife. He cannot recall the last day he did not spend at least an hour online viewing pornography.

To make matters worse, until recently his wife was clueless about his double life. His sick excuse for not telling her was that it would break her heart, and he wanted to spare her the pain, as if he were a concerned, loving husband. The hard truth is that he is afraid she will leave him and take his sons and half of all his considerable wealth with her.

Thomas has become so self-deceived that he actually thinks getting an occasional STD test to ensure that he does not infect his wife makes him a good husband. Occasionally his guilt overwhelms him and he responds by running to alcohol, which only makes matters worse, and he becomes more depressed, less discerning, and more reckless. Most often, however, his guilt compels him to work long hours for penance, as if he could do enough good things to counterbalance his sin.

As we sat together, he told me about his life of sin in great detail. When he was done, he told me I needed to hold it in confidence and pray for him so that he could feel better about himself. He actually thought that by confessing his sin without ever repenting of it, God would be pleased with him. He thought he could just keep sinning as long as he felt bad and once every few years sat down to tell a pastor his sin in confidence without taking any responsibility. However, the Bible knows nothing of using confidentiality as a cover for sinful irresponsibility, especially when it puts someone else in danger. So I told him I needed to get the full truth to his wife. After his initial shock and some arguing, he agreed that she deserved to know. So I told him to disclose everything to her and then have her call me to confirm that he'd been responsible. Not surprisingly, she demanded that he repent, and she walked out until he did.

This letter is written to Thomas in an effort to teach him that Jesus will be pleased with nothing less than redeeming him from being one kind of man to being an entirely new man and from a life of bondage to sin to a new life of holy freedom in Christ.

◎ ◎ ◎ ◎ ◎

## Dear Thomas,

This letter will be painfully pointed. We know each other well enough that I won't waste our time flattering you or softening you up with jabs of kindness. So, I will just launch in with a series of heavy blows of truth.

The bottom line is that you are absolutely out of control. During his life on the earth, Jesus' best friend was a young man named John. John went on to become a pastor who wrote five books of the New Testament. Two lines from one of his letters are poignant and worthy of your committing to memory: "Do not love the world or the things in the world. If anyone loves the world, the love of the Father is not in him. For all that is in the world—the desires of the flesh and the desires of the eyes and pride in possessions—is not from the Father but is from the world" (1 John 2:15–16).

Thomas, when the Bible speaks of "the world" here, it is referring to the various ways that people live in sin against God. Examples in your life would include your addiction to pornography, your adulterous sexual affairs, your drunkenness, your pride, your lying to your wife, and your pretending to be a decent Christian guy outwardly while in your heart you are more like Judas than Jesus. Furthermore, it says that you cannot simultaneously love the world and God because you cannot run to sin and to God at the same time.

True followers of Jesus sin, but they don't love sin as you do. Even as they sin, they hate what they do. Paul illustrates this well in Romans 7:14–25. There Paul speaks of his sin saying, "I do not do what I want, but I do the very thing I hate," and, "For I have the desire to do what is right, but not the ability to carry it out. For I do not do the good I want, but the evil I do not want is what I keep on doing." Were you truly a Christian, you would be aware of your own sin, thanks to the conviction of God the Holy Spirit, but like Paul you would also "hate" it and "desire to do what is right." Paul then goes on to say that he, like all true Christians, could only overcome sin by an ongoing trust in Jesus and reliance on the power of the Holy Spirit.

Because you have chosen years of repeated sin, you have run far from God, and I sincerely doubt if you ever were or currently are a Christian, although that is ultimately for Jesus to decide. You show no signs of being redeemed, because you love sin, and your deepest desire is to do what is evil. Furthermore, you are not compelled to live in relationship with Jesus or rely on the power of God the Holy Spirit. By your own admission you do not really love God, but rather merely fear hell.

John wisely describes your situation as a series of addictions (1 John 2:15–16). First, you are enslaved to the cravings of your physical body, which rules over you with sexual perversions of nearly every sort. Second, you are enslaved to the lust of your eyes and cannot stop looking at naked women on computer screens, in strip clubs, and in your bed. Third, you are enslaved to your pride. Your entire life is devoted to covering your tracks so that no one knows who you really are. This explains why you regularly erase the pornographic files on your computer as well as any history of which web sites you have visited, commit adultery while out of town so that your wife will not find out, and have a private phone number and e-mail address for your mistresses.

To use very biblical wording, you are a slave. Second Peter 2:19b explains it this way: "For whatever overcomes a person, to that he is enslaved." Because you cannot stop what you are doing, the fact is that you are a slave. You will likely scoff at the notion that you are a slave because you are a free man, able to do as you please. But in our meeting together you said, "I cannot stop looking at porn. I cannot stop committing adultery. I have tried. I have stopped for a few days only to start again. I cannot stop."

If you were free, you would be free to stop. Since you cannot stop, though, you are indeed a slave, who is not free at all. Like a prisoner locked in a cell who cannot escape, so you too are locked in a prison of sin and cannot get free.

To some degree, you so much as admitted in our meeting that you are a slave. You tried to convince me that your sin is in many ways out of your control because you are a victim. Because you were exposed to naked women in person and print as a young boy, you have simply decided that you are a slave to lust. Because you have a stressful job, you have decided that you are a slave to sin and the pressures of your job push you to sin. Because your parents were perverted, you have excused yourself as some sort of genetic victim who is sexually deviant. You don't see yourself as a willful rebel but rather as a slave to your DNA, as if there were some pervert gene that was passed on to you, thereby giving you permission to have sex everywhere from public bathrooms to hotel rooms with perfect strangers.

But you are a slave—a slave to sin. Because you are a slave, Thomas, I want to tell you a story of slavery from the Bible and then explain how it could be a prototype for your life.

In the book of Exodus, millions of people were enslaved to a king named Pharaoh who ruled over the most powerful nation on the earth, Egypt. He was worshiped as a god and he brutally mistreated the people whom he enslaved. Those people cried out to the real God for freedom, and he heard their pleas. God raised up a man named Moses to speak on his behalf to Pharaoh, demanding that the slaves be set free in order to live new lives in worship to the real God. God graciously but authoritatively called Pharaoh to righteousness, but Pharaoh became hard-hearted under God's provocation, just as God said he would, and he refused to release the people from their brutal slavery. As a result, God sent a succession of plagues as judgments and warnings upon Pharaoh, kindly giving him many opportunities to repent and do what God demanded.

Pharaoh repeatedly refused to repent of his ways and release the people, so God sent a terrible series of judgments upon the entire nation. The wrath of God was eventually poured out on the firstborn son of every household, all killed in one night. The only households spared from the death of their firstborn son were those families who, in faith, took a young, healthy lamb without blemish or defect and slaughtered it as a substitute and then took its blood and used it to cover the doorposts around the entry to their home. As a result, the wrath of God passed over them and was diverted, because of the lamb.

At this point, Thomas, I am sure you are wondering why I would tell you this story. It is because you also are a slave and, like the people in Moses' day, you are completely unable to free yourself from slavery and are facing both death and the wrath of God. Like the Israelites, you need God to show up in power and liberate you to a new life. Thankfully, no matter whether the powerful oppressor is Pharaoh or your lusts, nothing is more powerful than the living God.

Simply, as a slave, you need to be redeemed from your slavery. *Redemption* is synonymous with being liberated, freed, or rescued from bondage and slavery to a person or thing. The word *redemption* and its derivatives (e.g., *redeemer*, *redeem*) appear roughly 150 times in the English Bible with roughly only twenty occurrences in the New Testament. The prototype for redemption is the Exodus story. You can confirm this for yourself by looking up the many Bible verses that present Exodus as the prototype of redemption, including Exodus 15:1–18; Deuteronomy 7:8; 15:15; 2 Samuel 7:23; 1 Chronicles 17:21; Isaiah 51:10; and Micah 6:4.

Thomas, you need to be delivered from the sin that rules over you like a mighty Pharaoh. For this to happen, you need a redeemer to redeem you. The theme of God the Redeemer echoes throughout the Old Testament (Ps. 78:35; Isa. 44:24; 47:4; 48:17; 63:16; Jer. 50:34; Hos. 7:13; 13:14). At the birth of Jesus, it is prophesied that he is God the Redeemer (Luke 1:68; 2:38). Paul also speaks of Jesus as our Redeemer (Rom. 3:24; 1 Cor. 1:30; Gal. 3:13–14; 4:4–5; Eph. 1:7; Titus 2:13–14). In each case, redemption comes against the background of helplessness. In each instance we see human beings captured and held captive by forces they cannot overcome. Only by the intervention of a powerful third party can bondage be broken and the enslaved person be set free. The only redeemer available to you is Jesus. The Scriptures repeatedly and emphatically declare that the one true God, Jesus Christ alone, is able to liberate you from false little gods like lust and pride that rule over you.

Furthermore, in Exodus, people were spared the wrath of God because they were literally covered by the blood of the lamb. This clearly points to Jesus who was, like the Exodus lamb, young, healthy, and without defect, which symbolizes the sinlessness of Jesus (Heb. 9:12–14). Jesus' blood was shed for your sins. Echoing the Exodus, Jesus is called "the Lamb of God, who takes away the sin of the world!" (John 1:29). The Bible also declares, "Worthy is the Lamb [Jesus] who was slain" (Rev. 5:12).

Thomas, when Jesus was crucified and his blood was shed, he suffered and died in your place for your sins so that you could be redeemed from your slavery to sin. First Peter 1:18–19 says it this way: "You were ransomed from the futile ways inherited from your forefathers, not with perishable things such as silver or gold, but with the precious blood of Christ, like that of a lamb without blemish or spot."

Thomas, your only hope is to turn from sin to trust in Jesus so that he can be your redeemer who liberates you from your slavery. Even before his birth it was prophesied by both a man named Zechariah and a woman named Anna that Jesus was God coming into human history to redeem sinners from slavery (Luke 1:68; 2:38). In Paul's letter to Titus he says, "Jesus Christ . . . gave himself for us to redeem us," and to the Romans Paul wrote, "redemption . . . is in Christ Jesus" (Titus 2:13–14; Rom. 3:24). Many more examples of Jesus being offered as the redeemer of slaves are scattered throughout the New Testament (1 Cor. 1:30; Gal. 3:13–14; 4:4–5; Eph. 1:7).

During all of your foolish sin, you have been deceived into thinking that you are free to do as you please. However, the truth is that you have lived as a slave to Satan and demons, your sinful flesh, and the world; that is, the depraved aspects of culture that lure you to sin and away from Jesus. The other side of your deception is that you are helpless before your lusts. There's nothing you can do to get free, so you just give up.

The good news is that God is more powerful than anything, including your sinful desires. If you turn from sin and trust in Jesus, God the Holy Spirit will indwell you. As a result, you will receive a new power by which to say no to your sinful desires and yes to the holy desires of God. Unless you become a Christian, your sin will continue until it leads to death and the wrath of God being poured out upon you eternally in hell.

Satan wants you to sin, and he wants that sin to kill your marriage, kill your family, kill your health, and ultimately bring you to an eternal hell with him. Only through Jesus can you be redeemed from your slavery to Satan, sin, death, and hell. Colossians 1:13–14 says it this way: "He has delivered us from the domain of darkness and transferred us to the kingdom of his beloved Son, in whom we have redemption, the forgiveness of sins." Thomas, you have been living in darkness with Satan, doing evil and hiding from Jesus, your wife, and your own conscience. Jesus wants to forgive your sins so, as a redeemed man, you can be free to live a new life under his rule.

Currently it is your flesh, and not God your Creator, that is your ruler. When the Bible speaks of your flesh, it is not speaking of your physical body per se, but rather that seed of foolish rebellion in you that enjoys defying God and living as a slave to sin. You inherited that seed from your first father, Adam, and without Jesus saving you from yourself, you will continue to sin until God crushes you as he did Pharaoh. Only through the forgiveness of Jesus can you say no to sin and yes to God and walk away from your slavery to sin. Romans 6:6–7 says, "We know that our old self was crucified with him in order that the body of sin might be brought to nothing, so that we would no longer be enslaved to sin. For one who has died has been set free from sin."

In speaking with you, I was angered, shocked, and saddened that you did not really want to change but merely did not want to get caught.

Despite the absolute horror that is your life, you still believe the demonic lie that you are living a great life marked by power, wealth, and sex with lots of beautiful women. The hard truth is that your life is pathetic, demonic, empty, and dead. If you turn from sin to Jesus you will see that Jesus has "ransomed [you] from the futile ways" (1 Pet. 1:18).

There is nothing redeemed about your life; it is instead a very boring, typical, evil, and worldly way of existing. You started looking at porn and smoking weed in junior high. You started messing around with girls in your early teens. You dated multiple women in your twenties, having sex with all of them and being faithful to none of them.

In your late twenties you shacked up with some young woman whom you fooled into thinking you wanted to marry. By your thirties you thought it was time to get married, so you grabbed the youngest, hottest woman who would marry you and cheated on her until she left you.

After a few years you got bored with the bachelor life and married again so that you could have legitimate children. You left your wife at home to raise your kids while you went back to acting like a junior high kid some more.

Today, with your life more than half over, you have done nothing but drive around the same cul de sac of stupidity. Jesus needs to save you from your "futile" way of life before you end up divorced again, declaring war on your wife in court to keep your money and kids, and then heading out to do it all over again.

In conclusion, your sin of self-esteem is so high that you are as proud, hard-hearted, and stubborn as Pharaoh. You actually smirked when you explained to me all the women you have slept with, as if you were proud of all the notches on your bedpost, and as if I was supposed to be impressed. You need to be redeemed from the inside out. Your life is little more than your heart showing forth the sad truth that you are not connected to God but rather to Satan, demons, sin, and death. God is as angry with you as he was with Pharaoh.

My prayer is that you will come to your senses and give your sin to Jesus as the Lamb who shed his blood for your sins before it is too late and you find yourself bound in the chains of hell. Through his victory over Satan, demons, and sin, Jesus alone can and will redeem you. For this you need to follow five steps.

1) *Conviction.* God made you with a conscience to guide your decision making through life and make you feel guilty when you do wrong. Because of your ongoing life of sin, though, you have so ignored God's conviction that your conscience is broken, and you have no moral compass. You must no longer rely on what you think is moral or immoral, because your mind is completely corrupt. To renew your mind, you must spend considerable time reading the Bible. I would recommend that you start by reading Genesis to see how generation after generation of foolish men have brought so much sin and pain into the world by living in the same sort of sin that you do. I also want you to see how some of those men turned to God in faith and were transformed and blessed by God, so that you can see what Jesus alone can accomplish for you.

When you have finished Genesis you can then read Exodus to see how you will be either redeemed like God's people or crushed like Pharaoh. If you read your Bible accurately you will find that you end up feeling condemned, evil, and horribly messed up. This is not because the Bible is bad, but rather because you are bad and are not doing what the Bible says. God the Holy Spirit, through the Bible, needs to bring to you the gift of conviction so that you see and feel the gravity of your sin.

2) *Confession.* As the Holy Spirit convicts you of sin and renews your mind, you must then name your sin as God does and accept that you are a sinner, pervert, adulterer, drunk, and a hard-hearted, proud man enslaved to Satan and sin. Confession means agreeing with God and telling the truth about who we are and what we have done—something I'm not sure you have ever done. You need to confess all of your sins to Jesus. You also need to sit down with your wife and confess all of your sins to her. You must do this without blaming anyone else for your sin, excusing it, minimizing it, or only partially confessing it. While conviction is a gift God gives to you, confession is your response, which then prepares you for a life of repentance, restitution, and reconciliation. Lastly, you must contact any of the women that you are able to find and confess your sin to them and ask their forgiveness, along with their husbands', so that your confession can be complete.

3) *Repentance.* The heart of repentance is changing your mind about who is god in your life. You need to turn away from the pathetic gods of sex, power, and thrills and turn to Jesus, the true and living God, who alone loves you enough to die for you and your freedom. You must

learn to continually repent by turning your face to Jesus and your back on sin. You must stop trying to manage your sin but put it to death before it puts you to death. Colossians 3:5 says it perfectly: "Put to death therefore what is earthly in you: sexual immorality, impurity, passion, evil desire, and covetousness, which is idolatry." Repentance for you will include going to a biblical counselor for intensive help in stopping your life of sin and beginning a new life as a slave to righteousness. Repentance for you will also include setting up accountability software on your computer(s) so that a godly friend can see if you are living a life of repentance, traveling with a male assistant for business who ensures you are not doing evil, and getting into a rehabilitation program that is based upon redemption through the cross of Jesus, the truth of the Bible, and the support of the church.

4) *Restitution*. Your sin has stolen a great deal from others. For example, you have stolen trust, love, time, intimacy, oneness, and joy from your wife and children. Further, some of the women you slept with and knew personally were married, which was stealing something that belonged to their husband alone. Thomas, I want to make clear that restitution is not something you do so that God will forgive you. The Bible is clear that your redemption is a gift of grace from Jesus alone to be received by you through personal faith in him (Eph. 2:8–10). The result of this gift of salvation is a humility and an ongoing life of good works, not so that Jesus will redeem you but because he has.

These good works will include your seeking to make restitution for all that you have done to damage others. Parts of the Bible, for example, Exodus 22:1–17 and Numbers 5:5–10, speak of this kind of repayment, and men such as the rich people in Nehemiah and Zacchaeus in the New Testament modeled it when they repaid the people they had stolen from. For you, this may look like taking a job that does not require you to travel so much so that you can spend more time with your children and prayerfully considering how you can support your wife so that she can meet with a pastor and get the help she needs.

5) *Reconciliation*. Once the previous steps are undertaken, the sin that separated people is forgiven and taken away by Jesus with the hope that they can be brought back together in loving and trusting relationship. For you, this may take many years, if it is to happen at all. Your wife wants a separation from you because all trust is broken, and she will

likely pursue a divorce. I do not know if your wife, unlike Jesus, will forgive you, ever trust you again, or ever take you back. So, you must not turn to Jesus to use him to save your marriage. Instead, you must be reconciled to God through Jesus and see what happens next. Despite all that you have done, it is possible that, if you and your wife pursue Jesus, he could bring you together. No matter what, if you do become a Christian by committing yourself to the lifelong pursuit of the process I have outlined, then reconciliation with your Christian wife will happen, although it may not be in this lifetime.

Thomas, writing this letter to you has been painful for me. As I write I keep thinking of the beautiful, devoted wife and kids that God has given you. I also keep thinking of the health and wealth that you possess and cannot find a logical reason why you are not happy, content, and satisfied. There is just something sick, evil, and corrupt in you that must die.

What scares me most is that I am so very much like you. We both grew up poor. We both grew up as highly competitive jocks. We both grew up smarter and tougher than most of the people we knew. We both saw our first porn magazine at an early age. We both had sex with our first girlfriend in our teens. We both had violent tempers that intimidated other people. We both graduated with honors as good students and respected leaders. We both went to college intent on fighting, partying, and having a lot of sex with hot girls.

Yet, unlike you, Jesus grabbed me by the neck and redeemed me from the life I was pursuing. I thought I would get married some day, have a few kids, make a lot of money running some company, commit adultery and look at porn on the side (but seek to manage it so that it did not affect my family), lose my temper now and then to cuss out my wife and kids, and still attend church occasionally, because I considered myself a good spiritual person.

Since Jesus redeemed me from the life I was headed for, things could not be more different. To be honest, I am actually quite surprised that I have been faithful to my wife since I met her in 1988. I'm equally surprised that I have not been in a fight since Jesus redeemed me.

The truth is that you and I are exactly alike in every way but one. Despite the fact that I have not lived in sexual sin as you have, the Bible says that regardless of all the "good" things I did as a non-Christian, I was corrupt and dominated by sinful desires at the core. By redeeming me from one way of life and redeeming me to another way of life, though, Jesus has done something remarkable for me and has saved me from myself. My life is going well; much better, in fact, than the life I had planned for myself. He has given me a new heart so my deepest desires are like his. None of it, however, is the result of my own doing, because I am not a great guy; rather, Jesus is a great God.

Thomas, as I heard your story some weeks ago, as I have prayed for you since, and as I write this letter today, I have to confess that it has really troubled me that, apart from Jesus, I think we're basically the exact same guy. I don't like to admit it, but we are pretty much the same except for the one difference that makes all the difference—Jesus has redeemed me. So, I'm praying that you turn from sin to him so that he can redeem you as well. If you do, let me know. Until then, I will pray. It all comes down to you and Jesus. You are more evil than you have ever feared, and more loved than you have ever hoped.

# Answers to Common Questions about Redemption

*Is it true that the concept of redemption in Scripture was actually a concept borrowed from pagan religions?*

Sadly, it has been commonly taught by some Christian theologians, e.g., Origen, since the early days of the church that the concept of redemption was adopted from the pagan slave market where a price was paid to free a slave. This led to wild speculation that Jesus died to pay off Satan, which is preposterous because Jesus owes Satan nothing.

Present-day liberal theologians have wrongly argued that because redemption was a concept taken from paganism, the Bible endorses paganism. Therefore, to accommodate current paganism, they recast Jesus' work on the cross according to modern pagan thinking, such as goddess worship, radical environmentalism, feminism, postmodernism, and other religions.

*Redemption* is synonymous with being liberated, freed, or rescued from bondage and slavery to a person or thing. The prototype for redemption is not the pagan slave market, but rather the deliverance of God's people from slavery and tyranny under Pharaoh, also known as the Exodus. There, God liberated his people but in no way paid off the satanic Pharaoh. God simply crushed him. Exodus 6:6 is one of many Bible verses that present Exodus as the prototype of redemption: "Say therefore to the people of Israel, 'I am the LORD, and I will bring you out from under the burdens of the Egyptians, and I will deliver you from slavery to them, and I will redeem you with an outstretched arm and with great acts of judgment'" (see also, Ex. 15:1–18; Deut. 7:8; 15:15; 2 Sam. 7:23; 1 Chron. 17:21; Isa. 51:10; Mic. 6:4).

Redemption in the Old Testament is God going to Pharaoh, demanding he release the Israelites, destroying Pharaoh when he refused, and taking God's people to their home. You can see how this applies to the atonement. God never gives legitimacy to the Devil or pays a price to him. God destroys the power and finally the person of the Devil. This is called the triumph theory of atonement.

Lastly, the New Testament writers clearly learned their theology not from contemporary culture or religions but from God's revelation (Gal. 1:11–15). When you go to the Bible, you see a God very different from the gods of the religions and a salvation uniquely based on redemption in Jesus Christ.

### Isn't redemption pretty normal in the world's religions?

It is not. In fact, of all the world's great religious writings, only the Bible presents God acting out of his love and power to come and redeem humans from bondage. This unique theme of redemption portrays humanity helplessly entrapped in sin and reveals a God whose love moves him to intervene. At his own expense, he paid the price needed to win our release from self, sin, and Satan.

### What has Jesus redeemed us from and to?

Jesus has redeemed us from and to many things, including the following:

- Jesus has redeemed us from the curse of the law to live transformed lives by the power of God the Holy Spirit (Gal. 3:13).
- Jesus has redeemed us from Satan and demons to a new life made possible by the forgiveness of all our sins (Col. 1:13–14).
- Jesus has redeemed us from our sinful flesh to live a new life of freedom by the power of the Holy Spirit (Rom. 6:6–12).
- Jesus has redeemed us from being dead to God and alive to sin to being dead to sin and alive to God (Gal. 6:14–15).

Furthermore, Jesus has redeemed us to the following things, which we await:

- Life forever with God (Ps. 49:15);
- The return of Jesus (Job 19:25);
- A resurrection body (Rom. 8:23).

# CHAPTER THREE

# "My Wife Slept with My Friend": Jesus Is Luke's New Covenant Sacrifice

*You were ransomed from the futile ways inherited from your forefathers, not with perishable things such as silver or gold, but with the precious blood of Christ, like that of a lamb without blemish or spot.*

1 PETER 1:18-19

**Luke and his wife were relatively new Christians** who were trying hard to learn their Bibles and reorganize their lives to honor Jesus. They were only a few weeks away from the birth of their first child when Luke's wife confessed to him her darkest and most shameful secret.

She told him that before her recent conversion to Jesus, she had slept with one of his good friends. To make matters worse, much of their sin occurred in Luke's own home while he was away at work laboring lovingly to provide for his family.

Upon hearing what his wife had done, he was understandably filled with rage, humiliation, and panic. His rage was directed at his supposed friend and his adulterous liar of a wife. His humiliation was caused by the thought that he was oblivious to what was happening under his own roof and that he was intimate with his wife in the same bed where she had been with his friend, sometimes only hours prior. His panic was due to feeling trapped by the forthcoming birth of his child. As a new Christian, the last thing he wanted was to have his child grow up in yet another broken home, which meant he felt trapped in a marriage to a wife who had made herself his enemy.

Another pastor and I met with the couple immediately after his wife confessed her sin in deep repentance. Tears flowed down her face and soaked the front of her shirt. Her breathing was so heavy that I feared she would hyperventilate. She was a deeply broken woman whom the Holy Spirit had brought under deep conviction. She was panicked with fear as her mind raced through the various ways in which her husband could respond. Would he kill his friend? Would he divorce her and leave her as yet another single-mother statistic? Would she be stuck in a loveless marriage with a distant and bitter husband who tormented her by withholding forgiveness for the rest of her life?

We were in one of those moments in which they would each choose a path that would affect the rest of their lives and the lives of their child and grandchildren. I tenderly kissed her on the top of her head and told her I loved her and that she had done the right thing in confessing her sin. I also encouraged her to make a full and complete confession so that there could be hope for the wound to heal without having to be reopened later by further revelations of sin.

I took Luke into my office, and he sat down in the chair. He was as furious as I have ever seen any man. His hands clenched as he gripped the chair arms. He was breathing heavily and his heart rate was obviously high. His eyes were focused and not blinking. His teeth were clenched behind pursed lips.

I asked him the simple question, "What do you want?"

"I want blood," he replied.

"You deserve it," I said. "They both should die."

I then went on to explain the doctrine of new covenant sacrifice to Luke. I tried to explain that he got his blood at the cross of Jesus. This letter is a further articulation of this great truth to my dear friend and his lovely bride.

◎　◎　◎　◎　◎

## Dear Luke,

On that darkest of days when we sat in my office, you said, "I want blood." I have meditated on that desire for many months since our discussion and have come to a conclusion. Your answer was wonderful. As a new Christian, you possessed the raw masculine integrity that so many docile, neutered church guys have had pressed out of them under the weight of trying to be cheery in the hideous name of pleasantness, as if Jesus himself was little more than a well-medicated greeter at Wal-Mart.

Your desire for blood was in fact born out of your sense of justice as an image bearer of a just God. God continually feels righteous anger, as you did, because he too is continually sinned against. Throughout the Bible, our sin against God is often explained in terms of adultery. Our sin, in a very real way, is even more horrific than how your wife and alleged friend betrayed you.

God understands exactly how you feel. Though not to minimize what your wife has done in any way, your sin against God is even more painful for him to bear than your wife's sin against you. Therefore, I would encourage you not only to look at the sin of your wife but also to look at your own sin in other parts of your life to see where you too have betrayed God as your wife has betrayed you. In this you will not minimize her sin, but you will add to your sense of justice and heart of mercy as God teaches you to deal with her sin in a way that is patterned after the way in which he has dealt with your sin against him.

Because God is holy, good, and just, he not only feels angry about sin but also deals with it in ways that are holy, good, and just. One example from the old covenant that pertains to your situation is Leviticus 20:10, which says, "If a man commits adultery with the wife of his neighbor, both the adulterer and the adulteress shall surely be put to death."

Your statement, "I want blood," has got me thinking a lot about blood lately. It's not something I generally like to meditate on, but it is important because the Bible is one bloody book. One scholar says that blood is mentioned some 362 times in the Old Testament, most often in reference to bloody sacrifices and bloody, violent death. He also says that the New Testament speaks of blood some ninety-two times, also most often in relation to bloody and violent death.

One old British theologian I remember reading said that blood is spoken of in the New Testament three times more frequently than the cross of Jesus Christ. He went on to say that also in the New Testament blood is spoken of five times more frequently than the death of Jesus Christ. He further argued that blood is the most common means by which the Scriptures refer to the death of Jesus.

Most people get squeamish at the thought of blood and don't like to talk about it. I can still remember attending church as a new Christian and being completely confused as to how people could sing songs about blood with smiles on their faces.

Nonetheless, most folks don't even like to think about blood. This is understandable because when blood is outside the body, it is associated with suffering, pain, and death. We naturally find such things troubling, horrifying, and disturbing. This is in part because blood is a powerful reminder of our mortality; without blood we return to the dust of the earth.

Throughout Scripture, Luke, blood is inextricably connected with sin for two primary reasons. First, shed blood reminds us that sin results in death. Second, God is sickened by sin, which causes death, a connection first made in Genesis 2:17 and repeated throughout the Bible. So when God sees blood, it points to the sickening reality of sin and death. Leviticus 17:11 says it this way: "For the life of the flesh is in the blood, and I have given it for you on the altar to make atonement for your souls, for it is the blood that makes atonement by the life." Blood is sacred, epitomizing the life of the sacrificial victim given as substitute for the sinner's death. Practically every sacrifice included the sprinkling or smearing of blood on an altar, thus teaching that atonement involves the substitution of life for life.

The Old Testament makes frequent reference to the theme of blood to prepare people for the coming of Jesus to die for our sins. In fact, it was God who shed the first blood in human history in response to sin. In Genesis 3, when our first parents Adam and Eve committed the original human sin, it was God who slaughtered an animal to make clothes to cover their nakedness. From then on blood sacrifices were the standard way to worship God. Following the flood, Noah's first act was to shed the blood of an animal as a sacrifice to God, showing that he too was a sinner who deserved to die in the flood, but God had saved him by grace (Gen. 8:20). Immediately upon entering his new land, Abraham built an altar so that he could worship God with sacrifices (Gen. 12:7–8; 13:4, 8). Job, who probably lived in the same era as Abraham, offered sacrifices for his sins and the sins of his children (Job 1:5; 42:7–9). Other major biblical figures with bloody hands include Isaac, Jacob, and the priests.

One of the bloodiest books of the Bible is Exodus. There, God's people were enslaved to the godless king Pharaoh, and God saved them by shedding a lot of blood. The people were given two choices. One, they could repent of sin, place their faith in God, and demonstrate their faith by slaughtering an animal and covering the doorposts of their home in blood. If this was done, then God promised to pass over (hence the related feast of Passover) their house and not kill the firstborn son in the home, but rather accept the substitution of the life of the sacrificial animal. Two, they could fail to repent of their sin and to place their faith in God and see death come to their home. On that night in Egypt, much blood was shed and death came to every home, as either the blood of a substitute animal was shed for the sinners, or the firstborn son in each home was put to death by God.

One of the major functions of the Old Testament temple was the slaughtering of animals, as seen by the stream of blood that often flowed out of the temple. Blood is, in fact, a major aspect of Old Testament religion. There were some eleven different sacrifices that fit into one of four groupings (burnt offerings, peace offerings, sin offerings, or guilt offerings), and sacrifices were made both in the morning and evening, all of which involved blood.

The most holy day of the year was the Day of Atonement. On that day, the high priest would represent the sinful people and enter the Holy Place in the temple to atone for the sins of the nation through the shedding of blood. He would undertake a meticulous threefold process involving a lot of blood. First, the high priest would take a young bull and slaughter it as a sin offering for himself and his family. He took some of the blood into the Most Holy Place, sprinkling it before the Lord in a most careful process. Any mistake or omission meant instant death.

Once the high priest was cleansed, he took two goats, which together represent the two-part work of sacrifice for the people of Israel. Together they showed the horror of sin. He cast lots, choosing one to show that every person was a sinner deserving death. He slaughtered it and went once again into the Most Holy Place, sprinkling some of the blood on the sacred altar, just as he done with the bull. This was to deal with the offense sin brings to the Lord. Then he would lay his hands on the other goat and confess the sins of the nation, showing that they were filthy because of their sin. He would send that goat away, showing that God takes our sin away, cleansing us of our defilement.

Finally, he offered a ram as the normal sin offering, once again showing that sin leads to death. The slaughter of the innocent animals was to atone for the different dimensions of human sin.

Luke, this entire old covenant process was symbolic in that it ultimately pointed to Jesus' death. It was a preparatory, temporary teaching tool that God used to prepare his people for the coming of Jesus, who paid for our sin through his blood on the cross. Faithful Israelites put their faith in God and his promised Messiah, not in the mechanics of the sacrificial system; their faith was ultimately in the coming of Jesus to shed his blood for their sin.

Despite all of this bloodshed, the Old Testament sacrificial system was never meant to be something sufficient in itself. When Israel misunderstood the purpose of the sacrifices, putting their faith in the sacrifices themselves, there were major problems. The first problem was that the bloodshed of a substituted animal did not forgive human sin (Ps. 51:16; Mic. 6:6–8; Heb. 10:4). The second problem was that it enabled hypocrisy; people could undergo external rituals, such as offering a sacrifice, without truly repenting of sin and trusting in God internally (1 Sam. 15:22; Prov. 15:8; Hos. 6:6). The third problem was that it was only preparatory and therefore incomplete until the coming of Jesus, who made the better new covenant possible (Heb. 7:22; 8:5–7, 13).

This theme of blood, like every theme of Scripture, finds its fulfillment in the coming of Jesus Christ into human history. Early in Jesus' life, his cousin John saw Jesus coming and declared, "Behold, the Lamb of God, who takes away the sin of the world!" (John 1:29). This taking away, of course, would be accomplished when Jesus was slaughtered on the cross where his blood flowed freely.

The prophecy of John was echoed by Jesus at the Last Supper with his disciples:

> Now as they were eating, Jesus took bread, and after blessing it broke it and gave it to the disciples, and said, "Take, eat; this is my body." And he took a cup, and when he had given thanks he gave it to them, saying, "Drink of it, all of you, for this is my blood of the covenant, which is poured out for many for the forgiveness of sins." (Matt. 26:26–28)

Jesus promised that by going to the cross and shedding his blood, sins would finally be forgiven forever.

If we visualize the Bible's revelation of Jesus' crucifixion, it seems that Jesus must have been a bloody mess. Jesus likely began bleeding when an angry mob of thugs surrounded him, beat him, and punched him in the face so that blood flowed from his mouth and nose. The Bible records that Jesus was scourged. What that means is that a whip with multiple strands of leather with metal or bone hooks on the ends was repeatedly whipped across the entire body of Jesus. Those hooks dug into Jesus' back, thighs, and buttocks. As the hooks were ripped away, they took flesh, muscle, and possibly even bones with them. This scourging nearly killed Jesus and by this point he was a bloody mess, in fulfillment of the prophecy in Isaiah 52:14 that says, "As many were astonished at you—his appearance was so marred, beyond human semblance, and his form beyond that of the children of mankind."

Jesus' beard was then pulled from his face in fulfillment of the prophecy of Isaiah 50:6. This act of ancient disgrace caused even more blood to flow from the body of Jesus. The bleeding had only begun, despite the fact that Jesus' nearly naked body was covered in blood and he was a disgustingly horrifying bloody mess.

A crown of thorns likely a few inches in length was then pressed into the skull of Jesus and blood poured down his face. Nails were pounded through Jesus' hands and feet as he was hung on a wooden cross.

Hanging there, Jesus continued to bleed until he died. In addition, as if Jesus had not shed enough blood already, a spear was thrust into his side and blood along with water poured out of his heart sac.

Luke, the results of Jesus' shed blood are staggering. Hebrews 9:22 says, "Indeed, under the law almost everything is purified with blood, and without the shedding of blood there is no forgiveness of sins." First Peter 1:18–19 also says, "You were ransomed from the futile ways inherited from your forefathers, not with perishable things such as silver or gold, but with the precious blood of Christ, like that of a lamb without blemish or spot."

Today, in the new covenant, we no longer need a priest because we have Jesus, who is our Great High Priest (Heb. 2:17; 4:14–15). We no longer need to offer blood sacrifices because Jesus is our sacrifice for sin (John 1:29). We no longer need to visit the temple to be near to God because Jesus is our temple (Rev. 21:22). We no longer need to celebrate the Passover because Jesus is our Passover (1 Cor. 5:7). Finally, we no longer need to live in habitual sin because, through Jesus, we have been made holy and have been given new life (Heb. 9:26; 10:10).

Luke, you wanted blood and through Jesus you got it. Jesus shed his blood for your wife and her horrendous sins. He suffered in her place and paid the penalty that she should have paid. As a result, Jesus has forgiven your wife's sins, cleansed her from the filthy stain of her sins, and redeemed her from her sinful and empty way of life. As a Christian, her sins have been covered by the blood of Jesus.

Now, some years after her confession of adultery, I am profoundly glad for the blood of Jesus that has given you the wife you always dreamed of, even though your dream came true through the horror you always feared. Today you are a truly blessed man. Your wife belongs to Jesus and has become a new woman through her new covenant relationship with him. She is a lovely, devoted wife who has been faithful to you as a Christian and has given you a beautiful family. She sits at your side to worship Jesus with you in church and to teach the Bible with you as a fellow church leader. You and your wife have a depth of understanding and appreciation for the gospel that few Christians do.

I am reminded of this every time I see you and your wife standing together in church serving communion. As she holds the cup of wine that symbolizes Jesus' blood, it makes me glad because she truly knows what his blood has accomplished. She knows that she has been justified "by his blood" (Rom. 3:25), that the blood of Jesus "cleanses us from all sin" (1 John 1:7), and that Jesus "loves us and has freed us from our sins by his blood" (Rev. 1:5).

Luke, as your friend and pastor I am deeply grieved by the sins your wife and your former friend committed against you. I can only imagine the righteous anger that wells up in you on the occasions that you see in your imagination the things your alleged friend did with your wife in your own bed. When you are haunted by the thought of your friend betraying you with a kiss, it will be important for you to get some time to prayerfully talk it through with Jesus Christ. As Hebrews 4:15 says, Jesus can and does "sympathize" with you. You will remember that Jesus had a good "friend" named Judas who also betrayed him with a kiss. Rather than ever repenting of his sin and begging for forgiveness, Judas went out, threw a rope over a tree, and hanged himself. In Acts

1:18–19, Peter tells us that Judas's body burst open and his bloody intestines spilled out. Subsequently, the place where Judas hanged himself after betraying his friend with a kiss was called the "Field of Blood."

I am sure that, as a man who appreciates justice, the temptation to make your former friend bleed in his own "Field of Blood" for what he has done is very strong. I would encourage you not to let your anger lead you into sin but rather to remember that one way or another you will get your blood from him also. Either he will come to repentance of his sin and faith in Jesus so that he can be saved through Jesus' blood shed on the cross, or he will stand before Jesus to be condemned. On this point, Romans 5:8–10 is insightful:

> God shows his love for us in that while we were still sinners, Christ died for us. Since, therefore, we have now been justified by his blood, much more shall we be saved by him from the wrath of God. For if while we were enemies we were reconciled to God by the death of his Son, much more, now that we are reconciled, shall we be saved by his life.

Paul's words speak of what Jesus has accomplished for you through his shed blood. Conversely, they also speak of what your friend will not enjoy if he fails to repent of his sin and receive Jesus.

First, God does not have a heart of grace toward him, because he is an unrepentant sinner. Second, Christ's death has not applied to him and will not until and unless he repents of sin and receives Jesus. Third, he is not justified and, therefore, stands guilty and condemned before God. Fourth, he is an enemy of God. Fifth, he is not reconciled to God. Sixth, he is not saved from the penalties of sin such as death and hell. Seventh, the wrath of God remains upon him. Eighth, if he continues in unrepentance and unbelief, Jesus' blood will not cover him, and he will spend eternity suffering in conscious, eternal torment.

This is why the Scriptures also speak of a future day of bloodshed when unrepentant sinners will be thrown like grapes into a winepress, and Jesus will stomp them underfoot so that their blood flows as high as the bit in a horse's mouth for one hundred eighty miles (Rev. 14:19–20). Time will tell if your friend finds himself in that dreadful place under the boot of Jesus, but either way you will get your blood, brother.

In the meantime, I want you to move on with your life and seek comfort, hope, and joy in the covenant you have with your wife and the one you and your wife have with God the Father through Jesus Christ by the power of the Holy Spirit. In the Bible the word *covenant* appears more than three hundred times and is therefore essential to rightly understanding how God relates to us. A covenant is a particular relationship that binds people together as one (God and people, or people and people) by promised terms and loving grace. Furthermore, every covenant has a head, and that person is primarily responsible to ensure that the terms of the covenant are kept.

Both the Old and New Testaments speak of the new covenant (e.g., Jer. 31:31–34; Matt. 26:28; Luke 22:20; Rom. 11:27; 1 Cor. 11:25; 2 Cor. 3:6; Heb. 7:22; 8:8–13; 9:15; 12:24). The Bible tells us that a new epoch in human history has arrived with the coming of God into human history as the man Jesus Christ. In the new covenant, all of the prophecies, promises, foreshadowing, and longing of the old covenant are fulfilled.

In the new covenant it is Jesus Christ who serves as our covenant head (Eph. 1:10, 22; 4:15; 5:23; Col. 1:18; 2:10, 19). As I have already explained, it is Jesus who went to the cross to shed his blood in your place for your sins so that you could have a new covenant relationship with him. This also is true of your wife, which means that when Jesus shed his blood for her and all of her sins, that included her past, present, and future sins. In particular, this also means that Jesus shed his blood for her adulterous sin against you and God. Thankfully, because Jesus died for her sin, the sin of adultery has not killed your marriage.

As members of the new covenant, you and your wife are continually growing to be more like Jesus by the power of God the Holy Spirit working through your new heart, which is the center of your new identity and new desires. His work in you has been nothing short of amazing. Through your covenant relationship with Jesus you are continually learning how to love your wife and lead your family as a covenant head. The Bible speaks of your relationship with your wife in terms of covenant (Prov. 2:16–17; Mal. 2:14). I am seeing both you and your wife increasingly grow in your understanding of what it means to have a new covenant marriage. As a result, you rightly understand that you, as the husband, are the human covenant head as the Scriptures repeatedly command (Gen. 2:18; 5:2; 1 Cor. 11:2–16; 14:33–34; Eph. 5:21–33; Col. 3:18; 1 Tim. 2:11–15; Titus 2:3–5; 1 Pet. 3:1).

Unlike some foolish men who sinfully misrepresent and misapply this loving principle as a license to be harsh with their wives, an opportunity to rule over their wives in domination, or even to believe that their wives are somehow inferior to them, you have come to understand your role as covenant head in light of Jesus. You understand that just as Jesus suffered to be in covenant with you, you too have suffered to be in covenant with your wife—because you love her and continually seek her best. You also rightly understand that, as the covenant head, you bear a greater burden for humble service, love, care, protection, and provision so that Jesus can be experienced by your wife, in part through you.

I doubt you hear this enough, so I want to say it in masculine honor. I am incredibly proud of you as your Christian brother, friend, and pastor. I know that you have suffered greatly, but you have treated your wife according to Jesus' new covenant example. Although she sinned and was at fault for her sin, you took responsibility to ensure that God was honored, repentance was encouraged, gracious forgiveness was extended, transformation was occurring, and the relationship was reconciled through the blood of Jesus Christ. Simply, your wife treated you like God's people in the Old Testament treated him, which is why the Bible repeatedly calls Israel a whore. Yet Jesus lovingly pursues and redeems the church; you have responded to your wife as Jesus responded to his and in so doing have shown the gospel with greater precision and power than most theologians could ever articulate in mere words. For that, I praise Jesus and thank you, my new covenant brother.

## Answers to Common Questions about New Covenant Sacrifice

*All this talk of blood is gross. Why do we have to do that?*

It is gross. But not nearly as gross as the sin it deals with.

Remember that God warned Adam: "You may surely eat of every tree of the garden, but of the tree of the knowledge of good and evil you shall not eat, for in the day that you eat of it you shall surely die" (Gen. 2:16–17). When Eve and Adam decided to disobey and eat, God did not immediately kill them. Rather they chose the deadly course. So God, in his grace and wisdom, instituted sacrifice as a way for someone or something other than us to experience the death. The blood comes as a visible sign that death has occurred; blood is the result of death. So the sprinkling of blood on the altar in the Old Testament, which foreshadowed the shed blood of Jesus, showed the reality of death and that the penalty for sin had been paid.

*Why don't Christians do blood sacrifices today?*

Old Testament sacrifices did not have power to atone for sin. They were symbols of the coming reality of Messiah Jesus. Old Testament believers were saved by their faith in the compassionate grace of the Lord and his Messiah, just as we are today. They were waiting for Jesus' first coming as we are waiting for his second coming. Their sacrifices expressed that faith. You can see this in the Christological significance of the Day of Atonement (Leviticus 16) and in the Lord's refusal to accept sacrifices done without faith (Isaiah 1).

The theological answer to this question is well developed in the book of Hebrews, especially chapters 9 and 10. Now that Jesus has come and has offered the true sacrifice that the Old Testament sacrifices pointed to, there's no need whatsoever to continue doing them: "But when Christ had offered for all time a single sacrifice for sins, he sat down at the right hand of God. . . . For by a single offering he has perfected for all time those who are being sanctified" (Heb. 10:12–14).

*Isn't blood something that pagans use in
their rituals?*

Many do. Pagans understand the connection between sin and death better than many Christians. If you live around pagans, or animists, as they are often called, you may well see them kill animals and use the blood for rituals. However, they go a lot further, actually thinking the power is in the blood itself. For example, in the Roman times followers of the cult of Mithras would kill a large animal, preferably a bull, and drink the blood in a wild feast, thinking that they could receive the bull's power. Try doing a web search for a phrase like "bats' blood power," and you'll see that even modern American pagans still believe in using blood to get power. This magical use of blood has nothing in common with the biblical perspective. Power comes from the Spirit, not from blood.

Some Christians have gotten carried away with blood theology. For example, the Moravians, founded by Count Nicholas Ludwig von Zinzendorf, developed an obsession with blood. They were fascinated with the wound in Jesus' side, calling it the "side hole." All sorts of odd practices and songs came from "side hole" theology. William Cowper's famous 1772 hymn illustrates the fascination with blood:

> *There is a fountain filled with blood*
> *drawn from Emmanuel's veins;*
> *and sinners plunged beneath that flood*
> *lose all their guilty stains.*

The truth is that all sins are forgiven because of Christ's death, symbolized by the blood. But this sort of fascination with blood itself has no resonance with the Bible.

*But Christians drink blood in the Eucharist,
don't they?*

Not at all. Though Catholics mistakenly believe the essence of the Eucharistic wine becomes Jesus' blood, they still believe it is wine to the senses or to a chemist's test. Biblical Christians believe the wine or grape juice used in the Eucharist, or communion, is just that. It is a symbol of the blood Jesus shed on the cross paying the penalty for sin so that we can be completely forgiven. We drink as a sign of our "participation in the blood of Christ" (1 Cor. 10:16). It means we participate in the death of Christ and get the benefits: complete forgiveness of sin because the penalty was paid in full. By faith we join in the sacrifice by which Jesus instituted the new covenant. Joining in communion gives concrete expression of our faith in that sacrifice.

# CHAPTER FOUR

# "I Am a 'Good' Christian": Jesus Is David's Gift Righteousness

*For our sake he made him to be sin who knew no sin, so that in him we might become the righteousness of God.*

2 CORINTHIANS 5:21

**David is, by the standard of most people,** a "good" Christian guy. He shows up on time to his job every day and does what his employer asks of him. He comes home every night to eat dinner with his wife and children. He pays his bills on time every month. He cuts his grass every week and maintains his home like a good neighbor should. He eats healthy food, avoids tobacco and alcohol, and exercises regularly. He goes to church every Sunday without fail and even serves in his church faithfully. He gives 10 percent of his income to God. He votes Republican, pays his taxes, and thinks abortion and gay marriage are both sinful acts. By his own admission, he grew up in a Christian home, made a personal decision to be a Christian while in elementary school, and has been a moral, God-fearing, self-disciplined person his entire life.

Furthermore, the list of things he has not done is rather impressive. He did not have sex before he got married. He did not grow up looking at porn or flirting with girls. He has never tried drugs. He has never been drunk. He has never stolen anything. He has never cheated on his wife. He has never raised a hand in anger against his wife or children.

Yet his wife and children live miserable lives under his leadership. He is a controlling, insecure man who governs his family at a distance with rules instead of relationships. Functionally, his gods are control, comfort, and quiet. Subsequently, he is a distant and passionless Christian, husband, and father. To make matters worse, he is also incredibly self-righteous because he does not truly see himself as a sinner; rather, he sees himself as a mature Christian who avoids certain sins. He conveniently overlooks the fact that he does few of the things that flow out of love for God. He rarely reads his Bible, prays, serves anyone, or repents of any personal sin. He has never shown mercy to the brokenhearted as God does. His religious life has no need for God, but only need for God's rules.

Whether or not he is truly a Christian could be endlessly debated according to various theological traditions. One thing is for sure, though—he has no functional understanding of the gospel of Jesus Christ and, subsequently, no idea how someone can be seen as righteous before a holy and righteous God. This chapter is written to explain the gospel to Dave in hopes of compelling him to see that God not only calls sinners to repent of their unrighteousness, but also religious people like him to repent of their righteousness.

◎     ◎     ◎     ◎     ◎

## Dear David,

I suspect that the subject of this letter will come as quite a shock to you. Nonetheless, my hope in writing it is to articulate to you the good news of the gospel of Jesus Christ. Since childhood, you have thought you not only know but also live according to the gospel. Sadly, as your friend, I must tell you the painful truth that your life does not bear witness to a functional understanding of the gospel, and as a result I am concerned for you and your family.

Dave, you are a very religious man, but I'm not sure you are a Christian man. This was made quite clear to me in a recent discussion with your wife. She loves Jesus very deeply and is also deeply devoted to you and your children. She appreciates the fact that you work hard and provide financially for her and the children. However, she is, frankly, a very miserable woman.

As she spoke through her tears, it became clear that, in her eyes, you love control, comfort, and quiet more than Jesus, her, or the children. She explained how you run your life and your family by a rigid set of unbending rules regarding everything, including time of awaking, time of meals, the fact that meals can include only foods that you enjoy regardless of the desires of other family members, budgeting down to the penny despite the fact that you are financially secure, an exact bedtime every night, and even scheduled sexual activity, as if it were simply an extension of your regimented exercise routine. Meanwhile, your wife and children would occasionally like to deviate from your heavy-handed schedule because it chokes the passion, spontaneity, and joy out of life.

You have somehow lost sight of the fact that some of the objectives of a husband and daddy include having fun, building fond memories, and taking the moments of opportunity that God provides for joy, which is usually not according to schedule. Your dear wife is so constrained by your control mechanisms that she cannot even go out to coffee with her friends because the cash allowance you give her is solely for functional purposes such as groceries and gas, and she has no personal spending money. Your children are also starting to rebel against you when you are not present. They tell their friends and relatives that they enjoy spending time away from your home because they get to have some fun and occasionally eat a treat, and if they pull out blankets to make a fort or laugh really loud they do not get rebuked for making a mess or noise. At the risk of sounding harsh, I think that you are a sinful and spiritually abusive father.

Because of my love for Jesus, you, and your family, I need you to prayerfully consider what the gospel of Jesus Christ truly is because it is your only hope, and Jesus is your only help. I suspect that in hearing that you need the gospel, you may be offended because you would say that you already do know the gospel and have for many years. But I think the words of the great Reformer Martin Luther are helpful on this point. Commenting on Galatians 2:14, Luther wrote, "The truth of the Gospel is the principle article of all Christian doctrine. . . . Most necessary is it that we know this article well, teach it to others, and beat it into their heads continually." Luther's point is that we who have heard the gospel are prone to forget it quite easily and therefore must continually have it beaten into our heads.

Perhaps the most succinct summary of the gospel is found in 1 Corinthians 15:1–4:

> Now I would remind you, brothers, of the gospel I preached to you, which you received, in which you stand, and by which

you are being saved, if you hold fast to the word I preached to you—unless you believed in vain. For I delivered to you as of first importance what I also received: that Christ died for our sins in accordance with the Scriptures, that he was buried, that he was raised on the third day in accordance with the Scriptures.

Here we see that the gospel is continual, in that we must continually be reminded of it; proclamational, in that it must be preached to us often, including preaching it to ourselves; personal, in that we must personally receive it in faith; essential, in that we must continually cling to it alone for the assurance of our salvation; central, in that it is the most important truth in all the world; eternal, in that it is passed on from one generation to the next without modification by religion; Christological, in that it is about the person and work of Jesus Christ alone; penal, in that the wage for sin—death—was paid; substitutional, in that Jesus' death on the cross was literally in our place for our sins; biblical, in that it is in agreement with and the fulfillment of all Scripture; and eschatological, in that the resurrection of Jesus reveals to us our future hope of resurrected eternal life with him.

Furthermore—and this may surprise you—the opposite of the gospel is idolatry. Idolatry is worshiping someone or something other than God. By *worshiping* I mean that we make sacrifices (e.g., time, energy, money, emotion, thought) so that we can give ourselves to someone or something because it is our highest priority. Everyone is a worshiper for the simple reason that we were made by God to worship and cannot help ourselves. But because we are sinners, we are prone to worship created things rather than God the Creator. Romans 1:25 teaches that this is at the root of all paganism/idolatry, saying, "They exchanged the truth about God for a lie and worshiped and served the creature rather than the Creator." This is a complete inversion of the purpose of our creation, which is to worship God and rule over created things as shown in Genesis 1:26–28.

Martin Luther taught that idolatry is, therefore, not just a sin but rather *the* sin that is the cause of all other sins. He went on to argue that the first two of the Ten Commandments bear this out (Ex. 20:1–17). The first two commandments tell us that there is only one God and that we are to worship only that God, which is why we are forbidden from worshiping anything in place of or in addition to the one true God.

Therefore, Luther reasons, we break the other commandments and do such things as lie, covet, steal, or commit adultery only as a result of breaking the first two commandments. If we break the first two commandments, we become idolaters who then worship such things as our image, possessions, comfort, and pleasure instead of God.

The reason that idolatry is so alluring is that idols promise to make life worth living, bring us happiness, and provide for us a sense of righteousness. All of these desires are good, but they become evil when they become our focus rather than Jesus, who alone makes life worth living and gives true joy and righteousness. For you, it seems that control, comfort, and quiet are the idols that you are devoted to worshiping. While an organized home and occasional Sabbath and silence are good things, you have elevated them to a level of god-like status.

Subsequently, your functional concept of heaven is not eternal life with Jesus, but rather a manicured yard, money in the bank, a tidy house, obedient children, a wife without any needs, peace and quiet, eight hours of sleep, dinner on the table at 6:00 PM, time for your hobbies, and functional sex that meets your biological desires. To live in your functional heaven, you have made rigid scheduling, budgeting, rule-making, chart-keeping, silence, cleanliness, orderliness, routine, and predictability your functional saviors that will give you your functional heaven, which has become for your wife and children their hell on earth.

To make matters worse, Dave, you have made your idolatry into a religion that, although you call it Christian, is the exact opposite of the gospel of grace. Therefore, I will outline the ten basic differences between religion and the gospel because I do not believe you functionally understand the difference. Sadly, for the first nineteen years of my life, I lived as a "good," moral, religious person who was good at rule keeping. I never did drugs or drank; I got good grades and in high school was voted as most likely to succeed, man of the year, and student body president. I lettered in sports for four years, edited the school newspaper, and earned college scholarships, but I knew nothing of the gospel of Jesus' grace and how it operated in my life practically. I say this as a man who likewise fell into the trap of rotten religion and is sympathetic.

First, religion says that God will not love me until I obey his rules enough to earn his love. This is akin to my telling my five children, "If you obey all my rules for the next year, then I will be your daddy."

The gospel says that because God has already loved me and expressed this through the person and work of Jesus on the cross, I am now free from sin to live a new obedient life by the power of his love given to me as a free gift. In 1 John 4:7–10 we read:

> Beloved, let us love one another, for love is from God, and whoever loves has been born of God and knows God. Anyone who does not love does not know God, because God is love. In this the love of God was made manifest among us, that God sent his only Son into the world, so that we might live through him. In this is love, not that we have loved God but that he loved us and sent his Son to be the propitiation for our sins.

Jesus loved us through the cross before we loved him, and his love transforms us so that we can love him and love others. Thankfully, this obedience is not what we have to do because of duty, but rather what we get to do in delight. Therefore, unlike with religion, Jesus loves us so that we might obey him rather than demanding that we obey him so that he might love us.

Second, religion says that the world is filled with good people and bad people. Religious people like you then make checklists by which to judge other people and to determine if they are good or bad people. Conveniently, while the exact lists of religious people vary, the one thing they all share is that they generally condemn as bad those who are unlike them while condoning as good people who are like them. Curiously, this phenomenon is clearly seen in political talk radio, which I know you listen to a lot. On the liberal talk radio stations, the liberals are lauded as good people while the conservatives are vilified as bad people. Yet if you tune in to a conservative talk radio station, you will hear the liberals vilified as bad people and the conservatives lauded as good people—on exactly the same issues for exactly the same reasons.

My point is not to endorse a political ideology or issue but rather to say that religion is popular and comes in many forms. However, the Bible clearly says that everyone is a sinner except for Jesus (Isa. 53:6; Rom. 3:23; Heb. 4:15). Therefore, the world is not filled with good people and bad people but rather with sinners who are either repentant and trust in Jesus' death for their life, or sinners who are unrepentant and remain spiritually dead and separated from God under his wrath.

Practically, this means that you too are a sinner who needs to continually repent of sin and trust in Jesus.

Third, religion is about what you do. Because of this, religious people like you like to quantify their righteousness in measurable ways. Meanwhile, because such things as love, patience, kindness, and mercy are not easy to quantify, you do not pursue them as vigilantly as a clean house, regular church attendance, enforced bedtime, and a balanced checkbook. Conversely, the gospel is about what Jesus has done—for you, in you, and through you—by grace.

Fourth, religion is about getting from God. So, in various religious traditions Jesus is offered as the means to an end. Subsequently, the false gospel of religion says that if you come to Jesus, God will make you healthy, wealthy, happy, successful, and so on. In your brand of religion, God exists to give you rules by which you can live a life of sovereign control over your own little kingdom of home. But the real gospel is not about getting what we want from God. Rather, the goal of the gospel is to get God himself, who is our greatest treasure, highest joy, and source of life, whether we are rich or poor, healthy or sick, living or dying, happy or sad. This is perhaps most clearly seen at the cross of Jesus, where Jesus gave nothing less than himself as a gift to us.

Fifth, religion sees hardship as unloving punishment rather than sanctifying discipline. To be sure, God does deal with the sins of Christians. In Scripture we see that this may even include the consequence of death for a rebellious Christian who remains unrepentant. For example, Ananias and Sapphira die in Acts 5:1–11 as a result of stealing from and lying to God. Christians in 1 Corinthians 11:17–34 die as a result of partaking of the Lord's Supper without repenting of sin. Finally, James 5:13–18 indicates that some Christians become sick because of unrepentant sin, and 1 John 5:16 speaks of sin that leads to death.

We must always interpret such instances in light of the character of God. In Hebrews 12:5–13 God reminds us that he is the loving Father who disciplines, chastises, or punishes his children appropriately, sometimes painfully, because he love them. He does it for our good, so we can share his holiness. Some hardship comes from God's hand as a consequence for rebellious sin. However, when he disciplines or chastises, he never condemns us and never breaks relationship with us. He is never cruel, vitriolic, harsh, vindictive, or uncaring with his children.

The emphasis in God the Father's loving discipline is correcting us, which godly punishment does as well. But to punish is to impose a penalty on someone for an offense. For the Christian the eternal penalty is paid in full by Jesus, but the temporal penalty is not. Because of Jesus' death, our spiritual death is taken away completely. Subsequently, God will never break relationship with us either temporally or eternally. But he may well impose temporal penalty for unrepentant sin with the goal of our repentance and correction.

At the cross, the relational penalty of our sin was already paid in the body of Jesus. Consequently, our just God will never again punish us by condemning us or breaking off relationship with us. He imposed that penalty in full on Jesus at the cross. Therefore, when trials and hardship come, we can trust that God will not punish us by walking away and leaving us to do some good work or religious ritual to regain status as his child. His absolute promise is that he will never leave us nor forsake us and will always be with us (Matt. 28:20; Heb. 13:5). David even says, "Even though I walk through the valley of the shadow of death, I will fear no evil, for you are with me" (Ps. 23:4).

Because the Father is good and loving, and because of Jesus' finished work on the cross, God is not condemning us with suffering but will use suffering to sanctify us through affliction and make us more like Jesus, who "learned obedience through what he suffered" (Heb. 5:8). Hebrews 12:1–11 also says that when we are suffering, we are to find encouragement by reminding ourselves of the cross of Jesus so that we will not grow weary or give up. Furthermore, we are told that God is a loving Father who will use the hardships we face in life as opportunities for discipline to grow us in holiness to live lives of ever-increasing righteousness.

Practically, I must say that this truth needs to be immediately incorporated into your parenting. Because you, Dave, are a religious person who has wrongly seen God as someone who is supremely concerned with the rules, you have unmercifully punished your children for breaking rules. You have withdrawn your relationship and love from them, condemning them to make them pay for their wrongdoing. Your children are confused about the gospel because you teach them that Jesus was condemned on the cross for their sins, and then you also condemn them when they sin.

It is imperative that you explain to them that Jesus forgives their sins because he suffered punishment in their place for their sins, and that you are commissioned by God to discipline them when they sin because you love them and want to train them in righteousness. However, this corrective discipline should never be confused as condemnation or severed relationship or withdrawn love because that is a false religious gospel you are demonstrating. I know that you learned this from your religious father, and for that I am deeply sorry. But you must not let the sin of your father rest upon your children. Instead, you must begin parenting out of the gospel.

Sixth, religion is about you. Religion, which rules you, is in contrast to the gospel and very selfish. This explains why you are so difficult to live with. In a word, you think that God, your wife, your children, your friends, your family, and the rest of humanity should obey, honor, glorify, and serve you as a little god. Subsequently, you become very angry when someone drops by unannounced, your children show up to the dinner table late, or your wife's friend calls in the evening because she needs emotional support at the same time that you expect to be waited on.

However, because Jesus has lovingly served us, and we love him, we are to lovingly serve people as Jesus has us. Philippians 2:1–11 says that Jesus is the most unselfish person who has or will ever live, as exemplified by his willingness to live for God's glory and our salvation in spite of his own suffering on the cross. Jesus spoke of himself as our example of dying to self and living for others: "For even the Son of Man came not to be served but to serve, and to give his life as a ransom for many" (Mark 10:45).

Seventh, because, as Jesus said, religion focuses almost entirely on the external, visible life of a person and overlooks the internal, invisible life of the heart where motives lie, how one appears on the outside before people is far more important to the religious person than how one appears on the inside before God. You would never allow yourself to appear fat, disorganized, lazy, or even sinful. You have a hard time repenting of your sin to your wife and children because to confess sin would be to admit that your external, visible life is out of order and would thereby destroy the image you have worked so hard to uphold.

On the other hand, the gospel is concerned first with the state of our internal self. Colossians 3:5 is incredibly helpful on this point, saying,

"Put to death therefore what is earthly *in* you." God who alone knows your heart tells you that the key to your spiritual life is to put to death what is earthly or sinful "in you." Practically, if the gospel is your guiding principle rather than religion, you will not labor so hard to appear as a godly and righteous man on the outside but will humbly confess your sin and live in repentance. First you will be changed on the inside, which will enable you to live a new life on the outside.

Eighth, because religion is about what we do, the end result is that we lack assurance regarding our standing before God. When asked if you are certain that your sins were forgiven at Jesus' cross and that your eternal life is secure, you weakly replied, "I hope so." You are uncertain because if your standing before God is based on your life and good works, then you can never be certain that you have done enough to please God. You thus have no assurance that if you sin tomorrow you will not undo all that you have already done in an effort to make God save you. This kind of false gospel is a demonic cruelty that robs you of the joy that is to be yours through the cross.

The gospel tells us that because our standing before God is contingent on Jesus alone, we can know with assurance that we are secure as redeemed people. First John 5:11–14 says it plainly: "And this is the testimony, that God gave us eternal life, and this life is in his Son. Whoever has the Son has life; whoever does not have the Son of God does not have life. I write these things to you who believe in the name of the Son of God that you may *know* that you have eternal life. And this is the confidence that we have toward him." The gospel says that if you believe in the person of Jesus and his work on the cross, you can know with assurance that your standing before God is secure and therefore live in the joy of that gift.

Ninth, religion simply does not work, because it results in either pride or despair depending on if we think we have done well or poorly in earning our salvation through moral conduct and religious devotion. You have made a list in your mind of what it means to be a good person whom God will love. You have made it your life's ambition, through being rigorously organized and self-disciplined, to make God love you by being a "good" person who does good religious and moral duties as judged solely by external appearances. Because you feel you have done a good job being a moral and religious person, you are now an arrogantly proud man who has little compassion for people who openly struggle with sin. You speak with contempt about drunks and whores and the like who do not have the kind of orderly and godly life that you have.

The hard truth is that pride is the worst sin of all. While the culture we live in renames pride "self-esteem" and labels it a virtue rather than a vice, pride is what got Satan kicked out of heaven and can also keep us from heaven if we fail to repent and believe the gospel.

On the other hand, religion leads to despair for those with the humble honesty to admit that not only do they not fully obey God's laws, but they also break their own little rules all the time. Such people try so very hard to make Jesus happy by paying him back for their sins and by living like him. Yet, no matter how hard they try, they never quite measure up to Jesus' standard of perfection established in Matthew 5:48. I am guessing that there have been just such dark seasons of despair in the private moments of your own life when the Holy Spirit convicts you of your sin.

In addition, I assure you that your wife and children are living in a state of continual despair under your leadership because you rule over them as a religious man following the idolatrous precepts of his own gospel-less religion. Conversely, the gospel alone leads to a humbly confident, joyous obedience because it teaches us that our righteousness is not our own, but rather a gift from Jesus because of his work on the cross, which is my final point of distinction between religion and the gospel.

Tenth, the desire underlying your pursuit of religion is in fact a noble one. David, you simply want to have righteousness. But you have sinfully sought it by the power of your own self-righteousness and not the cross of Jesus, which enables gift righteousness.

The Bible repeatedly says that God is righteous in everything he does, and that there is no righteous God but him alone (Ps. 11:7; Isa. 45:21; Dan. 9:14). To clarify, Scripture uses "righteous" to indicate that God is straight, right, sinless, just, holy, perfect, and good.

As his image bearers, human beings were also made righteous, or what Genesis 1:31 calls "very good" and Ecclesiastes 7:29 calls "upright." However, through the sin of our father Adam in Genesis 3, all of humanity now has his sin imputed or reckoned to them. Romans 5:12–21 teaches that this is because Adam was both our father and our representative.

He voted for sin in our place, similar to a president who chooses to go to war and thus, in a very real sense, includes all of the citizens of his nation in that war since they are directly implicated. Subsequently, we are now conceived with a sin nature, and everyone sins by both nature and choice (Pss. 51:5; 58:3; Rom. 3:23; 1 John 1:10). The result, as Romans 3:10 teaches, is that "None is righteous, no, not one." "Not righteous" or "unrighteous" means that we are the opposite of God—crooked, wrong, sinful, unjust, and lawbreakers.

Because we were created as God's image bearers made for righteousness, we continue to yearn for righteousness. Yet, because we are sinners, we pursue it through self-righteousness. Romans 10:3 says that religious people, "being ignorant of the righteousness of God, and seeking to establish their own . . . did not submit to God's righteousness."

Much of this religious pursuit of self-righteousness is through our own attempts to live by God's laws in addition to our own, just as you have done. Regarding such vain attempts at self-righteousness, Jesus said that "unless your righteousness exceeds that of the scribes and Pharisees, you will never enter the kingdom of heaven" (Matt. 5:20). In the history of the world, it is arguable that no one has been more religiously devoted than the Pharisees who, for example, actually tithed out of their spice rack in an effort to be certain that they gave God a tenth of literally all they had. Our attempts at self-righteousness are as repugnant to our holy and righteous God as giving a bloody tampon to someone as a birthday present (Isa. 64:6).

The good news of the gospel is Jesus Christ, not self. Jesus is our glorious eternal God who humbly became a human being as the second Adam; he came to create a new humanity by taking back through obedience all that was lost through the sin of the first Adam, according to 1 Corinthians 15:45. On the cross, the righteous Jesus died in our place as a substitute for us unrighteous sinners, as 1 Peter 3:18 says: "For Christ also suffered once for sins, the righteous for the unrighteous, that he might bring us to God."

Amazingly, on the cross, Jesus gifted his righteousness to us who are unrighteous. The Bible is emphatic that righteousness does not in any way emanate from us, but rather is given to us by Jesus if we believe, or have faith, in his person and work alone.

Let me point out three things about this gift of righteousness.

First, it is through faith, not rule keeping. Because you have heard Scripture for years but apparently missed this incredibly important truth, I will list a number of very important texts and ask that you carefully and prayerfully read them so that God the Holy Spirit, who inspired them to be written, might illuminate your understanding of them.

> [Abram] *believed* the LORD, and he counted it to him as righteousness. (Gen. 15:6)

> But now the righteousness of God has been manifested apart from the law, although the Law and the Prophets bear witness to it—the righteousness of God through *faith in Jesus Christ* for all who believe. (Rom. 3:21–22)

> Now to the one who works, his wages are not counted as a gift but as his due. And to the one who does not work but *believes in him* who justifies the ungodly, his *faith* is counted as righteousness. (Rom. 4:4–5)

> For Christ is the end of the law for righteousness to everyone who *believes*. (Rom. 10:4)

> And because of him you are *in Christ Jesus,* who became to us wisdom from God, righteousness and sanctification and redemption. (1 Cor. 1:30)

> Indeed, I count everything as loss because of the surpassing worth of knowing Christ Jesus my Lord. For his sake I have suffered the loss of all things and count them as rubbish, in order that I may gain Christ and be found in him, not having a righteousness of my own that comes from the law, but that which comes *through faith in Christ,* the righteousness from God that depends *on faith.* (Phil. 3:8–9)

Dave, you have to give up the illusion of control, which earning God's love through rule keeping gives you. You simply have to trust that God is good to his word and accepts us totally out of his merciful character and the work of Jesus Christ.

My favorite verse on gift righteousness is 2 Corinthians 5:21, which says, "For our sake [God] made [Jesus] to be sin who knew no sin, so that in him we might become the righteousness of God." Martin Luther called this "the great exchange." Jesus took our sin to himself and gave his righteousness to us. Unlike the idolatrous self-righteousness of religion that you have been actively pursuing in vain, this righteousness is passive; it is not something we do, but rather something that Jesus does and we receive by personal faith in him alone.

Second, the righteousness God gives is a status that is imputed, reckoned, attributed, or granted to us. This means that all the sins that severed our relationship with God are forgiven solely because of Jesus' cross. This is a courtroom analogy where we are charged with sin and found guilty and under penalty of physical and spiritual death; yet Jesus takes our penalty to himself and pays our price in full.

Then Jesus' righteousness is imputed to us. This means God grants us the status of being his children. Incredibly, it is the same family status as Jesus'. We are accepted by God because we are in Christ, Ephesians 1 tells us. This is a relational picture, a family analogy where we, who were in the dominion of darkness, were transferred into the kingdom of light, the kingdom of the beloved Son (Col. 1:13). This is what the theologians call justification. It comes from the cross of Jesus Christ alone.

But that's not all, Dave. The gifted righteousness is, thirdly, imparted to us at the time of faith, at the same time as our justification. Not only does God give us family status, but he also gives us new power through the indwelling Holy Spirit. He also gives us a new heart. Biblically, the heart is the control center of the person. Proverbs 4:23 tells us that from the heart flow the springs of life. Because God gives us a new heart, there is a change of the deepest values from which our acts and attitudes come. It is a change of the basic disposition or direction of the person. This is what theologians call *regeneration*. It flows from the resurrection of Jesus Christ. Therefore, we not only have a new status by virtue of being justified, but we also have a new heart from which new desires for holiness flow and a new power through God the Holy Spirit to live like, for, and with Jesus.

This righteousness is not something we work up on our own. It is not something we earn by religiously keeping rules. It is completely a gift of God through Jesus Christ. Ephesians 2:8–9 makes this unmistakably clear: "For by grace you have been saved through faith. And this is not your own doing; it is the gift of God, not a result of works, so that no one may boast."

This passive righteousness from Jesus, which is both imputed and imparted to us, is the bedrock of our joy. On it we build lives of hope, joy, assurance, and obedience. When accused by our great adversary Satan that we are sinners without sufficient righteousness, we need not defend ourselves. We merely need to remind ourselves of Jesus' words from the cross recorded in John 19:30 that "it is finished." All we need is the gift of Jesus Christ to be adopted into the family of God.

Here's the bottom line, Dave. If you have status as a child of God with Jesus as your brother, and if you have a new heart and the indwelling Holy Spirit of God, there will be a change in your basic attitudes. Because God changes your heart, the fundamental values of your life change to the values of Jesus. Exodus 34:6–7, the most quoted verse in the Bible by the Bible, describes the values of the Lord as compassion, grace, being slow to anger, and being loving, faithful, forgiving, and just.

Those are the values I'm not seeing in your life. You are showing the values of religion, not the gospel. That's why I am so deeply concerned for you. In addition, I am seeing what your religion is doing to your wife and children, which is heartbreaking since they are increasingly losing love for and joy with you.

In closing, there are two things that I want to say plainly. First, it is far easier to bifurcate religion and the gospel in this letter than it is in our lives. We will both spend the rest of our lives under the sun learning this distinction in the moment-to-moment opportunities that God, in his providential care, gives us to live by the gospel instead of by religion.

Second, in telling you that righteousness comes from Jesus alone and by virtue of none of your own good works, I am not advocating a kind of lawless Christianity where we are permitted to live in unrepentant and ongoing sin, unconcerned about whether we are living righteously. Rather, I am saying that only by understanding the righteousness of Jesus Christ in us can we live out of his righteousness as our new status as Christians. This is accompanied by new insight into Scripture, which 2 Timothy 3:16 says is good for "training in righteousness," a new weapon of repentance, which 1 John 1:9 says because of Jesus' death on the cross can "cleanse us from all unrighteousness," and a new power for righteousness through the Holy Spirit. I commend Romans 8:1–4 to you for a lifetime of meditation and satisfaction regarding the cross of Jesus:

> There is therefore now no condemnation for those who are in Christ Jesus. For the law of the Spirit of life has set you free in Christ Jesus from the law of sin and death. For God has done what the law, weakened by the flesh, could not do. By sending his own Son in the likeness of sinful flesh and for sin, he condemned sin in the flesh, in order that the righteous requirement of the law might be fulfilled in us, who walk not according to the flesh but according to the Spirit.

# Answers to Common Questions about Gift Righteousness

*This sounds extremely judgmental. Didn't Jesus say, "Judge not"?*

He does tell us not to judge in Matthew 7:1. He is addressing the Pharisees, the outstanding religionists of that day, who condemned other people and blasted them for small sins (the speck in their eye) while they totally ignored their own sin (the log in their own eye). The Pharisees are the epitome of hypocritical, self-righteous, condemning people. Jesus does not want us to be like them. But what many miss is the irony in that he is exposing their sin, the very thing many think he tells everyone not to do. He wants us to discern their sin so we won't be like them or validate people who are like them.

We must distinguish sin from righteousness, evil people from righteous people, gospel people from religious people. A little later, in Matthew 7:15–20, he tells us to "beware of false prophets." He goes on to say, "You will recognize them by their fruits. Are grapes gathered from thornbushes, or figs from thistles? . . . You will recognize them by their fruits," such as love.

We must discern sin and sinful hearts. But furthermore we must do so in a godly way. We must repent of our own sin, especially our inner sins. When we see sin in someone else, instead of condemning harshly from a distance we must come close in love, pointing out the sin in a compassionate and gracious attitude. Because Jesus has cared for us so well, we are to follow his example and care for other people as we call them to repentance and Christlikeness.

*What is the difference between imputed and imparted?*

Theologians love to take words and play with them. So using two words that sound almost identical but have very different meanings is a delight to Bible teachers! *Imputation* may be defined as "to attribute (reckon) guilt or righteousness from another to me/us." It is to transfer the legal standing of one person to someone else. So it is about our status or our relationship. It is an objective matter that is external to us. Some scriptural imputations include Adam's guilt to humanity, humanity's guilt to Christ, and Christ's righteousness status (standing, not character) to us.

On the other hand, *impartation* may be defined as "to transmit a substance, character, or quality from another to me/us." So it is about our state or character. It is subjective matter that is internal to us. Some scriptural impartations include Adam's depravity to humanity, a regenerate nature to believers, and the indwelling Holy Spirit to believers.

Maybe an illustration will help. When Gerry's parents died, he became the legal owner of their worldly goods. That's imputation. He had the status of owner. But a while later a check arrived, and the funds were deposited in his account. That's impartation. Owning the money is a legal, imputational matter. Having the funds in the bank is impartation.

*Aren't we justified by grace alone through faith alone in Christ alone? Isn't the righteousness of Christ imputed to us? What are you doing adding imparted righteousness to the gospel of free grace? According to what Paul says in Galatians 1:8–9, you should be eternally condemned.*

What you say about justification by grace alone and imputed righteousness is completely true. However, it is not the complete story. The Lord does give us status as his children totally as a gift. All sin is forgiven. Colossians 2:13 is quite clear: "You, who were dead in your trespasses and the uncircumcision of your flesh, God made alive together with him, having forgiven us all our trespasses." But don't miss the point that not only are sins forgiven, but we are also made alive. That great truth is the promise of the new covenant. Ezekiel 36:26–27 promises, "I will give you a new heart, and a new spirit I will put within you. And I will remove the heart of stone from your flesh and give you a heart of flesh. And I will put my Spirit within you, and cause you to walk in my statutes and be careful to obey my rules." That promise began to be fulfilled with the coming of the Spirit in Acts 2.

Paul expounds on the new covenant in 2 Corinthians 3–6. A highlight is 2 Corinthians 5:17: "Therefore, if anyone is in Christ, he is a new creation. The old has passed away; behold, the new has come." In another place Paul summarizes this, saying, "For at one time you were darkness, but now you are light in the Lord. Walk as children of light" (Eph. 5:8). It's not just that we are *in* the light. Because of his work in us, we *are* light. So of course we live as creatures of light.

*It seems that this is just theologians splitting hairs.*
*Is all of this really important?*

It's important only if you care about being saved! If the other religions are right and we have to do enough good things to get the gods to accept us, then we'd better get to our religious duties! But if the Bible is right, then God accepts us as his children totally out of Jesus' work of dying and rising again so we can have forgiveness and new life. If we repent and change our mind about who is God—it's not us—and believe, trusting that God is good to his word, then we can have complete forgiveness of sin, the very life of Jesus, the new community of the Spirit, and the body of Christ, and we can spend eternity with him.

*Where can I learn more about the gospel in light of*
*this chapter?*

For more on the gospel listen to or watch Tim Keller's session, "Preaching the Gospel," from the 2006 Reform and Resurge Conference (http://theresurgence.com/reform_resurge_conference_2006). You can also read Keller's article "Preaching in a Post-Modern City" (http://theresurgence.com/tim_keller_2004_preaching_in_a_post-modern_city_part_1). Best of all, you can read and study Peter's sermon in Acts 2:14–47. There he gives an outstanding exposition of the gospel of Jesus Christ. It begins with what God did: he came, died, rose again, and was exalted; then it shows what we do: repent and believe, which is expressed in baptism; and concludes with what we get: forgiveness of sin, gift of the Spirit, new life, new community, and a new future.

# CHAPTER FIVE

# "I Molested a Child": Jesus Is John's Justification

*All have sinned and fall short of the glory of God, and are justified by his grace as a gift, through the redemption that is in Christ Jesus, whom God put forward as a propitiation by his blood, to be received by faith.*

ROMANS 3:23-25

**John was raised in a loving and supportive** Christian home. He did not suffer abuse of any kind as a child. His parents loved him well, encouraged him, and provided for him a life filled with opportunity. While growing up, his social life centered on church and private school.

Following graduation from college, he moved away from his parents to start his career. At the time, he was a moral man; however, while he retained a general belief that a god of some kind does exist, he did not have any real relationship with Jesus. He stopped attending church once he was no longer near his parents and instead focused his energies on building his career in business and enjoying his recreational activities. He also began dating women more actively and became sexually active.

Some years later, while still unmarried, he finally acted on a sinful desire that he had apparently been suppressing. Tragically, he had sexual contact with an underage girl. Eventually, the truth of his sin was made known to her parents, who proceeded to press legal charges.

John was left with what he found to be a tremendously difficult decision. If he denied the charges and held out for a trial, he might be able to avoid a guilty verdict and thereby narrowly escape state-sponsored treatment, jail time, and the humiliating prospect of being registered as a sex offender. Yet, to deny the charges would likely mean that the young woman whom he sexually abused would be forced to testify about the entire ordeal and be subject to even more pain than he had already caused her. Or, he could simply plead guilty and accept his fate, whatever that might be.

The decision was gut-wrenching for him. In time he concluded that, since he was guilty, he should plead guilty to the charges against him and suffer whatever fate he was handed.

As a result, he spiraled into a deep depression. He stopped going out with his friends, ceased participating in sports and other leisure activities, and retreated to the confines of his home. There, alone in silence, he began seriously considering how and when to end his life.

On the day his plea was made before the judge, he was nearly emotionally undone. Upon hearing the judge declare him "guilty," he felt as if his hope and life had come to a painful and premature end.

In this season, God in his providential kindness brought a few Christian friends into John's life. They were fearful that he would take his own life, and they actively pursued a relationship with him. They prayed for Jesus to remake this evil and broken man. John could no longer look anyone in the eye, spoke only in hushed tones, and even in a crowd stood alone in the corner, trembling with fear and gazing at his feet.

At the heart of John's despair was a deep sense of his sin and guilt without any hope of forgiveness or transformation. When I met John, it was apparent to me that unless he met Jesus, he would kill himself and spend eternity in the torments of hell. This letter is written to explain to John the fact that, through Jesus and his justifying work on the cross, he can stand before Jesus his Judge and be declared righteous.

                 ◎     ◎     ◎     ◎     ◎

## Dear John,

You are a despicable human being. Jesus knew you would be born and said that it would be better if a large millstone were tied around your neck and you were thrown into the sea (Luke 17:2).

The source of your despair and suicidal thoughts is that who you truly are has now been made known to both you and the world. In our brief conversation, it was apparent that a lot of stupid counseling jargon that contradicts God is already finding its way into your vocabulary. You are frantically searching for something good inside of yourself that you can tap into as the root of a new life as a good person. You are also trying to find someone to blame for what you have done. In a word, you are trying to justify yourself by recalling any seemingly good things you have done throughout your life. The only problem is that no matter how much good you might do, you can never undo the terrible thing you have done. There is no one who made you do what you did. You made the choice. There is no one to blame but yourself.

By your own admission, what has triggered your breakdown is not the fact of your sin as much as the public declaration by the judge of the sins and crimes you have committed, along with the verdict of "guilty." That word *guilty* continues to ring in your ears because it accurately defines you as a human being. You are no longer able to define yourself by your intellect, competencies, income, toys, car, clothes, or friends because your name and address are now listed on the sex offender web site for everyone to see. You are named among the sadists, predators, and pedophiles that comprise the lowest and most despised segment of society. To make matters worse, the cold, hard truth is that your day before the judge is only a foretaste of what is to come.

Throughout the Bible, God is referred to as both a king and a judge. As king, God is sovereign over all of his creation, and there is no authority above him. As judge, God is the one we will stand before on the final judgment day. Romans 2:16 speaks of this as "that day when . . . God judges the secrets of men by Christ Jesus." Much like your day in court, on the day of final judgment you will stand before God, and all of the secret sins of your life will be made known. All of your wicked thoughts, words, and deeds will be listed, along with all of the good that you failed to do.

Unlike imperfect human judges and human laws, God is a perfectly just judge with perfectly just laws. The Old Testament speaks of God's law on more than six hundred occasions, and the New Testament speaks of God's justice and righteousness on more than two hundred occasions. Moreover, unlike God, you are an unrighteous law-breaker.

In Romans, Paul says that because God made us in his image and likeness, his law is also written on our hearts through the conscience that he has given us (Rom. 2:15). Thus, although you are not a Christian, you do have some sense of your guilt due to your conscience. Subsequently, you are continually judging yourself according to your own conscience and rightly concluding that you are guilty, evil, and condemnable.

Imagine how much greater your judgment will be when you stand before God himself and see for yourself that "the heavens declare his righteousness, for God himself is judge!" (Ps. 50:6). On that day you will learn that your sinful condition and ensuing sinful actions have not been merely against people but ultimately against God himself. In Psalm 51:4, a man who was guilty of committing a sexual sin like yours rightly said, "Against you [God], you only, have I sinned and done what is evil in your sight, so that you may be justified in your words and blameless in your judgment."

John, you have sinned against the holy and righteous God who spoke creation into existence and created you to be like him. In rebellion, you have sinned against God. You sinned against God on the day you touched a girl with the hands God made for his service. But you have also sinned continually through your whole life. Your sins include sins of commission, in which you have done what God—through the conscience he gave you along with Scripture—told you not to do, as well as sins of omission, in which you have not done good things that God created you to do.

To make matters worse, even the seemingly good things you have done are sinful because God knows that the motives of your heart in doing good were often evil, motivated by human applause, affection, and approval. You have altogether neglected God by living solely for yourself. The first commandment is to love the Lord (Mark 12:30). You have loved yourself first. You have loved only yourself.

The reason for your sins is that, as the theologians say, you are totally depraved. This is not to say that you are utterly depraved, because you could do greater evil more often. But you are totally depraved because, although God made your first parents, Adam and Eve, perfect, upright, and good, you have become imperfect, fallen, and sinful because of sin. Subsequently, your mind is corrupt so that you do not think God's thoughts. Your will is corrupt so that you do not desire what God desires of you. Your emotions are corrupt so that how you feel about yourself, your life, and God are not trustworthy. The Bible says in Genesis 1:31 that God made mankind "very good." But now even the remnants of the good image of God in you are pervaded by sinful evil.

Being totally depraved, you are in a state completely contrary to the entire purpose for which God created you. Paul speaks of your condition in some very stark terms. In Ephesians 2:1–2 he says that you are spiritually dead to God and alive to Satan. Furthermore, in Romans 8:7 he says that your mind is so hostile to God that you will not and cannot obey God. In summary, you are depraved, dead, and at war against God.

In light of your sinful condition and ensuing sinful actions, your impending day in God's proverbial courtroom seems utterly hopeless for anything other than a guilty verdict and a sentence to eternity in the torments of hell. In light of your obvious guilt, if God were to declare you anything but guilty he would cease to be a just and good God. God himself says that he "will not acquit the wicked" (Ex. 23:7). Furthermore, Proverbs 17:15 says, "He who justifies the wicked and he who condemns the righteous are both alike an abomination to the LORD." As a guilty sinner, you would likely prefer that God simply overlook your offenses against him. To do so, however, would by definition render God unjust, unholy, and unrighteous, which is impossible because he is always just, holy, and righteous.

As guilty sinners we are prone to expect mercy when we commit sins against others, yet we hypocritically demand justice when others sin against us. Likewise, we overlook our own sins while we are clearly aware of others' sins. For that reason, looking at this situation from the perspective of the victim rather than that of the sinner can provide some clarity.

Imagine, for example, if someone broke into your home, violated your privacy, stole your possessions, and harmed someone you loved, such as your mother. Imagine that the evidence against that person was incontrovertible, yet he was simply released, and all the charges were dismissed, and to top it off he received an all-expenses-paid vacation for the rest of his life. Because you are made in God's image, something in you would cry out for justice.

Likewise, God himself is the person you have sinned against throughout your life, and he too deserves justice. Furthermore, since you are unjust and God is just, he would be an unjust sinner if he chose to overlook your sin and declare you to be a righteous person and welcome you into the eternal Sabbath rest of his perfect heavenly kingdom.

Clearly, John, God does not owe you anything. If you were to spend forever in the torments of hell as a guilty and condemned sinner, you would be getting what you deserve. Pondering this same point, Job asks one of the great questions of the Bible: "But how can a man be in the right before God?" (Job 9:2).

Thankfully, not only is God holy, righteous, and just, but he is also compassionate, willing to forgive, and incredibly patient. God revealed himself to Moses as "The LORD, the LORD, a God merciful and gracious, slow to anger, and abounding in steadfast love and faithfulness, keeping steadfast love for thousands, forgiving iniquity and transgression and sin, but who will by no means clear the guilty" (Ex. 34:6–7). Because God is merciful, gracious, slow to anger, loving, faithful, and willing to forgive you, the dilemma is this: how could God justify you and remain just?

The answer is what is commonly called the doctrine of justification. What is meant by this doctrine is that, according to the Bible, guilty sinners can be declared righteous before God by grace alone, through faith alone, because of the person and work of Jesus Christ alone. This truth was the watershed issue of the entire Protestant Reformation. The great Bible teacher John Calvin called justification "the principle of the whole doctrine of salvation and the foundation of all religion." Martin Luther also said that justification is the issue on which the church stands or falls.

The question of how a guilty sinner can be declared by God as righteous is so important that justification is mentioned more than two hundred times in various ways throughout the New Testament alone. Perhaps the most succinct summary of how justification is made possible is found in 2 Corinthians 5:21, which says, "For our sake he [God] made him to be sin who knew no sin, so that in him we might become the righteousness of God." Martin Luther called the truth of this great verse the "great exchange." On the cross, Jesus took your sin upon himself and, though sinless, took upon himself the very worst of what you are—a child molester, liar, and enemy of God—so that he would perfectly stand in your place to suffer your punishment for your sins.

Let me be as clear as possible: the penalty of sin is death. God warned Adam in the garden that "in the day that you eat of it you shall surely die" (Gen. 2:17). Paul confirms this: "They know God's decree that those who practice such things deserve to die" (Rom. 1:32). The amazing truth I am trying to say to you is that God himself, the second person of the Trinity, stepped up to take your penalty in your place. Because Jesus took your sins to the cross, where he took the blow for you, there is no penalty left for you or any of us who will accept his payment. God forgave "all our trespasses, by canceling the record of debt that stood against us with its legal demands. This he set aside, nailing it to the cross" (Col. 2:13–14). It is Jesus' cross that makes the difference.

Additionally, not only did Jesus take all of your sins (past, present, and future) on the cross, but he also gave to you his perfect righteousness as a faultless and sinless person. As a result, the answer to Job's question regarding how you can stand before God and be declared righteous is Jesus. This is why Paul says that Jesus alone is our righteousness (1 Cor. 1:30). Therefore, justification through the work of Jesus Christ in your place for your sins on the cross is only possible by grace from Jesus Christ alone, through faith in Jesus Christ alone, because of Jesus Christ alone.

You are justified by grace alone, which means that there is absolutely nothing you can do to contribute to your justification. Rather, when Jesus said, "It is finished" on the cross, he was declaring that all that needed to be done for your justification was completed in him. For this reason, Titus 3:7 speaks of "being justified by his *grace*." Furthermore, Romans 5:16–17 says:

> And the *free gift* is not like the result of that one man's sin [Adam's]. For the judgment following one trespass brought condemnation, but the *free gift* following many trespasses brought justification. For if, because of one man's trespass, death reigned through that one man, much more will those who receive the abundance of *grace* and the *free gift* of righteousness reign in life through the one man Jesus Christ.

This gracious gift of Jesus' righteousness and justification must be received by you through personal faith alone. In other words, to be justified is to trust only in the person and work of Jesus and no one and nothing else as the object of your faith, righteousness, and justification. On this point Acts 13:39 says, "By [Jesus] everyone who *believes* is freed from everything." Also Romans 4:3–5 says, "For what does the Scripture say? 'Abraham *believed* God, and it was counted to him as righteousness.'

Now to the one who works, his wages are not counted as a gift but as his due. And to the one who does not work but believes in him who justifies the ungodly, his *faith* is counted as righteousness." And Romans 5:1 plainly states, "We have been justified by *faith*."

Perhaps most importantly you need to believe, in the core of your existence, that the source of your justifying grace and the object of your justifying faith is Jesus Christ alone. Simply, Jesus is everything. You need to give your sins to Jesus in repentant faith and receive from him the gift of righteousness in humble grace.

On the centrality, preeminence, and magnificence of Jesus regarding your justification, Isaiah 53:11 says, "Out of the anguish of his soul he shall see and be satisfied; by his knowledge shall the righteous one, my servant, make many to be accounted righteous, and he shall bear their iniquities." Galatians 2:16 says, "A person is not justified by works of the law but through faith in Jesus Christ, so we also have believed in Christ Jesus, in order to be justified by faith in Christ and not by works of the law, because by works of the law no one will be justified."

Romans 5:9 and 4:25 further stress that your justification is made possible by both Jesus' death and resurrection, saying, respectively, "We have now been justified by his blood," and "[He] was delivered up for our trespasses and raised for our justification." John, despite all of your sin, God has provided a way for you to be justified and declared righteous in his sight: Jesus' death on the cross in your place for your sins.

A day is coming, John, when you will die or Jesus will return; on that day you will stand before Jesus. Speaking of that judgment day, Paul says, "For we must all appear before the judgment seat of Christ, so that each one may receive what is due for what he has done in the body, whether good or evil" (2 Cor. 5:10). That day will feel eerily similar to the day you stood in court before a human judge who read your sentence. Unlike the day of your condemnation in a human court, however, that day will be a glorious day in which your salvation is declared in the court of God if you become a Christian in this life.

Let me be clear. I am in no way saying that I am in any way a better person than you. Jesus' own brother James writes in the Bible that God does not see people as good and bad but rather as either perfectly sinless or imperfect sinners. We all stand guilty before God with the exception of the sinless Jesus. Subsequently, I too should stand before Jesus and be condemned forever to the fiery torments of hell. However, because of Jesus' work on the cross for me and his ongoing work in changing me from sin to obedience through the Holy Spirit, I have assurance of being declared righteous on my proverbial day in court. On that day, I will be declared righteous because my sin was taken by Jesus and his righteousness was gifted to me.

John, I know that much pain has come into your life as a consequence of your sin. Many of your friends, family members, and coworkers want nothing to do with you. Furthermore, you are no longer welcome anywhere there are children; and even whole neighborhoods would prefer that you, as a registered sex offender, not live there. Yet, it is God himself who is welcoming you to be justified through Jesus into an eternal transforming relationship with the God who died and rose for you, that one day you too might rise to live with him and his people forever. To many people, this sounds altogether preposterous, and the New Testament even uses the Greek word for *scandal* to explain the shockingly wonderful nature of God's saving grace poured out on sinners like you and me through Jesus Christ (John 6:61; Rom. 9:33; 1 Cor. 1:23).

So, John, I implore you to confess your sins in prayerful repentance to Jesus. Then ask him to apply his justifying work on the cross to you. Jesus will gladly welcome you as a friend so that you can live a new life by his power with a new joy by his provision. That new life will be marked by an ongoing increase in holy living because you will hate your sin for what it did to Jesus. In addition, you will love Jesus for what he has done for you, and he will give you a deep desire to be like him.

Before closing, I offer you two practical suggestions. First, it would benefit you greatly to commit to memory all of Romans 3:21–31. If you become a Christian, you will find that Satan will continually condemn you for the sins of your past, but the truth of that section of Scripture will prove to be an anchor for your soul throughout life's storms.

Second, I would encourage you to spend a considerable amount of time pondering Luke 18:9–14. There Jesus tells a parable about a man with whom you will identify. In the story, two men went into the Old Testament temple to pray to God. One man wrongly considered himself righteous and looked down on other people whom he considered to be far less holy and righteous than himself. The other man reminds me much of you. That man was so devastated by his sin that he stood alone in the corner, as you have in our church. He would look only at the ground in shame, unable even to make eye contact with other people, just as you do. That man earnestly repented of his sin, beating his chest in remorse and crying out, "God, be merciful to me, a sinner!" Jesus finishes the parable with an encouragement that should bring you untold joy, saying, "I tell you, this man went down to his house justified, rather than the other. For everyone who exalts himself will be humbled, but the one who humbles himself will be exalted" (v. 14).

The first man made the tragic error that religious people are prone to make. He wrongly thought he could get justification from his sanctification. He wrongly thought that if he lived a good life and sought to pay back God through giving money, fasting, praying, and doing good works, God would be obligated to justify him. The other man did not confuse his justification and his sanctification. He humbly understood that he could be justified only by God through grace as he repented of who he was and what he had done. Only through that work of justification could he live an ongoing life of sanctification, being continually conformed to the character of Jesus by the same transforming grace that flows from him to us because of the cross.

John, you have been condemned by the court and your conscience. A day is coming when you will be condemned before Jesus Christ unless you are justified by him alone. So, I am asking you to search your heart and conscience to be sure that you know Jesus, love Jesus, have placed your faith in Jesus, have repented of your sin to Jesus, have received saving grace and the gift of righteousness from Jesus, have been forgiven by Jesus, and have been justified by Jesus so that you may live a new life of ongoing sanctification, increasingly becoming more and more like Jesus.

In closing, I know that you have been giving serious consideration to killing yourself in light of what you have done. The truth is that what you have done is worthy of death. But the good news is that Jesus has already died for your sins. As a result, you can now put your sins to death by his power and live a new life as a new man. Scripture further states that Jesus also rose from death for your justification and, as a result, is alive today and ready to hear from you, speak to you, and walk with you through the rest of your life and into eternity as not only your judge but also as your justifier (Rom. 4:25).

# Answers to Common Questions about Justification

## If God wants to forgive, why doesn't he just do it?

God doesn't just forgive because sin is all too real. That Jesus would go to the cross is a demonstration of the dreadfulness of sin. We have a sense within us that we are worth saving because we are made in the image of God. But when we are honest, we know our sin is deep. We certainly know the sin of others is deep. Our wrath at sin is only a small echo of God's wrath. If God merely forgave, nothing in us would change. We would be like this forever. That would be a horror story for sure.

This question is best answered by considering it from God's perspective. He created a perfect environment for Adam and Eve. He loved them and provided everything for them. The Serpent provoked them to make their own judgments about things rather than trust God and his direction. They refused God's authority, putting themselves in his place as their own gods. If God had simply forgiven them, he would have vindicated them as sinners and accepted Satan as an equal.

Furthermore, God would be endorsing evil by passively accepting it. Simple forgiveness seems merciful at first. However, what it really does is give God's blessing to Satan and evil by approving such things as rape and murder. Because God is just, he must distinguish between good and evil by promoting the former and opposing the latter. Mere forgiveness would destroy God's holiness, justice, and righteousness by not distinguishing between good and evil. Because God is good, he cannot approve of or ignore sin and its consequences.

Basically, the debt of sin must be paid, or evil is vindicated. That debt is paid either by the sinner in the torments of eternal hell or by our eternal God Jesus Christ dying on the cross in our place for our sins.

The great reformer Martin Luther put it well: "Since [Jesus Christ] became a substitute for us all, and took upon himself our sins, that he might bear God's terrible wrath against sin and expiate our guilt, he necessarily felt the sin of the whole world, together with the entire wrath of God, and afterwards the agony of death on account of this sin."[1]

The cross demonstrates the loving desire of God to forgive and heal. When God was confronted with the first sin of humanity, he was really angry. But instead of destroying everyone and everything he had made and being done with us forever, God called to Adam and Eve, promised that Jesus their Messiah was coming, and mercifully made coverings for their shame (Genesis 3).

This desire to heal and forgive with compassion, grace, and total justice comes together only at the cross. James Denney put this very succinctly: "Nothing else in the world demonstrates how real is God's love to the sinful, and how real the sin of the world is to God."[2]

God "just did it" by providing the full solution in his death and resurrection. Will you "just do it" and receive his gift of eternal life?

*Proverbs 17:15 says, "He who justifies the wicked and he who condemns the righteous are both alike an abomination to the Lord." Yet, Romans 4:5 says God "justifies [acquits] the ungodly." Isn't that an abomination?*

You are asking how a just God can acquit a sinner, someone who remains sinful even after he is justified. God does not overlook sin or pretend that it did not happen. God is not to be confused with a sentimental grandfather who chuckles at the sins of his grandchildren. If God were to do that, it would be an abomination. That's why God executes the full penalty of sin on Jesus and, really, on himself. God's justice requires that sin be treated as sin. Yet, in his love God takes the penalty upon himself. At the cross we see the ultimate manifestation of his justice and love. Romans 3:25–26 summarizes it perfectly: "God put [Jesus] forward as a propitiation by his blood, to be received by faith. This was to show God's righteousness, because in his divine forbearance he had passed over former sins. It was to show his righteousness at the present time, so that he might be just and the justifier of the one who has faith in Jesus."

*I can see how a financial debt can be paid by a substitute. But it doesn't seem right that John's moral guilt can be transferred from him to someone else.*

Honestly, I do not know how this can occur, but I can say that God knows and that it does occur. There's nowhere in our legal system where moral guilt is transferred from one person to another. If you are guilty of the crime, you must do the time. I don't understand how it works. God did not explain the *how* of the transfer when he proclaimed the reality of it.

Still, there is an important point here. Truth is not limited to our comprehension. God can and does do things that are beyond our understanding. This is what is meant when the Bible speaks of faith. Biblical faith is not blind or uninformed. Rather, it is faith set on our sure knowledge of the character of God.

Sometimes we do not know how God achieves something, but we do know that God is good, and so we trust him. The same is true of all our relationships, to a lesser degree. For example, I cannot fathom how my wife loves me as deeply as she does because I know I am a sinner who can be difficult to live with. Nonetheless, while I do not fully know how she could love me, I do know that she does love me, and I live my life trusting in that fact. Similarly, I do not know how God could love me and forgive my sin. But I do know that God is just and good, and so I trust that he has transferred my moral guilt to Jesus because that is what he tells me in Scripture, and I know that he is not a liar.

# CHAPTER SIX

# "My Dad Used to Beat Me": Jesus Is Bill's Propitiation

*In this is love, not that we have loved God but that he loved us and sent his Son to be the propitiation for our sins.*

1 JOHN 4:10

**With a beautiful wife, cute kids, a solid career,** and a fruitful ministry, Bill seemed to be living the idyllic life. As we ate chicken wings, I inquired about his upbringing, expecting to hear that he was raised by godly parents who were responsible for much of his success.

He spoke lovingly of his mom and siblings but said nothing about his father. Curious, I asked him about his dad, at which point his countenance changed and he said, "My dad is a Christian." It was rather obvious that there was more to the story, so I continued probing and asked him to tell me about his dad.

Bill explained that his grandfather was a mean drunk who routinely beat his wife and kids, including his father when he was a boy. Apparently, Grandpa was so violent that he put his kids in the hospital on more than one occasion. When he came home drunk, the kids would run for their lives, seeking a place to hide in the woods near their home. As a result, the kids spent many nights sleeping in various hiding places outside, hoping their dad would not find them and beat them yet again.

Growing up with constant violence deeply affected Bill's father, who continued much of the abusive behavior. As a result, Bill grew up routinely watching his mother being dragged around the house by her hair. If any of the kids tried to intervene, they were also screamed at, slapped in the face, punched, thrown to the ground, and sometimes kicked while they lay on the floor . . . even the girls.

The violence could erupt at any time, which meant that Bill grew up under constant stress. To make matters worse, he so despised the violence done by his father against his mom and siblings that he was the one who would most frequently stand up to his father and take the brunt of the beatings. In his mind it was the honorable thing to do; it spared the others from being harmed if he took a beating in their place.

This abuse continued for many years, and Bill grew increasingly tough, with a strong sense of duty and justice. He channeled the bitterness he had for his father toward perceived good and was an overachiever in school, sports, work, religion, and anything else he committed himself to. Outwardly, he was a very self-sufficient and good young man. Inwardly, he was filled with rage and bitterness toward his dad.

Bill first moved out of his father's house as a very young boy, around the age of three or four. He so hated his father that he built a fort in the yard and decided he would live there alone. His mother eventually came out, crying, and asked him to move back into his father's house, and Bill did so out of love for his mother, but his heart was never in that home again. As Bill grew older, he spent less and less time around his family until he eventually moved out for good following high school graduation. In the first few weeks of college, he got into a few fights, but in his mind they were always justified because he was standing up to a bully or combating an injustice.

Later in college, Bill's whole life changed when Jesus saved him. For the first time he felt the father-hole in his heart being filled with the love of God, and he deeply desired to learn the Bible and honor God the honorable Father. God led Bill to a great church where the pastor, a very masculine and godly man, became the earthly father figure he had longed for. In many ways, the mentoring of that pastor was one of the most healing events in Bill's life and gave him a vision for how to become a lovingly protective Christian husband and father.

In the ensuing years, Bill married a lovely Christian woman with whom he had great kids. He was proud that the cycle of violence that had destroyed generations of his family ended with him; he never raised a fist against his wife or children. However, he conveniently overlooked the fact that, while he did not hit his wife with his fists, he did abuse his wife with his words. His anger would erupt much like his father's because, in part, he had not forgiven his father for being an unjust and violent man, and a root of bitterness remained in his soul.

Then one day God also saved Bill's dad. Bill was skeptical at first but over time was convinced that his dad had indeed met Jesus. His father demonstrated it with a life of repentance as a new man who, though not perfect, was not the mean, violent man that Bill had known growing up.

On one hand, Bill was truly glad to see his father meet Jesus and be transformed. On the other hand, Bill still felt unsure of how to respond. His friends told him to just forgive his dad and move on. To Bill, though, that answer seemed trite. As a husband and father himself, he would sometimes try to picture himself dragging his own wife around by her hair while cursing her out, punching his own sons in the mouth, and kicking his own daughters while they lay on the floor after he had thrown them to the ground, but Bill would simply weep, unable to conceive of how any man could do such things. To make matters worse, Bill had seen the effects of his father's sin on the entire family; no one had ever really talked about the torment he inflicted, and they lived broken lives as a result.

To Bill, simply erasing the past as if nothing had ever happened and moving on because his dad got saved seemed to ignore the injustice. His feelings on the matter were quite right, despite his sin of bitterness, and this letter is written to him.

◎ ◎ ◎ ◎ ◎

## Dear Bill,

I want to thank you for sharing your story about your upbringing and family because I know, as a tough guy, you are reticent to be so vulnerable and transparent. I know that God has used the sin that was committed against you by your father for his good and has made you a strong and courageous man with a keen sense of justice. However, it is truly awful that you suffered so violently at the hands of your own father.

As you told me your story, it became apparent that you sought to be the good boy that your father would love, embrace, and say he was proud of, but no matter what you achieved, his love was never evident.

The one story that was most painful for me to hear was the day when, as a little boy, you brought home a report card with straight A's and handed it proudly to your father, only to hear him say, "I'm sure you won't get straight A's next time. You'll screw up eventually, and some day I expect to have to bail you out of jail for being a screw-up." I am so sorry for the beatings you took from his fists and his words. As a daddy of five kids, I cannot imagine the damage I would do if I were to rebuke, mock, and discourage one of my children for getting straight A's.

In our conversation, you said that you had a hard time just letting the past go now that your father is a Christian and no longer violent. At first your comments seemed born solely out of your bitterness, but as I have reflected on them, I think I understand what you were trying to say. For a man to devastate his family like your father did means that his simply saying "sorry" is not enough to erase the list of sins he has accrued or the damage he has done. I hope to untangle some of this conflict you are living in, and to do so we must begin with the character of God.

First, the Bible says that God is our Father, which means that fathers are supposed to be analogous to God and to love, serve, protect, provide, encourage, and grow us in godly ways. Second, God the Father is holy and altogether without sin, and daddies, including you and me, are to follow in his example. Summarily, your father sinned against God, you, and the rest of his family and in doing so defamed the name "father," which God graciously bestows to men blessed with children.

The results of such sin include a great deal of grief and pain for you that were evident through the tears in your eyes and the tremble in your voice. As you spoke of your father's sin and the grief and pain that it caused you, I was reminded of the words of Genesis 6:5–6: "The LORD saw that the wickedness of man was great in the earth, and that every intention of the thoughts of his heart was only evil continually. And the LORD was *sorry* that he had made man on the earth, and *it grieved him to his heart*." Therefore, the way you have felt about your father is also the way that God has felt about your father.

Furthermore, as we spoke, you also mentioned how your father's sin had separated you from him so that you were not close with him; when you were a young boy you even told him that you hoped the day would come when you would never see his face or hear his voice again. Your statements reminded me of Isaiah 59:2, where God says, "Your iniquities have made a *separation* between you and your God, and your sins have *hidden his face* from you so that he does not hear." So, again, you reacted to your father in the same way that God responds to sinners.

Lastly, you spoke of building forts in the yard as a kid and pretending that you lived there instead of in the house with your father because you longed for the day that you could move out and never return. Bill, God feels the same way about sinners as you did. Psalm 5:4 says, "For you are not a God who delights in wickedness; evil *may not dwell with you.*"

So, your response to your sinful father was very similar to how God responds to sinners. As we spoke, however, it seemed clear that you are still conflicted about the anger you have felt toward your father. That is likely the result of poor Bible teaching you have received from flaccid men who wrongly believe that anger is always bad and that nice Christians don't get angry. The truth is that when evil, injustice, and oppression occur, the right feeling is anger that compels us to do all we can to defeat injustice and protect the weak and vulnerable, as you did with your mother and siblings.

As a little boy you rightly felt angry at your dad, and that anger rightly compelled you to confront his injustice and protect the rest of the family. Therefore, anger can be a righteous virtue, which explains why God gets angry at sin too. The Bible is filled with examples of God getting angry at sinners. A few examples will illustrate my point clearly, but a reading of Leviticus 26:27–30, Numbers 11:1, and Deuteronomy 29:24, for starters, speak of God's anger as being hostile, burning, and furious.

Flaccid church guys will often accept that in the Old Testament God did get angry, but they will say that Jesus was a nice, emotionless, flaccid church guy, just like them, who chose a hollow, fake smile over anger every day. But even Jesus got angry, furious, and enraged. Mark 3:5 says, "[Jesus] looked around at them with *anger*, grieved at their hardness of heart." Also, the Revelation 19 picture of Jesus coming again as a warrior with a tattoo down his leg and a sword in his hand, riding on a white horse to slaughter evildoers until their blood runs through the streets like a river, is hardly consistent with the common false portrait of Jesus that lacks any sense of righteous anger.

In speaking of God's anger, I want to be careful not to give permission for us to lose our temper and rage, because that is a sin—the very sin that your father committed repeatedly. However, because God is perfect, his anger is perfect and, as such, is aroused slowly (Ex. 34:6–8), sometimes turned away (Deut. 13:17), often delayed (Isa. 48:9), and frequently held back (Ps. 78:38).

Furthermore, God feels angry because God hates sin (Prov. 6:16–19; Zech. 8:17). Sadly, it is commonly said among Christians that "God hates the sin but loves the sinner." This is as stupid as saying God loves rapists and hates rape, as if rape and rapists were two entirely different entities that could be separated from one another. Furthermore, it was not a divinely inspired author of Scripture but the Hindu Gandhi who coined the phrase "Love the sinner but hate the sin" in his 1929 autobiography.

The love of God is in fact true but sadly has been so overly emphasized in most Christian teaching that one wonders if God is love or if love is now God. The blunt-edged truth is that God both loves and hates some sinners, as the following Scriptures illustrate:

> You [God] *hate* all evildoers. (Ps. 5:5)

> The LORD is in his holy temple; the LORD's throne is in heaven; his eyes see, his eyelids test the children of man. The LORD tests the righteous, but his soul *hates* the wicked and the one who loves violence. (Ps. 11:4–5)

> "Every evil of theirs is in Gilgal; there I began to *hate* them. Because of the wickedness of their deeds I will drive them out of my house. I will love them no more; all their princes are rebels." (Hos. 9:15)

> As it is written [Mal. 1:2–3], "Jacob I loved, but Esau I *hated*." (Rom. 9:13)

Additionally, God's anger at sin and hatred of sinners causes him to pour out his wrath on unrepentant sinners. This doctrine is not as popular in our day as it was in past times, but the fact remains that in the Old Testament alone nearly twenty different words are used for God's wrath, which is spoken of roughly six hundred times. The Bible also speaks of God's wrath coming upon both men and women because both genders are sinful (Ex. 22:22–24; Ezek. 16:38).

The wrath of God appears roughly twenty-five times in the New Testament, including passages such as John 3:36, Ephesians 5:6, Colossians 3:6, and 1 Thessalonians 1:9–10. Furthermore, Jesus will also pour out wrath on people who will call "to the mountains and rocks, 'Fall on us and hide us from the face of him who is seated on the throne, and from the wrath of the Lamb, for the great day of their wrath has come, and who can stand?'" (Rev. 6:16–17). Here we see that not only does God the Father pour out wrath upon unrepentant sinners, but so does Jesus Christ.

Regarding God's anger and hatred, it is commonly protested that God cannot hate anyone because he is love. But the Bible speaks of God's anger, wrath, and fury more than of his love, grace, and mercy. Furthermore, it is precisely because God is love that he must hate evil and all who do evil—evil is an assault on whom and what he loves.

Therefore, Bill, your anger toward and hatred of your father are justifiable and are the healthy response to seeing your dad beat the mother and siblings you love. However, in a mysterious conflict of deep emotions, you continued to love your father just as God continues to love unrepentant sinners whom he simultaneously hates.

Few Christians, even those deeply committed to Scripture, regularly speak of the wrath of God anymore. The assumption is that any wrath is harsh and irrational (though true anger is expressed against true evil and expressed with true righteousness). One of the most prominent pastors in the entire country has repeatedly said, for example, that he will not speak of such things as God's anger and wrath at human sin because he finds it too negative. This is due in part to both a lack of fearing God and a widespread misunderstanding of exactly how God's wrath works.

For starters, God's wrath is both active and passive. When people think of God's wrath, they generally think of God's active wrath, in which people are swiftly punished for their sin with something like a lightning bolt from heaven while they sit in front of their computer watching porn. God can, and I believe does, enact his active wrath upon occasion.

For example, I once met with a young man whose father, a pastor, suddenly left his ministry, wife, and teenage sons to have a homosexual affair with a man he had met on the Internet. He told his teenage sons that there is no God, Jesus did not rise from death, and that there is no such thing as punishment for sin. His sons experienced a profound crisis of faith, and since their dad kept saying that he was happy for the first time in his life, they wondered if God existed, and if he did, whether he cared. To make matters worse, the entire church he had been pastoring was experiencing the same sort of faith crisis. I prayed with one of the sons, asking God to either bring their father to repentance or pour out his wrath on the man as an example. Within days, the father died of an unexplainable, sudden explosion of his heart.

While we can't make a definitive connection of this timely death to the wrath of God, it is in keeping with what we see in instances like Genesis 38 where God kills the two sons of Judah because of their wickedness.

Indeed, God can work through active wrath but seems frequently to work through his more subtle passive wrath. Passive wrath occurs when God just hands us over to our evil desires and allows us to do whatever we want. Paul says it this way: "For the wrath of God is revealed from heaven against all ungodliness and unrighteousness of men, who by their unrighteousness suppress the truth. . . . Therefore God gave them up in the lusts of their hearts to impurity. . . . God gave them up to dishonorable passions" (Rom. 1:18, 24, 26).

When you were a little boy who would try to fight his own father in an effort to spare your mother and sisters, you were trying to pour your active wrath on him. Because you were smaller, though, his wrath continually overwhelmed yours, and you would take a beating at his hand. You would feel a seething rage because of the injustice. Part of your frustration with God regarding your father is that you deeply longed to see God's wrath poured out on him, and you feel that in some way God let you down.

You need to see that God's passive wrath was in effect for many years. Your father was living and acting separately from the transforming power Jesus gave through his death on the cross. As a result, all he could do was sin and cause damage and death to the relationships with his own wife and children so that everyone suffered and no one was blessed. This includes your father.

Furthermore, Bill, you must realize that not only could God's active wrath have been poured out on your father, but it just as easily could have been poured out on you. Like your father, you are a sinner who admittedly looked at pornography, had sex with girlfriends, and were unjustly violent on more than one occasion where you beat people just because they got on your nerves. In addition, though you admit to never hitting your wife, you agree that you have verbally and emotionally assaulted her in anger, beating her with your tongue instead of your fists, which makes you a guilty sinner along with your dad.

The truth is that everyone but the sinless Jesus merits the active wrath of God. Subsequently, none of us deserves love, grace, or mercy from God. An example of this is the rebellious angels who became demons, who are not given any chance of salvation but are only guaranteed the active wrath of God (2 Pet. 2:4). Joining demons, sinful people who fail to repent will have God's wrath burning against them forever (Deut. 32:21–22; John 3:36; Eph. 5:6; Rev. 14:9–11). The place of God's unending active wrath is hell, which Jesus spoke of more than anyone in the Bible. Hell is an eternal place of painful torment akin to taking a beating, getting butchered, and being burned by Jesus (Matt. 8:11–12, 29; 13:49–50; 18:8–9; 24:50–51; 25:41, 46; Mark 1:24, 5:7; 9:43–48; Luke 12:46–48; 16:19–31; Rev. 14:10).

However, God's active wrath is diverted from some people because of the mercy of God. This is made possible because, on the cross, Jesus substituted himself in our place for our sins and took God's wrath for us. Two sections of Scripture in particular speak to this matter pointedly:

> Since, therefore, we have now been justified by his blood, much more shall we be *saved by him [Jesus] from the wrath of God.* (Rom. 5:9)

> You turned to God from idols to serve the living and true God, and to wait for his Son from heaven, whom he raised from the dead, *Jesus who delivers us from the wrath to come.* (1 Thess. 1:9–10)

Scripture uses the word *propitiation* to designate how Jesus diverts the active wrath of our rightfully angry God from us so that we are loved and not hated. This word summarizes more than six hundred related words and events that explain it. The *American Heritage Dictionary* defines *propitiation* as something that appeases or "conciliates an offended power," and "especially a sacrificial offering to a god." Many Christians are not familiar with this word because various Bible translations use different words in an effort to capture its meaning. For example, the Revised Standard Version and the New English Bible translate the word "expiation." The New International Version and the New Revised Standard Version translate the word "sacrifice of atonement." The English Standard Version of the Bible has thankfully retained the original word, *propitiation*, from the Greek text of the New Testament. Therefore, I want to share the four primary occurrences of the word *propitiation* in the New Testament so that you can see them in their context.

> For all have sinned and fall short of the glory of God, and are justified by his grace as a gift, through the redemption that is in Christ Jesus, whom God put forward as a *propitiation* by his blood, to be received by faith. This was to show God's righteousness. (Rom. 3:23–25)

> Therefore [Jesus] had to be made like his brothers in every respect, so that he might become a merciful and faithful high priest in the service of God, to make *propitiation* for the sins of the people. (Heb. 2:17)

> He is the *propitiation* for our sins, and not for ours only but also for the sins of the whole world. (1 John 2:2)

> In this is love, not that we have loved God but that he loved us and sent his Son to be the *propitiation* for our sins. (1 John 4:10)

This final verse is incredibly important and is echoed in John 3:16 and Romans 5:8. It states that rather than seeing the cross as the place where love was absent as God's righteous wrath for sin was poured out on Jesus, the cross is precisely the place where God's love is shown in the propitiation of Jesus Christ.

I know that this will be difficult for you to comprehend, Bill, but Jesus has fully experienced what you have and much more. Jesus was mocked and beaten, though he was without sin. He willingly substituted himself for those he loved and wanted to save. I need you to see that even as a little boy you had some sense of the gospel because God made you as his image bearer. In standing between your father and your mother and siblings to take a beating that you did not deserve, you were in an imperfect way experiencing what Jesus did.

In saying this, I want to be clear that the correlation between Jesus' suffering at the hands of God the Father and your suffering at the hands of your father is not identical. Jesus was sinless and you are sinful. God the Father's wrath was just and your father's wrath was unjust. So, without wrongly presenting God the Father, I do want the horrible events of your childhood to help you more fully identify with the suffering of Jesus on the cross.

Furthermore, not only is your father a sinner who needs to have his sins propitiated, but you too are a sinner who likewise needs to have his sins propitiated. Not only did Jesus suffer like you; in a very real sense he also suffered at the hands of both you and your father on the cross. However, in Jesus' act, which you emulated as a little boy, the love of God was shown to both you and your father in the brutality endured by the crucified Jesus.

Therefore, you need not merely let your dad off the hook because he became a Christian. Further, you need not punish him for all the evil he has done. Instead, at the cross justice and mercy kissed; Jesus substituted himself for your father and suffered and died in your dad's place to forgive him, love him, and embrace him—not in spite of his sins but because his sins were propitiated and diverted from him to Jesus. Because you are a Christian, you can look to the cross to see that the demands of justice have been met for both you and your dad. Consequently, your father does not need to pay for his sins and neither do you, since Jesus has propitiated the sins of you both.

To help illustrate this point I want to explain to you one of the central events in the Old Testament, the act of atonement, including the annual celebration of the Day of Atonement (Yom Kippur), which was guided by the regulations of the book of Leviticus.

The Day of Atonement was the most important day of the year. It was intended to deal with the sin problem between humanity and God. Of the many prophetic elements on this special day, one stands out. Two healthy goats without defect were chosen; they were therefore fit to represent sinless perfection. The high priest would slaughter one goat, which acted as a substitute for the sinners who rightly deserved a violently bloody death for their many sins. The high priest treated the first goat as a sin offering. He slaughtered the innocent goat and sprinkled some of its blood on the mercy seat on top of the ark of the covenant inside the Most Holy Place. But the goat was no longer innocent after taking the guilt of the people's sin, because it had become their sin offering. Therefore, its blood represented life given as payment for sin.

As a result, the dwelling place of God was cleansed of the defilement that resulted from all of the transgressions and sins of the people of Israel, and God's wrath was satisfied. The bloody slaughter of the goat on the Day of Atonement represented propitiation and foreshadowed the coming of Jesus to shed his blood as the substitute for sinners.

I know that you appreciate Jesus as your propitiation of sin and expiation from sin. But I need you also to accept that what Jesus did for you out of love, grace, and mercy he also did for your father. Your father has come to a sincere faith in Jesus, has repented of his sins, has asked for your forgiveness with tears in his eyes, has sought counseling to change, and is a man who is living a new life in Jesus.

I know that what your father did to you was horrendously evil. But because Jesus has forgiven your dad and taken away his sin, you must also forgive your dad, because Jesus was his sacrifice, and let it go, because Jesus was his scapegoat. You have enjoyed those same blessings from Jesus, and it would be unjust for you to enjoy grace that you refuse to extend.

I know you fear that by forgiving your father, what you endured would be little more than a series of wasted painful abuses. However, because God is both sovereign and good, through that evil you have been given one of the deepest appreciations and insights of the doctrine of propitiation of anyone I have ever met. Just as you stood in the place of your own mother to suffer as an act of love for her, Jesus has done similarly for you. Subsequently, Jesus' cross makes perfect sense to you as it appeals to the very core of who you have been ever since you were a little boy.

Lastly, Bill, when life gets hard I am concerned that you will assume that God the Father is treating you the way your dad did and is punishing you unjustly. So, I want you to remember that God the Father will never punish you unjustly. Hardships come from living in this broken world and from our own sin, in addition to the sins that are committed against us. Thankfully, God uses even these hardships of life to strengthen you, the son he loves, for his service. While he may punish your rebellion, he will never do it harshly or irrationally. He does it to get you to realize the wrongness of your rebellion. Still, he will never stop loving you or abandon you, because God is the perfectly loving Father.

Bill, God the Father is the Dad you've always needed and the Dad your dad has always needed too. Because God's wrathful anger has been poured out on Jesus instead of on you and your dad, the two of you can now have a Christian friendship as men who are father and son through the cross of Jesus. I praise God that even though your father's father beat him and your father beat you, Jesus has saved you both; now your own sons have both a father and a grandfather who raise their hands in worship and in prayer rather than in violence and abuse because Jesus has propitiated their sin and has given his salvation.

## Answers to Common Questions about Propitiation

*Isn't propitiation a view held only by hard-hearted people who enjoy the thought of people they don't like suffering God's wrath?*

No one would accuse the noted theologian Karl Barth of being a hard-hearted fundamentalist. Yet even he believed that Jesus Christ "has not only borne man's enmity against God's grace, revealing it in all its depth. He has borne the far greater burden, the righteous wrath of God against those who are enemies of His grace, the wrath which must fall on us."[1]

It is true that as sinners, humans often manifest anger and wrath in sinful ways. Nonetheless, if something is wrongly used it should not necessarily be abandoned, but rather redeemed.

Likewise, *love* is a word that our culture often uses wrongly for such things as fornication, adultery, and perversion. Yet, the answer to such sins is not to abandon love but to redeem it.

The only way that something can be redeemed and used for the purpose God intended is by a repeated returning to Scripture. There, God patiently teaches us truth. In regard to such things as anger and wrath, the Bible reveals to us that God beautifully and perfectly becomes angry at unrepentant sin because he loves what is true, beautiful, and good, whereas sin is violence against such things. Nonetheless, Scripture also reveals to us that on the cross God not only poured out his wrath on sinners but also poured it out upon himself to lovingly suffer and die in the place of sinners. In so doing, God's angry wrath and loving mercy are exalted as altogether glorious and reveal a God that is anything but hardhearted.

*If good translations like the New International Version avoid the word* propitiation, *why do we have to use it?*

Scripture says that the very words of God, not just the thoughts of God, are inspired (Ex. 19:6; Deut. 32:46–47; Prov. 30:5–6; Matt. 4:4; Luke 21:33; John 6:63; 17:8; 1 Thess. 2:13; Rev. 21:5; 22:18–19). This is where we get the doctrine of verbal plenary inspiration, which means that God the Holy Spirit inspired not just the thoughts of Scripture, but also the very words and details. Therefore, how the original words are translated into English is very important for Bible readers.

One of the more popular arguments for thought-for-thought Bible translations (e.g., New International Version, Today's New International Version, New Revised Standard Version, New Living Translation, Contemporary English Version, Good News Bible) and paraphrases (e.g., Amplified Bible, Living Bible, The Message) over more literal word-for-word translations (e.g., English Standard Version, New American Standard Bible, New King James Version, King James Version) is that people do not understand the theological nomenclature that Scripture uses to express doctrinal concepts. Proponents of thought-for-thought translations and paraphrases argue that words like *propitiation*, which the original text of Scripture used, should be replaced with more modern vernacular that people can understand.

However, *propitiate* is the only English word that carries the idea of pacifying wrath by taking care of the penalty for the offense that caused the wrath. But it has the shortcoming that it is not a word people use today. That is why the New International Version and the New Revised Standard Version use "sacrifice of atonement," and the New Living Translation uses "sacrifice for sin" in such places as Romans 3:23–25, Hebrews 2:17, 1 John 2:2, and 1 John 4:10 where the original word was "propitiate."

Worse still are the Revised Standard Version and New English Bible, which use "expiation" instead of "propitiation." These latter two translations change the entire meaning of the verse because propitiation deals with our penalty for sin whereas expiation deals with our cleansing from sin. While the doctrines are related, they are very distinct. To confuse them is to make a major theological error.

Furthermore, the various words chosen to replace propitiation are no clearer to the average American, and they lose the aspect of dealing with God's wrath. Therefore, it is good for us to retain the language of Scripture and simply take the time to explain what the words mean. Sadly, many in our culture have no understanding of even the most basic of Bible words, such as *Jesus*, *sin*, and *truth*. If we start removing all of the words from the Bible that people do not understand, we may very well end up with blank pages.

*The New English Translation (NET) Bible uses the term mercy seat, the covering of the ark where the blood was sprinkled on the Day of Atonement, in place of propitiation in translating Romans 3:25. If these very conservative scholars repudiate the idea of appeasing divine anger, why do you hang on to it?*

If you read the NET footnote for Romans 3:25, you will see that it points out that the mercy seat is the place where propitiation was accomplished. So they don't deny propitiation at all.

*I know of all sorts of pagans who offer sacrifices to keep their gods from being angry. Is that what Christians mean by propitiation?*

What you say about pagans is true. For example, I (Gerry) was in Taiwan during Ghost Month, the seventh lunar month, during which the gates to the underworld are opened, and it is believed that the spirits are allowed to cross over into the world of the living. The Taiwanese people perform shows to entertain the ghosts and put out large, food-laden tables with hanging lanterns to guide the ghosts to the tables. They buy and burn huge piles of ghost money so the ghosts will have food and money for life in the other world.

They do this because they fear that the ghosts will get very angry unless they are well treated. Because of the fear of danger from the ghosts, people avoid weddings, burials, business deals, vacations, and childbirth. Being around water is considered particularly dangerous because the ghosts might grab your body away from you. For relief, the people must pacify the ghosts or suffer serious acts of retribution.

Propitiation is about Jesus, who is God come as a man to suffer and die in our place for our sins on the cross to divert the wrath of God from us. For many reasons Jesus' propitiation on the cross is nothing like the appeasement of false gods and demons that is found in other religions and spiritualities.

First, propitiation is not something we do to appease God, but rather something God did for us. Second, God is not petulant and evil but loving and good. Third, God's anger is not capricious but righteous. Fourth, in propitiation God is not demanding something from us but giving himself to us. Fifth, once we have received Jesus, the wrath of God is removed forever so that unlike the other religions and spiritualities, we no longer need to live under the fear of condemnation or do anything else to make God at peace with us.

*I read a commentary on the book of Romans by C. H. Dodd, which argued very persuasively that the wrath of God isn't a personal act or attitude but just something built into the structures of this world. Consequently, if you have unprotected sex, you are likely to get an STD. Isn't this idea of simple cause-and-effect a better way to understand God's wrath?*

Actually, no. We've seen from Bill's story that personal wrath against sin makes a lot of sense. But it is even clearer when we look at the Bible. Deuteronomy 29:18–29 describes God's reaction to the Israelites who reject him and instead worship and serve other gods. His wrath and anger burn against such a man. God curses him, blots out his name, and sends affliction on him. The Lord uproots the Israelites from their land in anger and fury and great wrath and casts them into another land. If any of those people had been asked if God's wrath felt personal to them, it is doubtless they would affirm it did.

This same wrath is also found in the Gospel of John, which is the Gospel of love. John 3:16, which says, "For God so loved the world, that he gave his only Son, that whoever believes in him should not perish but have eternal life," is followed by, "Whoever believes in him is not condemned, but whoever does not believe is condemned already, because he has not believed in the name of the only Son of God" (3:18). The chapter ends with verse 36: "Whoever believes in the Son has eternal life; whoever does not obey the Son shall not see life, but the wrath of God remains on him."

Therefore, God's love and wrath are both equally personal. Consequently, it is erroneous to say that God's love rests on us personally and individually while also denying that God's wrath rests on us personally and individually. God's love is as personal as his wrath.

*Many respected Bible commentaries argue that the Greek term for propitiation doesn't include the idea of propitiation but rather speaks of the expression of divine love. How do you know the term means appeasing divine anger?*

The best way to know is to look in the Septuagint, the Greek translation of the Old Testament, to see how the term is used. In Genesis 32 we read the story of Jacob's return to Israel. He is very worried about the anger of his brother Esau, whom he had defrauded years earlier. So, Jacob sends servants with large herds of fine animals ahead of himself. Jacob reasons, "I may appease him with the present that goes ahead of me, and afterward I shall see his face. Perhaps he will accept me" (Gen. 32:20). Jacob is seeking to appease the just wrath of his brother with an offering so that he will not be attacked for his sin against Esau.

The various Bible versions translate the *propitiate* verb as "appease," "pacify," "conciliate," or "propitiate." Therefore, those who exclude the idea of appeasing wrath with an offering go against its clear use in the ancient Jewish translation of the Bible.

*So you don't believe that* propitiation *means "expiation" or "the cleansing of sin and defilement"?*

We do. If you hold to propitiation, appeasing God's wrath, you also hold to taking care of sin. That means sin is cleansed and divine wrath is pacified as the penalty is paid.

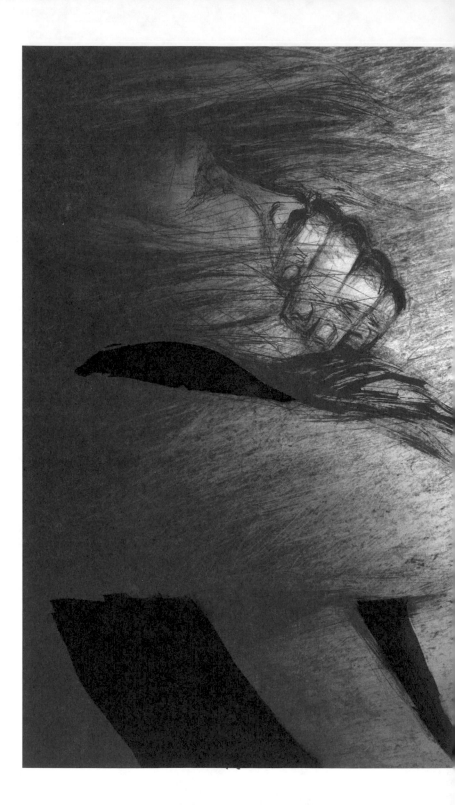

# CHAPTER SEVEN

# "He Raped Me": Jesus Is Mary's Expiation

*If we walk in the light, as he is in the light, we have fellowship with one another, and the blood of Jesus his Son cleanses us from all sin.*

1 JOHN 1:7

**As we sat together Mary told me the story of her life,** and it broke my heart. I wept uncontrollably for the first time in many years.

She was raised in a Christian home and walked with Jesus faithfully and joyfully until she had her first boyfriend in high school. He was a bit older and came from a deeply troubled family. Their relationship started out when they met in the church youth group, and he quickly grew more controlling of her. It began with him dictating her wardrobe, then her friends, and finally her schedule. He controlled where she could go and what she could do. He even transferred to her high school so he could keep an eye on her and ensure that she was not speaking to other guys or breaking any of his laws since he ruled her like a false god.

To make matters worse, he would physically abuse her by throwing her up against walls, locking her in his car while he cussed her out, and robbing her of her dignity. She grew to be so afraid of him that she would try not to be alone with him for fear of being physically or emotionally hurt. Understandably, she did not feel safe with him, loved by him, or attracted to him and subsequently did not want to have any sexual relationship with him. But he would have none of it and soon began forcing himself on her.

She would try and get away or would occasionally appease him with a sexual favor in an effort to be left alone. However, he began raping her and continued doing so for nearly two years, although she did not admit to herself that she was being sexually abused until many years later. Her shame grew as he forced sexual favors on her while they were on youth group retreats and church outings. His mother even walked in on them during a sexual act at one point, which only multiplied her shameful disgrace.

The relationship deteriorated and she was terrified because his physical, verbal, and sexual abuse continued to escalate. One day, he locked her in his car and told her he had a secret he would confess if she promised not to break up with him. She agreed, and he then told her that he had also been sleeping with another girl. Upon hearing of his betrayal, she decided in her heart to break up with him.

Amazingly, she did not consider the ongoing verbal, sexual, and emotional abuse reason enough to end the relationship, but for some reason his sexual infidelity seemed like sufficient cause for her to walk away from her abuser. Within a few days, she told him she did not want to date him any longer, and he grew increasingly violent and dangerous. He began stalking her, following her after school wherever she went and sometimes even jumping out of bushes late at night to terrify her and threaten her about what he would do if she did not return to him.

Around this time, another young man in her school befriended her. He came from an abusive family where his father was violent, and so he had a particular hatred for abusive men as well as the courage to fight them. The young man took her out on a date, during which her ex-boyfriend showed up on his motorcycle and nearly ran her over, terrifying her. The new young man in her life snapped and wanted to pull the ex-boyfriend off the bike and beat him, but the cowardly ex drove away in haste. He was willing to beat on a young girl but unwilling to stand toe-to-toe with a young man. From that day forward, the new boyfriend chose to be her defender and protector, ensuring that harm would never come to her again.

They dated for some years and eventually entered into Christian marriage, but they had a very hard marriage because of her shame. She was ashamed that she had been raped and controlled by a guy who was not handsome, smart, successful, or kind—in short, a loser. To make matters worse, the loser boyfriend had ended up cheating on her with another, less attractive girl, which added to her shame. Eventually she got out of the relationship with the loser cheating boyfriend, thanks in part to the intervention of the new boyfriend, her future husband, who cared for her.

However, while dating her husband, she had cheated on him, which only further added to her shame. To make matters even worse, she did not tell her husband of the rapes done to her or her cheating against him until they had been married some years. She knew that he would not have married her if he had known she had been unfaithful. She felt like damaged goods, and so she spent the first years of their marriage hiding her deep secrets from her husband and being ruled by shame.

She rarely looked her husband in the eye, rarely made love to him with any passion, rarely spoke to him at the heart level, and as a result he broke a little bit every day, not knowing the truth of her life's story and why he was not allowed to know or love her. He remained sexually faithful to her and was never physically violent, but he was verbally abusive as his frustration welled up, causing him to lash out in angry words that only contributed to her shame. Once she finally did confess her infidelity and admit to him the truth of her rape-filled first relationship, they both entered into a long process of learning the gospel and using it to heal their brokenness. This letter is written to her from me, as her pastor, with the hope of the gospel bandaging her soul wounds.

◎　◎　◎　◎　◎

## Dear Mary,

I have spent many hours since we last spoke praying through what I would say to you and what counsel I would give you. Before I begin, let me first say that, as your pastor, I love you very much and will seek to be pointedly honest with you. I ask that you not turn my words toward your shame; my goal is not to see you further shamed but rather cleansed. The theologians call this cleansing from the stain of sin on our soul *expiation*. I am certain that Jesus longs to expiate your soul from the filth that has defiled it, and I thank him for allowing me the honor of explaining how that is possible for you.

Your story, like so many, sadly begins with sins of omission. Your father failed to defend you as a young woman. He failed to teach you about young men so that you would be wise and safe. He failed to know your first boyfriend and prevent him from ever dating you. He failed to establish clear boundaries for your relationships with boys and to vigorously defend those boundaries. Worst of all, he failed to develop a heart-level, honest, and loving relationship with you, so you never did run to him for help, and he did not know you well enough to see that you were hurting and needed your daddy.

For that, with tears in my eyes, I would simply say that I am truly, deeply, and painfully sorry. As the daddy of two lovely girls, I realize that these kinds of sins of omission by a daddy are altogether devastating and leave the door open for sins of commission. I know you initially struggled to see your father's relationship with you as sinful because, as you said, "He never did anything." That is true. Your father did not abuse you, but by doing nothing he was sinning, and one of the worst sins a daddy can commit is simply doing nothing.

While your daddy was guilty of committing sins of omission against you, his sin allowed your boyfriend the opportunity to commit sins of commission against you. Your boyfriend took your virginity, he took your innocence, he took your freedom, he took your dignity, he took your joy, and he sinned against you in word and deed as a rapist, bully, and sadist of the worst kind whom Jesus will repay severely if he does not repent. You have spoken candidly of the sense of dirtiness and shame you feel because of his evil deeds. Leviticus speaks repeatedly about the defiling impact of sexual sins like this. You feel filthy even though you did nothing wrong in the rapes. To make matters worse, you were not only raped but also tormented. His locking you in rooms and cars, stalking you, and physically restraining you from escape was a life of torture that has broken your spirit and shaped every day of your life since.

I also want you to see that in all of this you too are a sinner. You began the relationship by having sex with the boy, which is in no way an excuse for his later sexual abuse, but it did cloud your judgment of him and distanced you from God and your family and set you up for the abuse. You lied to your fiancé and to your pastor during your premarital counseling, about your infidelity while dating your fiancé and your rape prior to meeting him.

I understand that you were filled with shame, but the fact remains that you have spent many years of your life keeping secrets, hiding, and lying. This has prevented you from getting help and has kept your husband from truly knowing you. Subsequently, you have denied your husband your heart, body, and soul for many years and have nearly destroyed him because he aches to be close to you.

Also, in cheating on him while dating and then lying about it until you were married, you robbed him of his right to know and decide if he actually wanted to marry you. Subsequently, he is struggling with the fact that you lied to him and feeling that you trapped him into marriage and then did not love him well. Your sin hurt both you and your husband. It also hurt the God who loves you and whom you love.

My point in all of this is to show you the destructive and deadly nature of sin. The hard truth is that we are all sinners who do evil to others, and you are a sinner who has done evil to your husband. We are also all victims of sin that has been done to us, and you are a victim of sins of omission by your daddy and sins of commission by your first boyfriend.

The tricky part of dealing with sin is that the typical Christian gospel presentation only deals with sins for which we bear responsibility and guilt. It only addresses wrong things we did (commission) or things we ought to have done but did not do (omission). What I mean is this: the typical gospel presentation is that we are all sinners, and if we confess our sins to Jesus he will forgive our sins through his sinless life, substitutionary death, and bodily resurrection. This is clearly true according to Scripture.

For you, however, this gospel addresses only the sins that you have committed (active sin) and neglects to deal with the sins that have been committed against you (passive sin). You cannot repent of being raped, beaten, tortured, and abused for two years of your life because those are not sins you committed, but rather sins that were committed against you. Thankfully, the gospel of Jesus does have something to offer you.

Throughout the Bible, some dozen words are used to speak of sin frequently in terms of staining our soul, defiling us, and causing us to be filthy or unclean (e.g., Ps. 106:39; Prov. 30:11–12; Mark 7:20). The effect of sin, particularly sins committed against us, is that we feel dirty. One rape victim explained to me, for example, that after being raped she took a shower because she just felt dirty. What she was referring to was much deeper than just her body; somehow her soul had also been stained by the sin committed against her.

Furthermore, the Bible gives a number of causes for our defilement, such as any sin and involvement with false religions and/or the occult (Lev. 19:31; Ezek. 14:11). Scripture also speaks of violence as a cause of defilement (e.g., Lam. 4:14).

Perhaps the most common cause of defilement in Scripture, however, is sexual sin. Genesis 34:5 speaks of a young woman named Dinah who, like you, was raped and was thus "defiled." First Chronicles 5:1 speaks of incest between a stepmother and her adult stepson and that "he [Reuben] defiled his father's [Jacob's] couch." Referring to adultery, Numbers 5:27 says, "She has defiled herself and has broken faith with her husband." Speaking of prostitution, which includes stripping and exchanging sexual favors for gifts, Leviticus 21:14 names such women among the "defiled."

My simple point in all of this is to show you, Mary, that your soul has been stained and defiled by the filth of sin that you have committed and that has been committed against you. I would also like to further explain how this defilement is tied not only to your identity but to your entire life in hopes that you begin to see what else has been defiled.

In Scripture there are three categories of defilement. First, places become defiled by sin (Lev. 18:24–30; Num. 35:34). For example, I know of a Christian family that awoke one morning to discover that some evil man had broken into their very young daughter's bedroom during the night to rape and molest her. The family was rightfully devastated and had to leave the home for a few days because it had to be secured as a crime scene. While staying in a hotel, the father decided that his home had been so defiled that they could never again return there. So, their church packed up their things and moved the family from the defiled home that they refused ever to enter again.

Thus, I must ask you, what places are defiled in your mind? For example, you mentioned that you avoid being alone in a room with your husband not because he is dangerous, but because when you used to find yourself alone with your boyfriend, he would grope you, demand sexual favors, and trap you until you gave in to his demands.

Second, things, such as the marriage bed, become defiled by sin (Heb. 13:4). For example, I know of one woman who would suffer panic attacks around bedtime at the prospect of going to bed with her husband. He loved her and was a kind, godly man, and he did not understand why she was so afraid of lying with him in their bed. She confessed to him that she had developed breasts at an early age and that her father, who had snuggled with her while reading bedtime stories and praying with her, began fondling her breasts and masturbating on her sheets nearly every night. She felt so disgusted that when he would leave her room she would take her pillow and doll and sleep under her bed because it had been defiled. Consequently, the thought of lying in bed with her husband and being intimate with him triggered for her horrifying memories of defilement.

What things are defiled in your mind, Mary? Is your body dirty because your boyfriend touched it? Do you prefer not to undress or bathe in front of your husband or let him see you naked because your body has been defiled?

Third, people are defiled by sin. The Old Testament and the Gospels are filled with people who were ritually unclean and were not to be touched or associated with. The commandments for ceremonial washings and such foreshadow the cleansing power of the death of Jesus. I have noticed that women who have been defiled either deny themselves sexual pleasure in an effort not to do anything they consider "dirty" or embrace their filth and become sexually loose women.

One such girl I spoke to many years ago had sex with so many partners she could not keep count and had been fired for having sex on the job at a retail store with five men at one time. When I asked her why she was so promiscuous, she explained that she had been molested by many men beginning at a very young age, and since she was a dirty girl she decided she was supposed to always do dirty things.

For you, Mary, the defilement has caused you to disdain your own body. Because you derived some occasional pleasure from your sexual abuse, you came to view your body as an enemy that caused your boyfriend to lust after you and that got you into trouble and mocked you with some pleasure as you were violated. Since that time you have guarded your desires and covered your body in an effort to drive your husband away from desiring you and to prevent you from experiencing joyous pleasure when the two of you are together sexually. Do you see that you consider yourself a defiled person?

The predictable result of defilement is shame, including the fear of being found out and known and having our deep, dark secret revealed.

This pattern is firmly established with the first sin of our first parents in Genesis 3. At the end of Genesis 2, God created our first parents to be naked together as a married couple, which displayed complete intimacy, knowing, and oneness without any shame. However, once sin entered the world, by Eve's commission of taking that which God forbade and Adam's cowardly sin of omission of doing nothing but standing idly by while Satan deceived his bride, everything changed.

Our first parents, filled with shame, covered themselves with fig leaves to hide from one another. They also hid from God and ran from intimacy and love toward isolation and death, propelled by shame. Additionally, they were filled with the fear of being found out and truly known for who they were as defiled sinners. Practically, I have noticed that people filled with shame cannot look you in the eye; shame seems to be revealed in the eyes. Your husband alluded to this when he said that you never really looked at him or gazed into his eyes.

Let me be clear that I am not defining shame as something altogether bad. Many counselors, even some Christian counselors, will speak of shame as if it were by and large a bad thing. I disagree. Shame exists where there is sin, and so feeling ashamed, particularly when we sin, is natural and healthy. A sinner that does not feel shame has a broken conscience and runs the risk of becoming an amoral sociopath. Therefore, shame is not bad, but unless the sin that causes the shame is redeemed, the shame will remain with devastating implications.

Tragically, this pattern of sin-defilement-shame-hiding continues through four possible roles that defiled people can assume. These roles are the fig leaves they and their secret hide behind, according to some experts I know in the field of sexual abuse. As I explain these, Mary, I need you to be honest about which fig leaf you are wearing—the role you are playing, the person you are pretending to be—so that you can repent of not only your sin but, as Romans 1:18 says, your efforts to suppress the truth of what you have done and what has been done to you, which contribute to your ongoing additional sin.

The first fig leaf is worn by the good girl. The good girl is successful, pleasant, and dependable. One friend described his wife as a lake with no waves, which is a fitting analogy. The good girl rarely, if ever, gets angry; she apologizes when anything goes wrong whether or not it is her fault and seeks to serve others and make them happy at the cost of her own health and well-being. The good girl is essentially dead, devoid of passion, and consumed with trying to smile, be good, and do the right thing, hoping to convince everyone that she is fine when she is really broken and devastated. The good girl fears conflict and pursues peace at all costs, even if that sometimes means she is sinned against or feels the need to sin to keep everyone happy with her.

The second fig leaf is worn by the tough girl. The tough girl has been hurt, and she projects to the world her confidence, anger, and toughness so that no one has the courage to hurt her again. The tough girl is respected by many but known and loved by few. What she really desires is intimacy and love, but she is so afraid of being hurt that she develops a hard outer shell that repels everyone. She thus achieves her goal of ensuring that she does not get hurt but is also left all alone and desperately lonely.

The tough girl often wishes she did not have to be tough, but her inability to trust anyone or feel truly safe in any relationship means that her guard rarely, if ever, comes down. The tough girl is also frequently the defender of the weak and hurting. She is keenly aware of those who are hurting, and she appoints herself as their protector and advocate. Sadly, the tough girl is truly not as tough as she appears and often suffers both anger and despair because she does not know how to be anything but a tough girl and feels trapped in an identity that not only keeps her from harm but also from love.

The third fig leaf is worn by the party girl. The party girl is the life of the party, the center of attention, fun to be with, and prone to self-medicate with drugs, food, and alcohol. The party girl has learned to mask her pain with laughter and is adept at making fun of even the most horrifying parts of her life. Thus, when she reveals to others who she truly is, it is done in a way that makes everyone laugh and overlook the painful hurt she suffers.

The party girl is also prone not to get visibly angry but rather to use her anger to cut others with biting irony and sarcasm, which is violence done through comedy. While the party girl is surrounded with people, the crowds only conceal her loneliness; few, if any, people truly know who she is and how she is feeling. This is because she so convincingly projects to others that she is happily enjoying her life and is surrounded by people who care. Sadly, it is all an illusion.

The fourth fig leaf is worn by the church lady. The church lady hides behind her religious piety, ministry work, and systematic theology. The church lady reads books and learns spiritual truth to help others but rarely uses it for her own healing. The church lady loves to pour herself out to help hurting people because it allows her to feel sorrow and grief vicariously while enabling her to avoid her own pain. The church lady is also prone to becoming rigidly moralistic and legalistic, judging other people and feeling hurt when people don't seem grateful for all she does.

The church lady often turns even a simple conversation into an opportunity to judge someone harshly, argues over the finer points of theology unnecessarily, or turns literally everything into a spiritualized discussion complete with lots of Bible verses, which are used as little more than a diversion from the matters of her heart.

The church lady is also often a phony optimist. While expounding the sovereignty of God, victory in Jesus, and power of the Holy Spirit with a legion of proof-text Bible verses, the church lady sadly treats Scripture as she would pagan mantras, hoping that if she says them frequently and confidently, somehow her problems will be fixed.

I suspect that you prefer to wear a good girl fig leaf and a church lady fig leaf. As you evaluate your life, I suspect you will find occasions with certain friends where you were also the party girl who went out for drinks and dancing.

Mary, having said all of this, I suspect you are feeling exposed. I have taken away your fig leaves and left you, in a sense, naked and known. My goal is not to shame you but to redress you in the righteousness of Jesus Christ.

The truth is that what is at stake is nothing short of the identity you have and, subsequently, the life you live out of that identity. You can no longer allow your identity to be shaped by what you have done by cheating on your fiancé, lying to him and your pastor, and denying your husband love and intimacy for so many years. You can no longer allow your identity to be shaped by what has been done to you by the failure of your father, the rape of your boyfriend, or the angry words of your bitter husband.

Mary, if I were preaching this to you, I would be shouting at this point; so please hear my plea for your stained soul. Your identity must be marked only by what Jesus Christ has done for you and no longer by what has been done by or to you. To explain this, the Bible uses terms such as atonement, cleansing, and a purifying fountain that washes away our defilement. The following verses illustrate my point well, that you are dirty but can be cleansed:

> For on this day shall atonement be made for you to cleanse you. You shall be clean before the LORD from all your sins. (Lev. 16:30)

> "I will cleanse them from all the guilt of their sin against me, and I will forgive all the guilt of their sin and rebellion against me." (Jer. 33:8)

> "On that day there shall be a fountain opened for the house of David and the inhabitants of Jerusalem, to cleanse them from sin and uncleanness." (Zech. 13:1)

On the cross, Jesus dealt with the sin that has stained your soul. Jesus both forgave your sins at the cross and cleanses you from all sins that you have committed and that have been committed against you.

These sins have resulted in great shame for you, which Jesus also dealt with on the cross. Sadly, one of the effects of sin is that it has made you feel contempt and disdain for yourself as a despicable person unworthy of love, intimacy, and joy, despite the fact that you are an image bearer of God. Through the cross, though, Jesus Christ has taken your sin and shame away forever.

This wonderful truth is perhaps most clearly illustrated by the Old Testament Day of Atonement, or Yom Kippur, which was the holiest day of the year. On this day, the sin problem between people and God was dealt with.

To represent the sinlessness of Jesus who was coming as the perfect substitutionary sacrifice, two healthy goats without defect were chosen. The first goat was slaughtered as a sin offering. That goat represented propitiation and foreshadowed the cross of Jesus, where the just wrath of God was satisfied through death as penalty for sin.

Then the high priest, acting as the representative and mediator between the sinful people and their holy God, would take the second goat and lay his hands on the animal while confessing the sins of the people. This goat, called the scapegoat, would then be sent away to run free into the wilderness, symbolically taking their sins with it. Theologically, we call this the doctrine of *expiation*, whereby our sin is expiated, or taken away, so that we are made clean through Jesus, who is our scapegoat.

Jesus not only went to the cross to die for your sin but also to scorn your shame. As Hebrews 12:1–3 says, "Let us run with endurance the race that is set before us, looking to Jesus, the founder and perfecter of our faith, who for the joy that was set before him endured the cross, despising the *shame*, and is seated at the right hand of the throne of God."

Mary, Jesus is the only way out of the mess that is your life and marriage. Jesus relates to the disgrace, shame, and defilement that you have suffered. Jesus was betrayed by someone he loved and considered a friend, just like you. Jesus' own friends did nothing for him in his moment of greatest need, just like your worthless friends. Jesus' family essentially turned their backs on him as yours did. Jesus was humiliated in degrading ways as you were. Jesus' body was stripped publicly, and his body was beaten even worse than yours was. He was mocked while he suffered torment, as you were. His beard was pulled out, which in that day was as disgraceful to a man as rape is to a woman.

Like you, he was held against his will to be tormented and defiled. As Hebrews 4:15 says, Jesus can sympathize with you in your weaknesses. Better still, Jesus scorned your shame, and because of Jesus you too can scorn your shame and regard it with the contempt and condemnation that it has imposed on you. In the expiating work of Jesus, your sin and shame have been fully taken away forever.

As a result, you can walk in the light with others who love you. I know you have longed for intimacy with your husband and Christian friends, but your shame has kept you from opening up and being fully known by others. On this point 1 John 1:7–9 says:

> But if we walk in the light, as he is in the light, we have fellowship with one another, and the blood of Jesus his Son cleanses us from all sin. If we say we have no sin, we deceive ourselves, and the truth is not in us. If we confess our sins, he is faithful and just to forgive us our sins and to cleanse us from all unrighteousness.

To begin, you must confess. That just means that you need to talk about the sins you did, along with the sins done against you, with Jesus, your husband, trustworthy female friends, and a trustworthy pastor or biblical counselor. You must journal out your sins and the sins committed against you and name what you have done and what has been done to you. This could take some time, as there are likely memories that you have worked hard to forget and hide because of your shame. There are secrets that you want no one to know that must be made known to Jesus, your husband, and a good pastor or biblical counselor.

This is what it means to walk in the light. Like children cowering in darkness, when we choose shame over Jesus we are hiding like our first parents, afraid of being known while dying in loneliness. However, if we confess our sin and shame, bring it into the light for others to see, and stop hiding behind our fig leaves, we can finally have deep and meaningful heart-level friendships with others, which is what the Bible means by the word *fellowship*. This begins with Jesus and your husband and will include some godly women from the church who have also scorned their shame and can meet with you to study the Bible and show you the work of Jesus in their life.

I know you may think that your sin and the sins committed against you are simply too gross and horrific to be made known, but Jesus' best friend, John, assures us that Jesus can and will purify us from *all* sin. Therefore, if we say that we are over our sin because it is in our past or make light of it because we are okay, then we are deceived like Satan and liars living lives of rebellion, not unlike demons who deny their wrongdoing and continue in a life of rebellion without honest repentance from sin. Yet if we name our sin and shame and come clean, we can enjoy two amazing accomplishments that Jesus secured for us on the cross.

One, Jesus will "forgive us our sin." Mary, this includes sleeping with your first boyfriend before the abuse started, cheating on your fiancé, denying him love and intimacy in marriage, lying to your pastor, lying to your husband, and living a fake life by pretending to be a godly woman while serving others for selfish reasons, and arrogantly judging others when they needed the gospel. You can and will be forgiven if you truly confess to Jesus and your husband and live a life of ongoing repentance.

I want to stress that your confession is not a work that earns Jesus' forgiveness. First John 2:1–2 clarifies this: "My little children, I am writing these things to you so that you may not sin. But if anyone does sin, we have an advocate with the Father, Jesus Christ the righteous. He is the propitiation for our sins, and not for ours only but also for the sins of the whole world." Jesus has already done the work on the cross to provide propitiation and forgiveness for every sin you have ever committed. No sin is beyond Jesus' work. There is no need for any sort of addition to his work. When he said, "It is finished," he meant it. Your confession merely opens you to the power of his work.

Two, Jesus will "purify us from all unrighteousness." Mary, this means that the filth that has come upon your soul by the failures of your father, violence of your boyfriend, and angry words of your husband can and will be purified, purged, and cleansed from your soul. Jesus shed his blood for you, Mary, to forgive your sin and cleanse your defilement. There is no one like Jesus, and no one who can accomplish what Jesus has done for you. Like John says, only Jesus is faithful and will not sin against you but will always help you. Only Jesus is just and will not allow any sin done to you or by you to be overlooked without being dealt with. This means that he died in your place for your sins justly. It also means that unless your rapist repents of sin and trusts in Jesus, he will experience a just eternity in torment like the hellish treatment he sadistically inflicted on you.

The beauty of this truth of the expiating or cleansing work of Jesus is poetically shown in symbolic acts throughout Scripture. I will leave them with you as images upon which to meditate in hopes that God the Holy Spirit would allow you to see yourself in these ways.

First, in washing after repentance of sin, we see that God has done to our soul what bathing does to our body. Exodus 19:10 says, "The LORD said to Moses, 'Go to the people and consecrate them today and tomorrow, and let them wash their garments.'" Mary, from this day forward I want you to remember the cleansing work of Jesus every time you do your laundry or dress yourself in clean clothes; use those opportunities as a visual reminder of the expiating work of Jesus for you.

Second, in baptism we identify with Jesus' burial and resurrection, which cleanses us from sin in the same way that water cleanses us from filth. Acts 22:16 says it this way: "Rise and be baptized and wash away your sins, calling on his name." I know that you have already been baptized, but from this day forward I would ask that every time you bathe, you remember how Jesus has cleansed your soul. Use the cleansing power of the water as a visual reminder of what Jesus has done to cleanse your soul.

Third, I want you to remember Jesus every time you wear white. Describing the marriage of Jesus and his bride, the church, upon his second coming, Revelation 19:7–8 says, "Let us rejoice and exult and give him the glory, for the marriage of the Lamb has come, and his Bride has made herself ready; it was granted her to clothe herself with fine linen, bright and pure." Certainly the church is not a bride who wears white because she is sinless and pure. Rather, the church is a bride who wears white only because Jesus has forgiven her sin and cleansed her filth.

In closing, I will share a story with you that illustrates this point well. A friend of mine had been married to a woman he dearly loved for many years. Yet they were never as close and intimate as he desired, and he could not figure out why. It was because his wife was, like you, filled with shame. She had been molested as a girl, raped as a young woman, and promiscuous throughout much of her teen years. She even cheated on her husband during their engagement and did not share these shameful, dark secrets with him. After many years, she finally told her husband who she truly was, what she had truly done, and what had been truly done to her.

The truth devastated her husband, who would have never married her had he known of her infidelity during their engagement and possibly would have walked away from her as damaged goods had he only known about the many times she was molested as a young girl, raped as a young woman, and promiscuous in her teens. At this point she feared that her husband would leave her and want nothing to do with her. Then he did the unthinkable: he left their home, and she did not know where he was going or if he would ever return.

Because he knew the gospel of Jesus Christ, though, he went to the store and purchased for her a new, clean white nightgown. He returned home and asked her to undress in front of him and clothe herself in white, which she did. He then said that he had chosen to see her not by what she had done or by what had been done to her, but instead solely by what Jesus had done for her to forgive her sin and cleanse her filth. He embraced her and prayed for her, and she wept tears that purified her soul as her sin was scorned by the love of Jesus and her husband, who was filled with the Spirit of God. This is what God the Father intends for you, his daughter. Because of Jesus, your husband will view you that way soon, as he learns to see you not by what you have done or what has been done to you, but rather solely by what Jesus has done for you. As an act of worship, I ask you to remember the expiating work of Jesus every time you wear white.

# Answers to Common Questions about Expiation

*I've heard that liberals are the ones who believe in expiation rather than propitiation. Didn't the Revised Standard Version of the Bible distort the gospel when it translated the word* propitiation *as* expiation?

To translate the word *propitiation* as the word *expiation* is a serious error that leads to theological problems. For example, there are those who deny propitiation, the satisfaction of God's wrath by the pouring out of that wrath on Jesus. In so doing, they deny an essential part of the gospel and need to be labeled as false teachers. But the Bible is just as clear that, through the cross, Jesus cleanses sin. That is what we mean by expiation.

Those who deny this aspect, often in a reactionary response to liberal error, also truncate the gospel. When we look at the Day of Atonement in Leviticus 16, we see that there are two goats. One is the propitiatory sacrifice and the other, the scapegoat, is the expiatory sacrifice. That is the goat that takes the sin and defilement away. For a complete view of atonement, you must have both goats.

P. T. Forsyth put it this way: "The blood of Christ stands not simply for the sting of sin on God but the scourge of God on sin, not simply for God's sorrow over sin but for God's wrath on sin."[1]

*Isn't the cross about forgiveness and getting to go to heaven?*

It is. But it is also about a lot more, such as cleansing and new life now. The work of God in the cross of Jesus Christ is both objective (forensic and external) and subjective (personal and internal). The Bible is very clear: it is Jesus Christ who "loves us and has freed us from our sins by his blood and made us a kingdom, priests to his God and Father, to him be glory and dominion forever and ever. Amen" (Rev. 1:5–6). In another place it says that "the blood of Christ, who through the eternal Spirit offered himself without blemish to God, [will] purify our conscience" (Heb. 9:14).

As Christians, we should never settle for enjoying only part of what Jesus has accomplished for us. Eternal life is a new life lived in relationship with Jesus, which begins in this life, grows throughout this life, and culminates in our eternal life in heaven with him.

# CHAPTER EIGHT

# "My Daddy Is a Pastor": Jesus Is Gideon's Unlimited Limited Atonement

*He is the propitiation for our sins, and not for ours only but also for the sins of the whole world.*

1 JOHN 2:2

**Gideon Joseph is the youngest of my five children.** At the time I am writing this chapter, he is one-and-a-half-years-old. He has blond hair and blue eyes like his mamma, and broad shoulders and a thick frame like his poppa-daddy.

Gideon is incredibly cute and fun. One of his first words was "ball," and he likes to put on his baseball glove and join his two big brothers, Zachariah Blaise and Calvin Martin, as we play together in the yard. He can already hit off a tee and has a good right-handed arm, though his defense admittedly needs work. His big brothers are both Christians who love him very dearly and are very kind to their little brother. In their words, Gideon is part of the posse known as "the Driscoll boys."

Gideon's oldest brother, "buddy Zac," began praying on his own before he was even two and was baptized at the age of four after meeting with one of the pastors in our church to share his testimony and answer the same theological questions that the adults who want to be baptized answer. Now, at the age of seven, he has a few translations of the Bible in his top bunk because he's decided to read through the entire Bible as a first-grader.

On the bottom bunk under Zac is "buddy Calvin," who is five-years-old. Zac led Calvin in the sinners' prayer on Zac's seventh birthday while they were lying in their bunks at night. Zac had secretly been asking Jesus for a birthday present: he'd like his brother to become a Christian. Every night, Gideon's older brothers pray for his salvation. During the day, they look after him and love him well as they eat snacks, pretend to be Ultimate Fighters, build forts, pee in the yard, and try to figure out how to throw a curveball.

Gideon has two older sisters who are lovely girly-girls, enamored with shoes and anything creative from food to music to art. Three-year-old Alexie Grace loves hanging out with her family and singing and dancing around the house in various princess dress-ups. She loves Gideon, whom, for some reason, she has nicknamed Pooka, and makes sure that he has plenty of snacks and kisses every day.

Gideon's other sister is our oldest, Ashley, who is nine. She too loves Jesus and spends regular time in Scripture and likes to write out what God is showing her each night in her prayer journal before she falls asleep. Gideon's sisters are jewels and super fun, which is why he lights up around them. The girls also pray for "Giddy" every night and are very sweet to him, constantly tending to him and looking after him.

My wife, Grace, and I love Gideon and thank God for him often. My wife is petite, and I have a big head, which resulted in C-sections with the birth of each of our children. Having endured one miscarriage and four C-sections, Grace was ready to be done with pregnancies. But I was not yet ready to do anything to prevent God from giving us a child. So, we left it in God's hands and were given Gideon, whom I affectionately refer to as Guppy, for being the youngest, and as Flip Flop, because at a very young age he decided he only wanted to wear flip-flops on the wrong feet for the rest of his life. To her credit, Grace often gives me a hug and thanks me for not stopping at four children, because Gideon has been an absolute blessing and joy to our family.

Grace and I first met at the age of seventeen in high school. By God's grace, Jesus saved me and made me a Christian when I was nineteen, and at the age of twenty-one Grace and I were married. I do not believe I would have been a good father before my salvation because I was prone to moments of rage.

My upbringing included violence and, not knowing Jesus, I began to adopt some of the very same sins, such as anger and violence, that surrounded me. Had Jesus not saved me from myself, Satan, sin, and death, I am certain that I would not have married a Christian woman like Grace. Without the cross I am also certain that I would not have an enduring and forgiving marriage, and I would be prone to outbursts of anger and rage toward my children. However, because of Jesus' powerful transforming grace, Gideon's dad is a Christian with a marriage in which the gospel is doing its work every day.

I am no longer an angry, violent man, but rather a daddy who is very physically affectionate and likes to wrestle and snuggle with his kids, including Gideon. Gideon and I are so close that he wants to spend literally every moment of every day with me; if I even step out of the house for a minute to get something from my car, he has a complete meltdown, weeping bitterly with his face pushed up against our glass door, as if I were heading to war with little hope of ever returning.

Both sides of our family live near us in the greater Seattle area and see Gideon often. Gideon's grandfather on his momma's side has been a pastor for roughly fifty years, and his grandmother has been a Christian most of her life. The aunts and uncles on Grace's side of the family are all Christians who are actively involved in their local church and very kind to Gideon.

Similarly, my dad and Gideon's grandpa (from whom Gideon gets his middle name, Joseph) has become a Christian in more recent years. He and my mom, who has been a Christian for many years, are really wonderful grandparents who shower Gideon with love and affection. Additionally, my four siblings are also very kind to Gideon, and he is well loved by everyone and is a very affectionate boy as a result.

In addition to all of that, Gideon is surrounded by our church family at Mars Hill where I pastor. There, many families are involved in his life, and he receives much encouragement, prayer, and love from more people than we can even name. Furthermore, our house is often filled with Christian leaders from a wide variety of ministries from whom my children glean a great deal about Jesus. In summary, Gideon's life is filled with the effects of God's grace. My fear is that as he gets older he may take for granted all of the work Jesus has done to create the world that he was born into. This letter is written to my son Gideon so that when he gets a little bit older he can come to fully understand and appreciate Jesus' cross as the source of the blessings he enjoys.

◉   ◉   ◉   ◉   ◎

## Dear Gideon,

Because sin has entered the world, nothing is perfect. There are no perfect parents, perfect siblings, or perfect families. But because Jesus died for sin, we can put to death our sin and live new lives patterned after his by the power of God the Holy Spirit. As a result, because of Jesus you have parents, siblings, and a family that, while not perfect, are far better than would have ever been possible apart from Jesus.

For example, before I met Jesus I was guilty of sexual sin. I was sexually active prior to marriage and also occasionally looked at pornography. But because Jesus died for those sins and saved me from them, I have been able to put those sins to death. As a result, you were brought into a family where your mom and I truly love one another and have been faithful to one another in every way. We know that apart from Jesus, dying for our sin, sin would have killed our marriage. You would have been either raised by a single mother or trapped in a home of sin and bitterness, marked by unrest and hostility between your mother and me, if it were not for Jesus' death on the cross.

Furthermore, because Jesus has been at work in your siblings, you have been greatly blessed by how they have treated you. In no way have they been sinless in their interactions with you, but the work of Jesus in them is evident in how they treat you. For example, from a young age when you would frustrate your older brothers by messing up a picture they were working on, breaking their toys, or throwing their action figures in the toilet, they would often lovingly instruct you rather than beat you up as big brothers are prone to do. Also, your sisters routinely thank God aloud for bringing you into their lives, and just yesterday I walked into the room to see your three-year-old sister with her hand on top of your one-year-old head, praying to Jesus for you and thanking him for "my little Pooka."

Jesus has been at work in your extended family. Your grandpa Joseph, from whom you get your middle name, has been used by God to change the entire course of our family. His family history included a lot of drunken domestic violence, and, because Jesus died for the sins he has committed and those committed against him, your grandpa has been able to put to death the sins that have plagued men in our family for generations. In many ways, your grandpa is a bit of a patriarch, and our family history has made a great transition because of Jesus' work in his life in recent years.

Were it not for Jesus, it is certain that the sins of previous generations of men would still be at work. I likely would have been a violent daddy whom you feared, and you would have grown up to be a bitter and angry man yourself, who simply repeated the cycle of sin and death with your own wife and children. Thankfully, Jesus died so that we could live new lives.

First Peter 1:18–19 beautifully explains what Jesus' death means for you: "Knowing that you were ransomed from the futile ways inherited from your forefathers, not with perishable things such as silver or gold, but with the precious blood of Christ, like that of a lamb without blemish or spot."

Because I did not grow up with a Christian father or as a Christian, I am deeply aware of the difference Jesus has made in our family and how blessed you are to have been born into a family where Jesus has already been so diligently at work to forgive and cleanse sin. My fear is that, having lived only in a family where Jesus has already worked, you will not fully appreciate or even recognize the many benefits that come to you through his death and resurrection. I am writing this when you are little in faith so that one day, when you are old enough to understand it, Jesus will use it to help grow you in your love and appreciation for who he is and what he has done for you.

My focus here is to answer the enormous question, "For whom did Jesus Christ die?" This question, as much as perhaps any other, has generated some of the most heated and varied answers in church history. To help you understand these varying answers, I have compiled the following chart (which I'm assuming won't surprise you, as you know your pop is a bit of a theological neatnik).

|  | Heresy of "Christian" Universalism | Heresy of Contemporary Pelagianism | Unlimited Atonement | Limited Atonement | Unlimited Limited Atonement |
|---|---|---|---|---|---|
| **View of Sin** | We are born sinful but guilty for our sins, not Adam's. | We are born sinless like Adam but follow his bad example. | We are born sinful but guilty for our sins, not Adam's. | We are born sinners guilty in Adam. | We are born sinners guilty in Adam. |
| **Who Jesus Died For** | Jesus took all the sin and pain of the world onto himself. | Jesus lived and died only as an example for sinners. | Jesus died to provide payment for the sin of all people. | Jesus died to achieve full atonement for the elect. | Jesus died to provide payment for all, but only in a saving way for the elect. |
| **How Atonement Is Applied** | God's powerful love in Jesus will overcome all sin. | Anyone can follow the example of Jesus by living a good life. | God will apply the payment to those who believe in Christ. | God designed the atonement precisely for the elect. | While God desires the salvation of all, he applies the payment to the elect, those whom he chose for salvation. |
| **Heaven & Hell** | Everyone will be saved and will go to heaven. There is no eternal hell. | Those who live a Christlike life will be saved and go to heaven. Those who reject goodness will go to hell. | All who accept the gift go to heaven. Everyone else gets to follow their free will and choose to go to hell. | God does not need to save anyone from hell, but chooses to save some. | God does not need to save anyone from hell, but chooses to save some. |

Before we examine the final three answers to the question, "For whom did Jesus Christ die?" I need to eliminate the first two answers because they are unhelpful, unbiblical, and therefore unacceptable. I often pray that you and your siblings will not be universalists or Pelagians, who turn from the clear teachings of Scripture to follow what the Bible calls false teaching. As I am writing this chapter to you, I am reminded of a few well-known children of Bible preachers who have wandered from the truth and are presently promoting universalism and Pelagianism. They are gaining a hearing because they are wrongly using the influence they have inherited from the success of their fathers.

I need you to know that I desperately love you and would gladly lay down my life for you. But if ever you were to promote such false doctrines, I would also vigorously oppose you with tears of grief in my eyes, because I love Jesus more than I love you, and the best thing I can do for you is remain devoted to him. You have been born into a family that has gladly given itself to the service of Jesus. While I do not expect you to be a pastor and will not pressure you in any way to follow in my footsteps, I do long with all my heart for you to be a faithful Christian, which means you cannot be a universalist or a Pelagian.

To begin with, the cross of Jesus will make no sense to you or be any treasure for you if you do not first acknowledge your need for a Savior. Jesus died in the place of sinners so that they would be forgiven and saved from Satan, sin, death, wrath, and hell. Therefore, recognizing your own sin is vital. Scripture repeatedly states that you are a sinner by both nature and choice (Pss. 51:5; 58:3; Rom. 3:23; see also Ps. 53:3; Isa. 53:6; 64:6; 1 John 1:18). Despite depravity, you retain dignity because you are an image bearer of God, even though that image is marred by sin. Universalism erroneously contradicts the clear teachings of Scripture on human sinfulness and hell (e.g., Dan. 12:2; Matt. 5:29–30; 10:28; 18:9; 23:23; 25:46). If you subscribe to the false teaching of universalism, you will break my heart, live as a non-Christian who is at best a vaguely spiritual person, and die to spend eternity in the torments of hell as the just consequence for not responding to the grace made possible by Jesus' death on the cross for sin.

Pelagians also deny human sinfulness. Pelagianism is named after the ascetic monk Pelagius who lived in the fifth century and taught that people begin their life morally good, like Adam, and through the decision of their own will can live a holy life that will obligate God to take them to heaven upon death. Pelagius was condemned as a heretic at the Council of Carthage in 418, thanks in part to his opponent Augustine, who taught the doctrines of human sinfulness and salvation by grace alone. Likewise, I would implore you not to be a Pelagian because it is of no help in overcoming sin and will ruin for you both this life and the life to come.

We are left with three remaining options for Christians regarding the question of whom Jesus died for. I would rejoice if you held any of these three positions because they are faithful evangelical beliefs within the bounds of evangelical orthodoxy. My hope, though, is that you will be compelled to embrace the third option, along with your daddy, because I believe it is most faithful to the teaching of all of Scripture.

First, some Christians (e.g., Nazarene, Assemblies of God, Foursquare, Calvary Chapel, Mennonite, Christian and Missionary Alliance, Methodist, Christian Church) believe that Jesus died for the sins of all people. This position is commonly referred to as Arminianism, after James Arminius; Wesleyanism, after John Wesley; or Unlimited Atonement. As an aside, James Arminius was John Calvin's son-in-law and greatly appreciated Calvin. He said that, after the Scriptures, he believed Calvin's writings to be the most profitable study for God's people. Therefore, the acrimony that sometimes flares up between Calvinists and Arminians need not be so if the examples of Calvin and Arminius are followed by their followers.

Arminians appeal to those Scriptures that speak of Jesus dying for all people (2 Cor. 5:14–15; 1 Tim. 2:1–6; 4:10; Titus 2:11), for the whole world (John 1:29; 3:16–17; 1 John 2:2; 4:14; Rev. 5:9), for everyone (Isa. 53:6; Heb. 2:9), and of his not wanting anyone to perish (1 Tim. 2:4; 2 Pet. 3:9). Arminians, then, teach that to be saved one must make the decision to accept Jesus' atoning death and become a follower of Jesus. Furthermore, it is said that anyone can make that choice either by inherent free will (Arminians) or by God's universal enabling, so-called prevenient grace (Wesleyans). Subsequently, Christians are God's elect because, before the foundation of the world, God chose to give every spiritual blessing to those whom he foreknew would receive his free gift of salvation. God never forces anyone to make that decision through so-called irresistible calling or through regenerating people prior to their decision to repent and believe. Neither does God hang onto people who choose to turn away from Jesus. Lastly, they teach that all who fail to receive Jesus will suffer just condemnation for the guilt of their sins.

Second, some Christians (e.g., Presbyterians who follow the Westminster Confession of Faith, Reformed Baptists, some Independent Bible churches) believe that Jesus died only for the sins of the elect. Election means that before the foundation of the world God chose certain individuals to be recipients of eternal life solely on the basis of his gracious purpose apart from any human merit or action. He calls them effectually, doing whatever is necessary to bring them to repentance and faith (Isa. 55:11; John 6:44; Rom. 8:30; 11:29; 1 Cor. 1:23-29; 2 Tim.

1:9). This position is commonly referred to as five-point Calvinism, after John Calvin; Reformed theology; or limited atonement, which is also sometimes called particular redemption.

These Calvinists commonly appeal to those Scriptures that speak of Jesus' dying for some people but not all people (Matt. 1:21; 20:28; 26:28; Rom. 5:12–19), for his sheep (John 10:11, 15, 26–27), for his church (Acts 20:28; Eph. 5:25), for the elect (Rom. 8:32–35), for his people (Matt. 1:21), for his friends (John 15:3), and for all Christians (2 Cor. 5:15; Titus 2:14).

They disagree with all proponents of unlimited atonement, pointing out that if Jesus died for everyone, then everyone would be saved, which is the heresy of universalism. Likewise, they teach that since Jesus died to propitiate the holy wrath of God, universal atonement would mean all God's wrath was poured out on Jesus. They emphasize the sovereignty of God's grace and his commitment to glorify himself through a completely grace-based salvation of those whom he chose solely for his purpose. Because of the depths of total depravity and total inability, they also teach that people are dead in their sin and are completely unable to know or respond to the gospel. Consequently, God must regenerate people before conversion. They believe in eternal security of the elect saints since God's sovereign will cannot be frustrated.

Looking at everything in these views gets very complicated. One vital point of debate is the intent of Jesus when he died on the cross. Did Jesus intend to provide payment for all sins of all people, opening the doorway to salvation for all? That would be unlimited atonement, or what the Wesleyans and the Arminians believe. Do we accept it at face value when Paul said in 1 Timothy 2:6 that Christ Jesus "gave himself as a ransom for all"? Or did Jesus die to complete the purchase of our pardon on the cross, which is limited atonement, or what five-point Calvinists believe? Do we accept it at face value when Jesus said, "It is finished," in John 19:30?

At first glance, unlimited and limited atonement appear to be in opposition. But that dilemma is resolved by noting two things. First, the two categories are not mutually exclusive; since Jesus died for the sins of everyone, that means he also died for the sins of the elect. Second, Jesus' death for all people does not accomplish the same thing as his death for the elect. This point is complicated, but it is, in fact, taught in Scripture. For example, 1 Timothy 4:10 makes a distinction between

Jesus' dying as the Savior of all people in a general way and of the Christian elect in a particular way, saying, "For to this end we toil and strive, because we have our hope set on the living God, who is the Savior of all people, especially of those who believe."

Additionally, 2 Peter 2:1 speaks of people for whom Jesus died as not being saved from heresy and damnation by Jesus: "But false prophets also arose among the people, just as there will be false teachers among you, who will secretly bring in destructive heresies, even denying the Master who bought them, bringing upon themselves swift destruction."

By dying for everyone, Jesus purchased everyone as his possession, and he then applies his forgiveness to the elect, those in Christ, by grace, and he applies his wrath to the non-elect, those who reject Christ. Objectively, Jesus' death was sufficient to save anyone and, subjectively, efficient only to save those who repent of their sin and trust in him. This position is called unlimited limited atonement, or modified Calvinism. Or, as your daddy calls it, biblical.

On one side of this often heated debate are Bible-believing, Jesus-loving Arminians who have a pile of verses that state that Jesus died for more than just the elect Christians. On the other side of the debate are Bible-believing, Jesus-loving Calvinists who have a pile of verses that state that Jesus' death was to forgive sin and save people, which therefore cannot mean that he died for all people, because unrepentant, unelect sinners are going to hell—a fact which Jesus himself speaks of more than anyone else in the Bible.

In order to retain every verse of Scripture without disregarding one pile of verses for the other, I would urge you to be consistent with Scripture and believe what the Arminians believe and more, as well as what the Calvinists believe and more. If you do, you will find yourself in good company, as this is the position that I would argue John Calvin himself held as a very able Bible teacher and the namesake of your brother Calvin Martin Driscoll.

In his commentary on Galatians 5:12, John Calvin wrote, "It is the will of God that we should seek the salvation of all men without exception, as Christ suffered for the sins of the whole world." In his commentary on Colossians 1:14, Calvin wrote, "By the sacrifice of his death all the sins of the world have been expiated." In his commentary on Romans 5:18,

Calvin wrote, "Though Christ suffered for the sins of the whole world, and is offered through God's benignity indiscriminately to all, yet all do not receive him." Likewise, Calvin said:

> The word "many" is often as good as equivalent to "all." And in fact our Lord Jesus was offered to all the world. For it is not speaking of three or four when it says: "God so loved the world, that he spared his only Son . . ." Our Lord Jesus suffered for all and there is neither great nor small who is not inexcusable today, for we can obtain salvation in him. Unbelievers who turn away from Him and who deprive themselves of Him by their malice are today doubly culpable, for how will they excuse their ingratitude in not receiving the blessing in which they could share by faith.

Calvin also wrote in his commentary on Hebrews, "To *bear the sins* means to free those who have sinned from their guilt by his satisfaction. He says 'many' meaning 'all,' as in Romans 5:15. It is of course certain that not all enjoy the fruits of Christ's death, but this happens because their unbelief hinders them." Elsewhere Calvin wrote, "By His mediation God is satisfied and appeased, for He bore all the wickedness of all the sins of the world."

Let me state this in a different way so you can grasp the complexity of Jesus' work on the cross. First, Christ died for the purpose of securing the sure and certain salvation of his own, his elect. This is the intentionality that the five-point Calvinists rightly stress.

Second, Christ died for the purpose of providing payment for the penalty of all sin of all people. This is the universality the Arminians rightly stress. If the five-point Calvinist is right and no payment has been made for the nonelect, then how can God genuinely love the world and desire the salvation of all people?

Third, there is a genuine open door for salvation for anyone who believes in Jesus. It also makes the sin of rejecting the gospel of grace all the more inexcusable. Who could blame God for his holy wrath against those who despise the infinitely painful sacrifice both God the Father and God the Son had to endure to make the salvation of the despisers possible?

Fourth, this both/and approach of unlimited limited atonement explains the biblical statements about Jesus' dying to reconcile all things to the Father. For example, Paul says in Colossians 1:18–20 that Jesus "is the beginning, the firstborn from the dead, that in everything he might be preeminent. For in him all the fullness of God was pleased to dwell, and through him to reconcile to himself all things, whether on earth or in heaven, making peace by the blood of his cross." Furthermore, the sinfulness of believers will be covered by the blood of Jesus the Lamb, and they will come into fellowship with the triune God in his eternal kingdom. But nothing impure will ever enter heaven.

John tells us, "As for the cowardly, the faithless, the detestable, as for murderers, the sexually immoral, sorcerers, idolaters, and all liars, their portion will be in the lake that burns with fire and sulfur, which is the second death" (Rev. 21:8). God will overcome all rebellion through Jesus' blood and the triumph of the Lamb who is the Lion. In this sense, all those in hell will stand reconciled to God, but not in a saving way as the universalists falsely teach. In hell unrepentant and unforgiven sinners are no longer rebels, and their sinful disregard for God has been crushed and ended.

On this point, a friend named Dr. Bruce Ware has been helpful to both your daddy and his friend Dr. Breshears as we studied this doctrine together.

Summarily, it can be argued that even Calvin himself believed that Jesus died for all people in general so that they obtain some general benefits, and for the elect Christians in particular so that they would enjoy additional specific benefits regarding salvation. Having grown up in our home, you know that your daddy is a big fan of the great Reformed Bible preacher Charles Haddon Spurgeon. As is often the case, I believe he articulated this well. In a sermon titled, "General and Yet Particular," Spurgeon said, "There is a general influence for good flowing from the mediatorial sacrifice of Christ and yet its special design and definite object is the giving of eternal life to as many as the Father gave him."

Jesus' life, death, and resurrection have so radically changed human history that in a very real sense the whole world has benefited from his death and resurrection. You too have lived under this common grace that Jesus has showered upon the world. Because of Jesus and the influence of his teaching, you were born into a nation where religious freedom is valued, human dignity is cherished, the rule of law protects you from the rule of tyrants, and education is available for all.

You have seen the positive influence the church has had on Seattle. Mars Hill Church is a city within the city to love the city for Jesus. Because of Jesus you are free to worship; you are treated with dignity, protected by law, and educated so that you can grow in your understanding of God and the world he made for you to enjoy and steward.

Jesus also died in a saving way for the elect. The general benefits of Jesus are given to all people in this life. However, the general benefits they enjoy as a result of Jesus' death end with this life, unless they have personally turned from sin to trust in Jesus' work on the cross to forgive their sins. Practically, this means for Christians that this life is as bad as it gets because heaven awaits them, while for non-Christians this life is as good as it gets because hell awaits them.

Gideon, your mother and I love you with all of our hearts. As we discussed early in our marriage how large our family would be, we decided to take it one child at a time and see how things went. Deep down we both wanted a big family, but with the rampant infertility our siblings suffered, we did not know how many children God would enable us to conceive. Ever since your mom was a little girl, she always thought she would have four children. After a miscarriage, which still brings tears to my eyes when I think about it, we were blessed by God with four healthy, beautiful children.

I was sure Ashley was going to be a boy and was shocked when I held her for the first time. I prayed that she would turn from sin to trust in the finished work of Jesus on the cross for her, and she did so at a young age.

As I held your oldest brother Zac for the first time and prayed the same for him, he proceeded to poop all over my foot, protected only by an open-toed sandal. He too came into a truly saving relationship with Jesus at a very young age.

I prayed that same prayer over Calvin when he was born. Calvin gave his life to Jesus on Zac's seventh birthday under Zac's leading in their bunk bed late that night, because what Zac really wanted for his birthday was to know that his brother was saved.

Likewise, I prayed for Alexie's salvation upon holding her for the first time. Ever since she was very little, her heart for Jesus comes forth in her constant singing of praise songs. Her connection to Jesus seems to be tethered in large part by worship.

After four children, we thought we were done having babies because your mom suffered through painful C-sections with each birth, and we feared for her health. Yet, as I prayed, I believed that someone was missing from our family. Your mom prayed a lot and trusted me to lead our family. Out of our love you were conceived, and we were both thrilled because we believed that God had chosen you to be a blessing to our family and to the world in some way. Throughout the pregnancy, your mother and I and your siblings prayed daily for your physical, mental, emotional, and spiritual health.

Upon holding you for the first time, I thanked Jesus for all the benefits and blessings that have come into your life and mine through his death and resurrection. I also prayed, as I have every day since, that you would place your faith in Jesus and also benefit from his saving work on the cross, which he suffered in your place for your sins. I pray you will live in the power of his resurrection with the new heart and all the newness of life that it brings. I pray that you would be not only my son but also God the Father's son with whom I can pray, read Scripture, and serve Jesus in joy. For this to happen, you must live as a Christian man under the lordship of Jesus, because the line to heaven is single file.

Your mother and I are walking the path of faith into eternal life with Jesus and want nothing more than to see each of our children with us walking personally with Jesus. Therefore, as your pastor-dad, I am imploring you not to take for granted the person and work of Jesus, merely enjoying his general benefits while neglecting his saving benefits, or borrowing the faith of your Christian family without having your own. I cannot mediate between you and God, but Jesus can. He can and will forgive your sin and give you a new heart and a new nature with new appetites for holiness, and he will not only bless you in this life but also in the life to come.

For me, one of those blessings would include baptizing you in this life and seeing you rise from death to be with Jesus, forever freed of sin and all its effects, and to throw the ball around with your brothers in heaven.

In some ways, you were born into a family and a nation that is akin to the Old Testament nation of Israel. There, the most holy day of the year was the Day of Atonement, which foreshadowed the death of Jesus on the cross. On that day, the entire nation was called to repent of sin and trust in God for salvation from sin and its effects. In many ways, everyone who was a member of that nation was blessed by living among a people who worshiped God. Yet, in addition to that there was an expectation that each individual would also confess his own sins and have his own personal faith in God. In this way the Day of Atonement was a blessing to all in a general way, and a blessing to those who repented of sin and trusted in God in a particular way.

As a member of our family and church and nation, you have been born into a world with many blessings that are the consequence of Christ and Christianity, just like the Old Testament Israelites. But those blessings will be in vain if you are merely part of a Christian family and church without yourself being a Christian who has received Jesus' death as the source of your life.

Giddy, you know your daddy loves you with all of his heart. You need to know that Jesus loves you even more, and he showed it on the cross. You need to live in light of that defining, transforming, illuminating, and empowering truth.

## Answers to Common Questions about Unlimited Limited Atonement

*Isn't anyone who believes in election logically compelled to believe in particular redemption, so-called limited atonement, as well? If God's election means he chose specific individuals for salvation, doesn't unity in the Trinity also imply Jesus died for specific individuals on the cross?*

This is a very perceptive question. There are some key clarifications that will help you understand where we are coming from.

First, all Jesus-loving Christians believe in divine election. Arminians, Wesleyans, and Calvinists all read Ephesians 1:2–4 and agree that before the foundation of the world, God decided to give every spiritual blessing to those in Christ. This election is individual, in that God knew, loved, and predestined individuals to conformity with Christ that we might be to the praise of his glory. He also called each of us to come together in the company of the elect, the body of Christ, and the community of the Spirit in order that we might together, as the church, be a blameless bride for his precious Son.

But there is huge difference of opinion about how we get to be "in Christ." Wesleyan-Arminians believe we make the choice to be in Christ. While God knew we would choose to receive the totally gracious provision of salvation by the cross, his knowledge in no way determines or pre-decides our choice.

Calvinists, on the other hand, believe it is God who sovereignly places us in Christ. If salvation depended on our own choice, we would all end up in hell because as Romans 3:11 says, "No one seeks for God." There are other evangelical Christians who believe God makes the choice in cases such as Saul on the road to Damascus (Acts 9, especially v. 15), while in other cases people make a grace-enabled choice for Christ such as with the Ethiopian eunuch or Lydia (Acts 8:27–39; 16:13–16). These people believe God works in different ways with different people, but always by grace alone, through faith alone, in Christ alone.

If you believe in a version of election other than the Calvinist one, you do not believe God is the one who decided which specific individuals would be saved. In non-Calvinist views, God genuinely wants all persons to be saved. Jesus died to provide atonement for all persons, which enabled them to choose to accept God's gift of salvation by grace alone through faith alone.

Second, many who affirm the Calvinistic definition of election also affirm that Jesus provided atonement for all persons. This position is often called four-point Calvinism. They believe Jesus' work on the cross follows the pattern of the Day of Atonement (Leviticus 16). On that day, the high priest presented the propitiatory blood of the first goat for "the sin offering that is for the people. . . . Thus he shall make atonement for the Holy Place, because of the uncleannesses of the people of Israel and because of their transgressions, all their sins" (Lev. 16:15–16). The two goats provided propitiation and expiation on behalf of all the people, even though these benefits were applied only to God's elect, a remnant within the larger group.

Third, rationality and logic are precious gifts from God, a vital part of the image of God. These gifts are particularly helpful in interpreting Scripture, our supreme authority. Logic works only when we take every possibility into account. Yet, Scripture reminds us that we do not know everything about God (Deut. 29:29; 1 Cor. 13:12). Therefore, we must be very careful and humble when we use logic to go beyond God's self-revelation and even reluctant if we find ourselves explaining away the natural meaning of Scripture. Therefore, when we find "illogical" things in the Bible, it may simply be that we are not considering all of the biblical data.

*This kind of debate upsets me. It only divides the body of Christ. Why do we have to argue about such things?*

You are absolutely right that we must not argue about such things. Paul warns us: "Have nothing to do with foolish, ignorant controversies; you know that they breed quarrels. And the Lord's servant must not be quarrelsome but kind to everyone, able to teach, patiently enduring evil, correcting his opponents with gentleness" (2 Tim. 2:23–25).

When Jesus-loving people wrestle with issues like this, our attitude must be one of hearing each other rather than of winning debate points, and our goal must be finding God's truth by working together toward it rather than protecting personal beliefs. Because these are differences among believers in Jesus, we must discuss with our Bibles open and smiles on our faces, always seeking to understand more deeply. When people close their Bibles and defend personal positions, citing only their favorite verses, then it is time to stop the discussion and turn to humble prayer.

On the other hand, most people today make the opposite error. They never do the hard work to understand the things God has revealed. They keep on being satisfied with infant formula when God has a banquet of truth on which to dine (1 Cor. 3:1–3; Heb. 5:12–13). Their mantra is "keep it simple." According to P. T. Forsyth, "The lazy cry for simplicity is a great danger. It indicates a frame of mind which is only appalled at the great things of God, and a senility of faith which fears that which is high."[1]

There's a balance to be kept in our discussion between wrestling and submitting.[2] The Bible puts it this way: "'The secret things belong to the LORD our God, but the things that are revealed belong to us and to our children forever, that we may do all the words of this law" (Deut. 29:29).

*Who are some of the better-known proponents of the various views in this chapter?*

Sometimes in the process of understanding a doctrine it is helpful to know the identity of those who support that position. Therefore, in an effort to help you understand the proverbial teams, we offer the names of some men who are proponents of the various positions we discussed on this issue. Admittedly, such broad categories are not precise, and there are also variations within each broad category.

Among those holding the heresy of "Christian" universalism are Doug Pagitt, Brian McLaren, and Spencer Burke, who are all connected to the Emergent Village project. Among those holding to the heresy of contemporary Pelagianism are many teachers and preachers in the mainline liberal denominations. Those holding the Christian position of unlimited atonement include Jack Cottrell and Kenneth Grider. Those holding the position of limited atonement include Wayne Grudem, John Piper, and R. C. Sproul. Lastly, perhaps the most noteworthy person holding the Christian position of unlimited limited atonement is Bruce Ware.

## HELPFUL INFORMATION

In the letter to Gideon, there are six comments attributed to John Calvin. The first three are taken from Bruce Demarest, *The Cross and Salvation* (Wheaton, IL: Crossway Books, 1997), 162; the remaining three comments are taken from G. Michael Thomas, *The Extent of the Atonement: A Dilemma for Reformed Theology from Calvin to the Consensus* (Carlisle: Paternoster, 1997), 27, and 29, respectively. The quotation from Charles Haddon Spurgeon's sermon is taken from Bruce Demarest, *The Cross and Salvation*, 163.

# CHAPTER NINE

# "I Am Going to Hell": Jesus Is Hank's Ransom

*For there is one God, and there is one mediator between God and men, the man Christ Jesus, who gave himself as a ransom.*

1  T I M O T H Y  2 : 5 - 6

**At first glance, he is an intimidating, burly guy,** standing well over six feet tall and weighing in somewhere near 300 pounds. The years have not been kind to him. Though he is in his sixties, he could pass for much older because of the heavy bags under his eyes and his labored breathing from decades of constant smoking. The faded tattoo on his arm serves as a constant reminder of his days as a young man in the military when his heavy drinking, hard living, and constant fighting peaked.

As we sat down to talk, he began by telling me he was having significant financial trouble brought on by his escalating health-related bills and inability to earn an income. As he spoke, it seemed as if he was neglecting to reveal to me the hard truths he needed help with, which threatened to waste our time together. So, figuring he was a rather blunt, masculine guy who could handle it, I interrupted him, told him I sensed he was being a coward and wasting my time, and he needed to get to the point. He did, and it was horrifying.

He had started having sex in his early teens and had lost count of all the women he had been with over the years, including a long list of prostitutes. Most of his life was spent either in the military or working hard-labor jobs that broke his body. Sadly, there are also enormous gaps in his memory because he spent much of his time drunk.

What he does remember is being married multiple times to troubled younger women whom he would often abuse verbally, physically, and sexually until they left him. He also remembers having multiple children with various women and being an evil father. He routinely beat his sons to, in his words, "toughen them up," which only broke their spirits and took their dignity. They self-medicated with drugs and alcohol beginning in junior high, even attempting suicide more than once just to be rid of their father. Worse still, when he was drunk Hank would force his little girls to perform oral sex on him. He began fondling and raping them once they started developing physically. The girls ended up living brutal lives, being treated by a legion of men in the same manner as they had grown accustomed to by their father.

To be honest, everything in me wanted to cuss out the haggard old man and give him the beating of his life. I know that the Bible says that Jesus died to forgive sinners, but I had a hard time sharing the gospel with this guy because, truth be told, I wanted him to face Jesus for justice in hell. I would have enjoyed whipping him like Jesus did the moneychangers much more than telling this man anything about the grace of God poured out through the death of Jesus.

Nonetheless, I did my job and decided to assault the old man with my words instead of my fists. I called him a drunkard, bully, rapist, fornicator, adulterer, pedophile, liar, wife-beater, and some other words I won't write here because some good church folks could not handle it. I then told him he was the sorriest and most pathetically evil man I had ever met and that, as a father of five kids myself (two little girls and three young sons), I felt he had lost the right to breathe.

I was assuming he would cuss me out and leave, never to return, which would have been perfectly fine with me. But he began crying like a baby, which only made me angrier. The broken old man wanted me to feel sorry for him, but that was not going to happen. I told him to stop crying, because if I was going to feel sorry for anyone it would be his victims. He pulled it together and said, "You got me. I am an evil guy and I should die and go to hell, and I know that is where I am going. So, I need you to tell me how to pay everyone back so that I don't have to go to hell."

The pathetic old man had some strange concept of karma and did not understand grace, and his answer was to earn his own salvation by spending the very short remainder of his life trying to make up for the hell he had wrought on others. In short, he was an evil, tangled mess who still believed there was enough good in him to spend the final breaths of his life undoing a lifetime of evil.

When it comes to sin, people are tricky. We are prone to confess our sin but not repent of it. What I mean is this: people commonly say that they have done wrong but lack a deep remorse for who they are in addition to what they have done. The old man was at the point of confession but had not yet come to a place of repentance where he despised himself and wanted to become a new person, not just the same old person trying to do new good things. So, he needed to sit in his own feces for a season until he smelled his filth.

To get him there, I told him to get a notebook and draw a line down the middle of every page from top to bottom so that there were two columns side by side. His assignment was to spend a few weeks carrying that notebook around with him, writing down in the left-hand column every evil thing he could remember ever thinking, saying, or doing. I told him I would call him to see how it was going.

Some weeks later I called him and was surprised to discover that he had actually done what I told him and had basically filled up an entire notebook. He asked me what I wanted him to do next, so I told him to go back over his list of sins and, in the other column, write down next to each entry what he thought was an appropriate way to repay everyone for everything he had done.

Some weeks later I called him again, and he told me that he had been in and out of state-sponsored care centers because his health was quickly declining and he was penniless. He sounded terrible, and it seemed obvious that his death was imminent. I asked him how his assignment was going.

He said, "I cannot pay everyone back that I stole from and ripped off because I don't have any money. I can't make up for the things I have done because it is too late. I can't even call the people I have hurt to say I am sorry because I don't even know where to find them and some are dead. I tried calling my daughters and they refused to even talk to me. I am so sick that I can't even leave my bed to try and make anything right."

I asked him, "So where do you think you are going when you die?"

"I am going to hell," he said.

"Yes, you are," I said, "and Jesus will meet you there and repay you for everything you have done and everything you have failed to do. Since you cannot repay your evil, you have hell to pay."

He was silent and the phone line remained quiet for some time as reality sunk in for him. He then thanked me for my time and was going to hang up when I began explaining to him the work of Jesus on the cross in his place for his sins according to the doctrine of ransom. The following letter is for Hank and is a summary of what I told him.

◎    ◎    ◎    ◎    ◎

## Dear Hank,

When we first spoke, you said that you were in great financial debt because of all your sin and folly. You admitted that your financial debts are enormous and more than you will ever be able to repay. You mentioned that each month you receive statements from your debtors who have seized your home and almost everything you ever had of value, yet they are demanding more because your debts continue to compound every minute of every day. Understandably, this is causing you tremendous distress. But I have even worse news for you.

You, like most people, are unaware of the debt you also owe God. You keep an eye on your financial debts while neglecting to keep track of your spiritual debts. God made you to love, honor, and obey him in thought, word, and deed. Every time you have failed to do that perfectly you accrue a debt to God. Hank, stop for a moment and ask yourself, how in debt are you to God? Imagine that every time you sinned throughout your life—in thought, word, and deed—a rock was added to a pile. How big would that pile be today? Would it be a mountain?

Hank, sin happens when we think, believe, say, or do something we are not supposed to or do not do something we are supposed to do. Imagine the mountain of spiritual debt you have accrued to God every time you got drunk, acted violently, stole, or committed sexual sin. Now add every time you thought an evil thought, from lust to greed to violence. Then add every word you should never have spoken, including lying, vulgarity, and cruelty, and ask yourself how big your mountain of debt to God is.

On top of that, add every time that you failed to do what you were supposed to do. Throw a rock on your debt pile for every one of your sons' games you failed to attend because you were getting drunk at the bar, every meal you were supposed to eat with your family that you never showed up for because you were at the strip club, every time you simply ignored your wife and kids when they were speaking to you, every opportunity you missed to hug your daughters and encourage your sons, and ask yourself how big your mountain of debt to God is.

Hank, every time you sin, you sin against both people and God. You told me, after making the list of all the people you have sinned against, that there is no way you could possibly pay them back.

But what about God?

Throughout your life you have sinned against God, and you owe him as well. As it stands right now, you are on your way to hell, which is the eternal prison for spiritual debtors like you who have ripped God off by living sinful lives. There is not any way that a good, holy, and just God could possibly endorse or even overlook your pathetic life.

There is, however, good news. The good news is that your spiritual debt is owed to someone far more gracious, kind, and merciful than the people to whom you owe your financial debt. While the credit card companies and debt collection agencies continue to hound you, demanding payment in full, Jesus is willing to actually pay your entire spiritual debt to God the Father.

For your spiritual debt to be forgiven, you need three things. First, you need a mediator to stand between you and God to establish your total debt and come up with a resolution that God the Father, to whom you are indebted, will find acceptable. Second, you need a redeemer willing to intercede for you and pay your debt to God the Father. Third, you need a ransom, which is a repayment sufficient enough to erase your debt to God the Father.

Your mediator will be a middleman of sorts who will go between you and God to work out a resolution. This role is much like an arbitrator who mediates a conflict between parties in our legal system, a credit counseling service that works between someone in debt and the company they owe to work out a payment plan, or a counselor who works out relational differences between people. This person must be impartial and able to represent both you and God fairly.

In the Bible, a man named Job longed for just such a mediator and lamented, "For [God] is not a man, as I am, that I might answer him, that we should come to trial together. There is no arbiter between us, who might lay his hand on us both" (Job 9:32–33). Job rightly understood that he, like you, needed a mediator who is both God and a human being so that he can accurately represent both sides of the conflict, or, in Job's words, put a hand on both you and God to bring you together.

Amazingly, the answer to Job's longing and your need is Jesus Christ. Jesus is God who became a man. Jesus alone can mediate between you and God the Father, representing you both fairly, because he is the only one who is both God and man. This is why the Bible repeatedly speaks of Jesus as our only mediator: "For there is one God, and there is one mediator between God and men, the man Christ Jesus" (1 Tim. 2:5; see also Heb. 9:15; 12:24).

The words of Scripture here are plain and important. Your spiritual debt is to God, and there is only one possible mediator between you and God who can work out the dangerous mess you are in. No religion but Christianity is of any help to you at this point. Some will tell you to go to purgatory to pay God back by suffering. Others will tell you to reincarnate and pay God back through suffering. Both are wrong because you cannot repay God no matter what you do, and any more life would only add to your debt because you would continue sinning.

Soon you will die. And you will die because you are a sinner. In Genesis 2:16 God promised our first parents, Adam and Eve, that when they sinned, death would be the consequence. Romans 6:23 says it this way, "For the wages of sin is death." Romans 5:12 also says, "Death spread to all men because all sinned." Because of sin, more than 6,300 people die every hour, according to a recent report I read. Soon you will be among their number.

You should be gravely concerned about what will happen to you. My fear is that you are gullible enough to believe that everyone wins after death, or that everyone can win after death.

Universalists say that essentially everyone who dies goes to heaven, and annihilationists teach that everyone who dies simply ceases to exist. However, Daniel 12:2 clearly refutes both alternatives and says that everyone who dies experiences one of two options, "some to everlasting life, and some to shame and everlasting contempt." Basically, you will die and live forever; the only question is where. Will you go to heaven for eternal joy or to hell for eternal pain, which Jesus describes as wailing, weeping, and grinding your teeth in unending agony?

I also fear that you are actually naïve enough to believe that after death God will give you a second chance. Reincarnation teaches that you can have another shot at life and pay God back after you have wasted this one. Similarly, purgatory teaches that you can suffer for a while after you die to pay God back and thereby merit heaven, as if doing what you are supposed to do is enough to overcome what you have done. Hank, you've already believed a lot of dumb things throughout your life, and I am asking you to not believe the vain and foolish hope offered in reincarnation and purgatory. The Bible refutes both second-chance options, saying, "It is appointed for man to die once, and after that comes judgment" (Heb. 9:27).

God has appointed a moment for your death. If that moment were now, your immaterial soul would separate from your physical body. While your body would go to the grave, your soul would go to a place the Bible calls Hades. There you would experience great pain, suffering, and torment, as Luke 16:19–31 graphically depicts.

Worse still, some time later you would come before Jesus for a final eternal judgment (Rev. 20:13–14). On that day you would join these multitudes: "At the name of Jesus every knee should bow, in heaven and on earth and under the earth, and every tongue confess that Jesus Christ is Lord, to the glory of God the Father" (Phil. 2:10–11). Hank, you will stand before Jesus and you will honor him. The only question is whether it will be today for salvation or that future day for damnation. Will it be today on your way to heaven or tomorrow on your way to hell?

After judging you on that final day, Jesus (who speaks of hell more than anyone in the Bible) will send you to hell unless you repent of sin and trust in him as your ransom. Hell is also called "Gehenna" twelve times in the Bible, including eleven times by Jesus. That was a place outside the city of Jerusalem where people had actually performed human sacrifices, even murdering their own children in worship to false religions empowered by demons. God's people rightly considered that place defiled and turned it into the town dump where the garbage and rotting corpses were thrown. In that place both the worms who feasted and the fires that burned did so continually. This imagery is used to explain the hell that awaits you if you die today apart from faith in Jesus Christ.

If that were not enough, in Revelation 14:10 we see that it is Jesus who oversees the execution of perfect justice and condemning punishment on the other side of the grave for non-Christians. Hank, you will be with Jesus forever as either friend or foe.

Hearing you labor to breathe on the phone recently, I can assure you that your day of death and judgment is fast approaching. Upon that day, you will stand before Jesus Christ in all his glory. Revelation says that today Jesus is sitting in heaven on a throne as the mighty King of the universe with his name tattooed down his leg, wielding a sword and waiting to justly punish men like you. The Bible says you get to die once and once only. There is no universalism and no annihilationism. There is no purgatory and there is no reincarnation. There is, however, the throne of Jesus, which you will be seeing any day now.

Yet there is good news in the Scriptures: Jesus "has appeared once for all at the end of the ages to put away sin by the sacrifice of himself. . . . Christ, having been offered once to bear the sins of many, will appear a second time, not to deal with sin but to save those who are eagerly waiting for him" (Heb. 9:26, 28). Hank, the good news is that Jesus is the sacrifice, the mediator, and the redeemer.

A redeemer is a person who pays the debt of someone else. Job also longed for a redeemer to pay his debt to God, but that redeemer had not yet come to the earth when Job lived. Job longed to see the day of the earthly birth of his redeemer, and he cried out, "For I know that my Redeemer lives, and at the last he will stand upon the earth" (Job 19:25). Job knew that in his day, which was thousands of years before the birth of Jesus Christ, his redeemer was already alive as eternal God and just awaiting his entrance into human history.

That entrance occurred with the birth of Jesus Christ, our God-man mediator who can put a hand on you on earth and on God the Father in heaven, and our Redeemer who can pay our debt to God. Paul speaks of "our great God and Savior Jesus Christ, who gave himself for us to redeem us from all lawlessness and to purify for himself a people for his own possession who are zealous for good works" (Titus 2:13–14). He also says that "Christ redeemed us from the curse of the law by becoming a curse for us—for it is written, 'Cursed is everyone who is hanged on a tree' [Deut. 21:23]" (Gal. 3:13).

Because of his sinless life, death in our place, and resurrection in victory over sin and death, Jesus alone can forgive sin. One such example is found in Mark 2:5 where Jesus told a paralytic, "Son, your sins are forgiven." Because your sins, Hank, are against God, only God can forgive your debt of sin. Jesus is God who paid your debt on the cross in order to forgive your sin. This makes Jesus altogether distinct from and superior to every other religion and philosophy.

Sin is *the* human problem. Jesus is God who came down from heaven and lived without sin so he could forgive your sin and take you to heaven (Matt. 26:63–65; Mark 2:5; John 6:41–58; 8:46, 58–59; 10:30–33; 11:25; 14:6, 8–9; 16:28). Hank, no other religion claims anything like this. Their founders were only humans. Their founders taught people what they had to do to make themselves better people, vainly hoping somehow it would be okay. Only Jesus really dealt with sin.

Therefore, Jesus is both your mediator and your redeemer. However, you still need a ransom or price to be paid for your spiritual debt to God. Your problem, though, is that your sins are against a completely holy and perfect God and therefore require a perfect payment. Since all human beings are sinful, we cannot be a ransom for another. We have to pay our own debt with our own death. There is no way that any other sinful human can ever repay God for our spiritual debt. Psalm 49:7–8 says it this way: "Truly no man can ransom another, or give to God the price of his life, for the ransom of their life is costly and can never suffice."

The story of Jesus is often called the gospel, which means "good news" and, once again, Jesus is your good news. Although you can never pay your ransom debt to God other than by your own death in hell, and no other human being can ever pay it for you, Jesus can because, although he is God, he alone lived as a perfectly sinless human. Hebrews 7:26–27 says Jesus was "holy, innocent, unstained, separated from sinners, and exalted above the heavens. He has no need, like those high priests, to offer sacrifices daily, first for his own sins." He is even more than just a perfect human. He is also God. Furthermore, since nothing less than the death of God Jesus Christ was required to ransom your spiritual debt, you should be able to see how deeply indebted you are.

Referring to himself in Mark 10:45, Jesus said, "For even the Son of Man came not to be served but to serve, and to give his life as a ransom for many." Paul also speaks of "the man Christ Jesus, who gave himself as a ransom" (1 Tim. 2:5–6).

192 \\                                       **"I AM GOING TO HELL"**

Hank, here is the bottom line. You should die and you should go to hell and Jesus should torment you there forever, just as you have tormented others. Jesus should repay you for every sadistic evil you have done. Every day of your eternity should be spent crying, like you made your girls cry when you violated them, and gnashing your teeth in pain, like your boys did when you beat them. You were made by God with dignity but have sunk so deep into depravity that your life is nothing short of a disgraceful tragedy.

However, Jesus is willing to be your mediator, redeemer, and ransom. There is no reason for him to do so much good to a man like you who has done so much evil. Hank, Jesus is nothing like you. He is sinless. Furthermore, he is gracious, loving, merciful, and kind. He is also tougher than you, but he did not beat those who were weak and vulnerable. Rather, he took a beating for the weak and vulnerable at the hands of evil thugs just like you. He did not cry like a baby, like you did in my office, but took his beating like a man with his dignity intact because he was thinking of other people, including you, and not himself.

Through his sinless life, substitutionary death, and bodily resurrection in victory over Satan, sin, death, wrath, and hell, Jesus has redeemed evil men like you and me from allegiance to darkness by paying our ransom to God. Colossians 1:13–14 says, "He [Jesus] has delivered us from the domain of darkness and transferred us to the kingdom of his beloved Son, in whom we have redemption, the forgiveness of sins."

This is all accomplished solely by grace, which is a kind gift that God gives undeserving people like us. This may shock you, but of all the things that you have ever done, I believe that thinking you are good enough to pay God back with a few tears, apologies, dollars, and kind deeds is the most offensive.

I want you to sincerely wrestle with the hopeless situation you are in. What can you possibly do to unmolest your daughters? How do you expect to unrape your ex-wives? How can you possibly unbeat your sons? Do you really think a few tears, a few apologies, and a few canned goods to the local food bank can pay back God and people for all the sin you have done and all the good you have failed to do?

Even if you never sinned again for the rest of your life, which is impossible, you would only be doing what you are supposed to do. Although not accruing any further debt, you'd be doing nothing to pay off the mountain of spiritual debt that you have already accrued. It is insulting to hear you talk about paying God back, as if he needed anything from you or there was anything you could give him that he could not obtain for himself. You are a pathetic man who remains proud and arrogantly thinks he can somehow barter with God. I assure you that you have no idea who you are dealing with or how much trouble you are in and how little time you have.

Jesus knew you were going to end up in the mess you are in. While hanging on the cross, Jesus prayed that your debt of sin would be forgiven, and then Jesus answered his own prayer by dying in your place for your sin (Luke 23:34). Jesus has paid your debt and by grace will apply that to your account if you pray the words of repentance in faith that Jesus taught you to pray—"Forgive me my debts" (see Matt. 6:12).

Jesus has done the unthinkable and the scandalous and is willing to give you the one thing you have never given others—grace. Ephesians 1:7–8 says it this way: "In [Jesus] we have redemption through his blood, the forgiveness of our trespasses, according to the riches of his grace, which he lavished upon us."

Hank, it all comes down to you and Jesus. Either you will pay God back in eternal hell, or Jesus your eternal God will pay your debt, forgive your sins, and grant you eternal life with him. He will give you a new heart and his own Holy Spirit so you can live what's left of your life being like Jesus by his power and your new desires (Phil. 2:12–13; Titus 3:4–8). Through the cross, Jesus has made a way for your spiritual debt to God to be paid. Now it is your opportunity to respond by turning from sin to trust in Jesus. You'd better make up your mind quickly because you'll be on your knees before Jesus real soon, and one way or another your debt will be paid.

If you die as a non-Christian, this life will be as close to heaven as you will ever experience, and nothing but hell awaits you. But if you die as a Christian, this life will be as close to hell as you will ever experience, and nothing but heaven awaits you. This is why Paul says to Christians in Philippians 1:21 that "to die is gain."

So, rather than arguing whether or not it would be cruel of Jesus to torment you justly, you should thank him for suffering so that you do not have to. Run to him as a friend before your time is up, and you find yourself bowing before him as a foe.

# Answers to Common Questions about Ransom

*Ransom is what you give a kidnapper. Are you saying that somehow God gave a ransom to the Devil, our kidnapper?*

According to the so-called ransom theory of the atonement, sin put us under the ownership of the Devil. God wanted to set us free, but the only way to do so would be to pay the full price to the Devil in order to release us from his legal ownership rights. So God paid the price to the Devil, which was the life of Jesus. The Devil accepted the payment and let humans go free, wisely preferring Jesus to all of humanity. What the Devil didn't know was that Jesus was too strong to be held down. Jesus broke free and resurrected, justice was satisfied, and humans were free from the Devil's grip.

It is often asserted that this was the view of the ancient church. In fact, however, most early theologians held the triumph view, that God in Christ destroyed the power of the Devil through the cross (see, for example, Col. 2:15). There was no price paid to the Devil because that would have legitimized the Devil's claims.

We reject this form of the ransom theory of atonement. We do not believe that Jesus paid Satan. Satan does not rule over Jesus, and Jesus owes nothing to Satan. Furthermore, Jesus would never pay off Satan because that would validate Satan's false claim to also be a god. Jesus in no way paid off Satan for our salvation.

Origen (185–254), one proponent of the ransom view, creatively argued that God hid his deity in a cloak of humanity in order to deceive the Devil. Origen said that the Devil swallowed the bait of Jesus' humanity and was caught on the hook of his deity, and just as with contemporary narcissists, the Devil was deceived by his vision of his own greatness.

*Does the Devil really own those who do not believe in Jesus?*

He does. For example, Colossians 1:13–14 says, "[the Father] has delivered us from the domain of darkness and transferred us to the kingdom of his beloved Son, in whom we have redemption, the forgiveness of sins." This makes it quite clear that before we came to Jesus, we were in the domain or the authority sphere of darkness, which is the Devil's realm. Similarly, Jesus says in Matthew 12:29, "How can someone enter a strong man's house and plunder his goods, unless he first binds the strong man? Then indeed he may plunder his house." Sinful humans are plundered, taken, and redeemed from the house of the strong man (the Devil) by Jesus.

*Ransom is a price paid to someone. To whom is it paid?*

The Bible does speak of a price. Matthew 20:28 and Mark 10:45 say, "For even the Son of Man came not to be served but to serve, and to give his life as a ransom for many." Jesus spoke of his life as the ransom price. What an incredibly high price! The intriguing thing is that the Bible never tells us whom it is paid to. It is paid neither to the Devil nor to God nor to anyone else. It simply says our salvation was extremely costly.

It is the theologian who tries to complete the analogy by inferring the recipient of the payment. Most borrow from the propitiation motif and say the price is paid to God. That could be, but the Bible doesn't complete the analogy when it speaks of the motif of ransom. Ransom simply helps us see the great price: "You were ransomed from the futile ways inherited from your forefathers, not with perishable things such as silver or gold, but with the precious blood of Christ, like that of a lamb without blemish or spot" (1 Pet. 1:18–19). Therefore, all we can say with certainty is that Jesus did pay the price for our salvation on the cross.

*Does the price Jesus had to pay reflect how valuable I am?*

Sadly, some teach that since Jesus died for us we must be incredibly valuable. While we do have value as image bearers of God, the death of Jesus should not fill us with pride because we are so valuable, but rather fill us with horror that our sin is so terrible that it required the death of Jesus to atone for it. Therefore, at the cross we are to see the depth of our sin and love of our Savior so that we are humbled and he is praised.

# CHAPTER TEN

# "My Wife Has a Brain Tumor": Jesus Is Caleb's *Christus Exemplar*

*Christ also suffered for you, leaving you an example, so that you might follow in his steps.*

1 PETER 2:21

**The first time I met Caleb was over a decade ago,** just as we were gathering the core group to plant Mars Hill Church. At the time he was the lead singer for some cool band, out playing the clubs on weekends after working long hours at his regular job during the week. His free time was spent playing video games and looking at porn. He eventually got married, but things with his wife were brutally unpleasant, and before long they were divorced.

Caleb had no interest in Jesus whatsoever. His brother, who attended a different church, had become a Christian and was actively involved in leading worship there, but no matter how hard he tried, he could not get Caleb interested in anything spiritual. Some of Caleb's friends were members of our church and also reached out to him, hoping to bring him to Jesus and church, to no avail.

One of the few exceptions was a really cool gal he had met and was hoping to sleep with because his divorce was final. It turned out that she was a Christian and would not sleep with him but did want him to attend church with her. Hoping he could still find a way into her bed, he attended church with her, only to confirm his fears that she was totally into Jesus and totally not into sleeping with anyone but her husband when she got married some day. So, as he puts it, he "carefully put her in the friend zone" and planned to move on, pursuing other women for casual sex and "fun."

Upon occasion I would pray for Caleb to become a Christian, but over the years I must admit that my prayers for him became less and less regular. Nonetheless, Jesus in his perfect timing and faithfulness did a miracle and made Caleb a Christian. He took out Caleb's old hardened heart of selfish pride and gave him a new heart that was tender toward Jesus and people. He took out Caleb's old rebellious nature and replaced it with a deep desire to honor God in holy living. In short, Caleb seemed like one of those guys that God got hold of all at once.

Shortly after becoming a Christian, Caleb started regularly attending our church. Those of us who knew him were thrilled to see his rapid life transformation. He was baptized after giving his testimony to more than a thousand people at one of our church services. He began studying the Bible with great enthusiasm, started listening to Bible teaching on his iPod every morning during his run, and read through a pile of Christian books on theology at a rapid pace. Through it all he was very honest about his old way of life and how excited he was about Jesus. His passionate love for Jesus, combined with his outgoing personality, hilarious disposition, and brutal honesty, made him a natural evangelist.

Before long he was a leader in our church, running fast after Jesus without looking back. The woman he had carefully put in the friend zone became his fiancée and then his wife. Together they are serving as key leaders in our church. They are dear friends whom my wife, Grace, and I absolutely enjoy. They have even babysat our kids upon occasion. Our kids love Caleb because, as my sons report, the rock band front man puts on loud music with them and teaches them how to perfect rock star moves to look uber-cool.

The one difficult part of their life is his wife's health. He married her knowing that she had an ongoing battle with a brain tumor and as a result may not be able to bear children or live a long life. Nonetheless, he loves this woman so deeply and enjoys her so much that he chose to marry her anyway. He trusts God to enable him to love her well by caring for her, whatever the future might hold. This letter is written to my friend about how Jesus' death on the cross is exemplary and is the place to which he must continually look to know how to live his own life.

⊚  ⊚  ⊚  ⊚  ⊚

## Dear Caleb,

I want to thank you for being so honest with me and the other people who are in community with you about your journey with Jesus. You may not be aware of what a great encouragement and breath of fresh air you are, with your brutal honesty and seemingly endless passion.

Now that you are a Christian, I know it is your deep desire to pattern your life after Jesus. You want to be like him in this life, and you want to be with him in the life to come. I would wholeheartedly encourage you to continue to look to Jesus, because he alone lived without sin and is therefore exemplary in every way and is the man you should want to pattern your life after.

Further, while a seemingly infinite amount of wisdom could be gleaned from Jesus' earthly life in everything from learning Scripture to respecting women, working a job, and resisting sinful temptation, in this letter I want to help you understand how, when Jesus was dying on the cross, he served as your example for how to live your life in the most painful and difficult moments, particularly those regarding your very great wife.

The revelation of any person's true character occurs most often in their seasons of greatest suffering, hardship, loss, injustice, and pain. It is in those dark seasons that who we truly are deep down in our core is pushed to the surface for all to see. In Jesus' life, that revelatory darkness was the hour of his murder by barbarous crucifixion. Therefore, to best learn the character of Jesus so that you can pattern your life after his, it is imperative that you become intimately aware of how Jesus responded to his suffering, hardship, loss, injustice, and pain on the cross. Sadly, a lot of books you will read and teaching you will hear regarding the cross of Jesus fall into three erroneous categories, and so you must be discerning in your continued learning.

First, non-Christians look to Jesus as a great man, which he is, but neglect to see anything more significant happening on the cross than a great man suffering a tragic injustice with great courage and dignity. On this point, the Hindu Gandhi tragically said, "[Jesus'] death on the cross was a great example to the world, but that there was anything like a mysterious or miraculous virtue in it my heart could not accept."

Therefore, before I explain how Jesus is your example, I want to clearly articulate that while Jesus is a great man and example, he is also far more than just one of many great men who inspire us to live great lives. As you know but must always remind yourself, Jesus is also God. During a series of Christian theological councils beginning in Nicaea (325), continuing with Constantinople (381) and Ephesus (431), and concluding with Chalcedon (451), the early church met to wrestle with the confusion that surrounded the divinity and humanity of Jesus. Their deliberations culminated in the Chalcedonian Creed, which cleared up many heresies that wrongly defined the humanity and divinity of Jesus. In sum, the creed declared that Jesus Christ is one person with two natures (human and divine) who is both fully God and fully man.

Theologically, the term for the personal union of both natures in a single concrete, historical person named Jesus Christ is *hypostatic union*, which is taken from the Greek word (*hypostasis*) for "person." The reason I bring this up is that while I want you to look to Jesus as the example for your own life, you must always remember that he is more than just a great man; he is the God-man. Many people look to Jesus as an inspiring example, but you cannot forget that you should not only look to Jesus on the cross as your example, but also worship him as your God who saved you through the cross.

Second, more fundamental Christians bypass the self-emptying of the eternal Son. In fear that they will give comfort to heretics, they so overly emphasize the divinity of Jesus the God that they are prone to overlook and underestimate the humanity of Jesus the man. Therefore, when the Bible records that Jesus was tempted to sin, suffered great emotional anguish in the garden of Gethsemane in the hours leading up to the cross, and suffered on the cross, there is a tendency to see those events as fakery. The idea is that what appeared to be hardship did not truly affect him as it would a normal, average person. Subsequently, their erroneous picture of Jesus is more akin to Superman than to the God-man.

The practical implication of such error is that when you are suffering and hurting, looking to Jesus is pointless. If he was not truly human and merely a faker in times of trial, then he is ultimately not anyone who can sympathize with us, which means we are alone, without an example of how to live in our moments of darkest crisis. However, as Hebrews 4:15–16 says, "We do not have a high priest who is unable to sympathize with our weaknesses, but one who in every respect has been tempted as we are, yet without sin. Let us then with confidence draw near to the throne of grace, that we may receive mercy and find grace to help in time of need."

Third, more liberal Christians so overly emphasize the humanity of Jesus as man that they are prone to overlook and underestimate the divinity of Jesus the God. As a result, they will affectionately speak of Jesus' feeding the hungry, clothing the naked, and defending the marginalized, while failing to truly embrace the fullness of Jesus' death on the cross. On the cross, Jesus put himself in our place to suffer and die for our sins.

Yet more liberal Christians do not see anything objective, such as the remission of sin or securing of salvation occurring at Jesus' cross. Rather, they see Jesus on the cross as only an example to inspire you to live a humble, meek, and tolerant life. He is merely one more helpless victim who suffered at the hands of the rich and powerful. The problem with this view is that, like a lot of false teaching, it is half true. Jesus is our example on the cross, but he bled and died not just as our example but also for our salvation.

Had Jesus died only as your example, he would be of no help to you at all. You would see from his life how to live, but you'd get nothing from him to make that possible. However, because Jesus died in your place for your sins, and because he rose to conquer death and bring life, both as your divine Savior and human example, you now have a new identity, new provision, and new process. Your new identity is now in Christ, which has given you new potential for a new life in every area of your existence.

You now have new provision so that your resources for living a life like Jesus' are bigger than your experience, wisdom, and strength; this is because Jesus does not give you merely an example of how to redeem yourself, but he actually redeemed you. You are now in a new process of ongoing personal transformation called sanctification. Though forgiven, you are experiencing what the Puritan Christians called a "holy frustration" about not settling for a life that is anything less than what Jesus intends for you; he died for your sins so that you could put your sins to death.

You are already walking this path with Jesus. As you consider the cross of Jesus, I need you to know that your objective is to glorify God, your power to do so is the Holy Spirit, your community in which to do so is our church, and the means to do so is humble suffering. Apart from reading dead guys like the Puritans and other guys who read those dead guys, such as my hero Charles Haddon Spurgeon and friend John Piper, you will be unlikely to find these themes expounded in any great detail in our present age of Christianity Lite. In Christianity Lite the cross of Jesus is overlooked by people seeking a Christianity in which the objective is to glorify Self, the power to do so is Self, and the means to do so are self-sufficiency, victorious living, pride, and comfort, which together commingle as a false gospel that is of no help when the dark seasons of life envelope you.

The great Reformer Martin Luther distinguished between the Christianity Lite theology of glory and the theology of the cross. The theology of glory celebrates what human beings can do based on their personal vision, self-discipline, and hard work. The theology of the cross celebrates what Jesus alone can accomplish for us, through us, with us, and in spite of us. The theology of glory seeks to know God directly in his power, wisdom, success, and glory. The theology of the cross seeks to know God through the seeming weakness, folly, failure, and shame of the crucified Jesus. The theology of glory seeks to use God to avoid suffering, hardship, pain, shame, loss, and failure. The theology of the cross seeks to see suffering, hardship, pain, shame, loss, and failure as opportunities to grow in an understanding, appreciation, and emulation of the crucified Jesus. The theology of glory seeks to use God to obtain health and wealth. The theology of the cross seeks Jesus, even if that should mean experiencing pain and poverty like Jesus.

Caleb, without being overly harsh, I would warn you that the vast majority of Christian books I have seen and Christian preachers I have heard promote a theology of glory rather than a theology of the cross. As a newer Christian, you must be careful what teachings you believe since not all teachings that are "Christian" are truly Christian. To keep your head clear, keep looking to Jesus on the cross as both your Savior and example so that you can glorify God not through a theology of glory, but rather through a theology of the cross.

To help you understand the theology of the cross as more glorious than the theology of glory, let me begin by explaining who God is according to the Bible. God is glorious (Ex. 15:11; Ps. 145:5). Glory is one of the great mega-themes of Scripture, appearing nearly three hundred times in most English translations and roughly fifty times in the Psalms alone. The definition of the word *glory*, however, is tough to nail down; it includes splendor, beauty, magnificence, radiance, rapture, weightiness, transcendence, holiness, honor, excellence, and majesty. In the most basic of terms, glory is akin to glowing.

For example, if you put a metal poker in a raging fire and remove it some time later, you will notice that the poker is literally glowing, or glorying. The glory in the poker is the presence of the fire's heat having been transferred into it. The poker continues to glow, or glory, so long as the fire's heat is present in it.

Similarly, when Moses was in the presence of God, he was filled with the glory or fire of God. He literally glowed (Ex. 34:29–35; 2 Cor. 3:7). Likewise, the glory of God shone out of Jesus for a few moments during the transfiguration (Luke 9:29–31).

In Scripture, when people experience the glory of God, their responses include fear, awe, wonder, worship, dread, respect, conviction, repentance, and humility. In the Old Testament, when Mount Sinai gloried, the people trembled and stayed away, fearing they would die (Ex. 19:16; 20:18–19). When Moses glowed with the glory of God the people were afraid to be near him (Ex. 34:30). When Jesus gloried, the disciples were terrified (Mark 9:6). In Revelation Jesus comes glowing with his present glory, and John, the disciple who felt so comfortable with Jesus at the last supper, fell at his feet as if he were dead upon seeing Jesus in glory (John 13:23–25; Rev. 1:17).

In the New Testament, the glory of God is repeatedly connected to Jesus:

> [Jesus] is the radiance of the glory of God. (Heb. 1:3)

> And the Word [Jesus] became flesh and dwelt among us, and we have seen his glory, glory as of the only Son from the Father, full of grace and truth. (John 1:14)

> None of the rulers of this age understood . . . for if they had, they would not have crucified the Lord of glory. (1 Cor. 2:8)

> For God, who said, "Let light shine out of darkness," has shone
> in our hearts to give the light of the knowledge of the glory of
> God in the face of Jesus Christ. (2 Cor. 4:6)

Throughout Jesus' life he repeatedly stated that his purpose on earth was to glorify God the Father. That means his purpose was to make the Father's character visible. Jesus' glorifying God the Father included dying on the cross. In the week leading up to the cross, Jesus made the following statements connecting the Father's glory and his cross:

> Jesus answered them, "The hour has come for the Son of Man
> to be glorified. . . . Now is my soul troubled. And what shall I
> say? 'Father, save me from this hour'? But for this purpose I
> have come to this hour. Father, glorify your name." Then a voice
> came from heaven: "I have glorified it, and I will glorify it again."
> (John 12:23, 27–28)

> So, after receiving the morsel of bread, [Judas] immediately
> went out. And it was night. When he had gone out, Jesus said,
> "Now is the Son of Man glorified, and God is glorified in him. If
> God is glorified in him, God will also glorify him in himself, and
> glorify him at once." (John 13:30–32)

> When Jesus had spoken these words, he lifted up his eyes to
> heaven, and said, "Father, the hour has come; glorify your Son
> that the Son may glorify you." (John 17:1)

Having established that Jesus is both your Savior and example, I want to explain to you five great truths regarding the theology of the cross and your life.

1) You were made for God's glory (Isa. 43:6–7).

2) Everything in your life is an opportunity to glorify God (1 Cor. 10:31).

3) Rather than glorifying God, you will have a sinful tendency to do what you think will make you happy, and you will end up sinning (Rom. 3:23).

4) When you choose happiness over God's glory, enduring joy is impossible. You wind up pursuing things besides the glory of God (e.g., life, friends, comfort, pleasure—ironically, all gifts from God) rather than God himself.

5) Your pleasure is found in God alone; as God is glorified, your joy is satisfied. My friend John Piper has stated it this way in his book *Desiring God*,

which I know you enjoyed reading: "The chief end of man is to glorify God by enjoying Him forever." Phrasing it another way, he also said, "God is most glorified in me when I am most satisfied in Him."

Practically, this means that there is joy not only in your comfort and success but also in your suffering and hardship, just as there was for Jesus when he suffered on the cross. Hebrews 12:1–6 is worth memorizing as an anchor for your soul when the storms of life roll in and you find yourself drowning in a sea of tears:

> Let us also lay aside every weight, and sin which clings so closely, and let us run with endurance the race that is set before us, looking to Jesus, the founder and perfecter of our faith, who for the joy that was set before him endured the cross, despising the shame, and is seated at the right hand of the throne of God. Consider him who endured from sinners such hostility against himself, so that you may not grow weary or fainthearted. In your struggle against sin you have not yet resisted to the point of shedding your blood. And have you forgotten the exhortation that addresses you as sons? "My son, do not regard lightly the discipline of the Lord, nor be weary when reproved by him. For the Lord disciplines the one he loves, and chastises every son whom he receives."

When you suffer, Caleb, you can press forward through your pain and tears like Jesus because there is joy on the other side of whatever cross it is you must bear. We will all suffer, and as we suffer we must continually ask if we will suffer in a way that is purposeful or purposeless. As you and your wife suffer in your battle with her brain tumor, I don't want you to waste something so valuable. You have paid too high a price to have such a gift to simply waste it. By seeing your suffering as a valuable gift that you have paid much for, you can suffer well in a way that is joyful because the suffering is purposeful.

There is joy in knowing that through suffering God is at work in you to sanctify you and make you more like Jesus. There is also joy in knowing that through suffering God is at work to use your life as a witness and testimony of the difference Jesus is making in how you live your life, especially the most painful parts. In his opening chapter to the Philippians, Paul promises that the testimony of suffering well will both encourage and build up fellow Christians and will also result in non-Christians becoming Christians.

A quote that I often return to on this point is from an American missionary to India named E. Stanley Jones. He said, "Don't bear trouble, use it. Take whatever happens—justice and injustice, pleasure and pain, compliment and criticism—take it up into the purpose of your life and make something out of it. Turn it into testimony."

The joy that compels you is the glory of God in all things, and the joy that awaits you is the face of Jesus in the end and his commendation, "Well done, good and faithful servant" (Matt. 25:21, 23; Luke 19:17).

At the cross of Jesus, we learn that to be like Jesus means we pick up our cross and follow him as he commanded (Matt. 16:24). Practically, this means that we glorify God by allowing hardship, pain, and loss to make us more and more like Jesus. The false teaching of American Christianity Lite is that comfort is a virtue and pain a vice. As Christians we neither run to suffering as the early Christian ascetics did, nor run from it as modern Christian Americans do. Instead, we receive suffering when it comes as an opportunity for God to do something good in us and through us. We rejoice not in the pain, but rather in what it can accomplish for the gospel.

When your wife suffers, and you suffer with her, I anticipate you will suffer well in a way that is purposeful for the progress of the gospel both in and through you. For that to occur, you must continually remember Jesus Christ, of whom Scripture says:

> In the days of his flesh, Jesus offered up prayers and supplications, with loud cries and tears, to him who was able to save him from death, and he was heard because of his reverence. Although he was a son, he learned obedience through what he suffered. And being made perfect, he became the source of eternal salvation to all who obey him. (Heb. 5:7–9; see also Matt. 16:21; Heb. 2:9–10; 12:2; 13:12; Rev. 1:9)

At the cross of Jesus, we learn that we will suffer because of the sins other people commit against us. Peter spoke of Jesus' cross as your example when suffering injustice:

For what credit is it if, when you sin and are beaten for it, you endure? But if when you do good and suffer for it you endure, this is a gracious thing in the sight of God. For to this you have been called, because Christ also suffered for you, leaving you an example, so that you might follow in his steps. He committed no sin, neither was deceit found in his mouth. When he was reviled, he did not revile in return; when he suffered, he did not threaten, but continued entrusting himself to him who judges justly. He himself bore our sins in his body on the tree, that we might die to sin and live to righteousness. By his wounds you have been healed. (1 Pet. 2:20–24)

At the cross of Jesus we learn that we will suffer at the hands of those we love most, like Jesus did. In particular, Jesus suffered most for his bride, the church. As a Christian husband, Caleb, you too will suffer most to love, serve, and redeem your own wife. In taking her in for treatment, facing the possibility of never having children with the woman you love, and knowing that there could come a day when you stand over her coffin as they place her dead body into the ground, your life will be marked with dark seasons. In that darkness, which will feel like the darkness that covered the earth when Jesus died, you must not pursue a Christianity Lite theology of self-glory and comfort by which you become embittered against God. Rather, you must vigorously and continually pursue a theology of the cross like Jesus did, by suffering well for the glory of your God and the good of your bride. Jesus has saved you to be a masculine man like him, who weeps, loves, serves, and mourns as a cross-centered son of God.

To live a cross-centered life like Jesus will require humility and continually swinging your ax at the root of pride. You are living in a stupid culture where pride is a virtue, not a vice, and even the Christian bookstores have books dedicated to self-help, self-esteem, and self-glory.

As a result, all of the Bible's teaching that the last shall be first, that the weak are used by God to confound the strong, that life can be found only in losing ourselves, and that God opposes the proud but gives grace to the humble makes no sense at all to many. Again, however, when we look to the cross of Jesus, we see that he was able to glorify the Father and suffer well because he was humble. Though fully God, Jesus humbly entered human history as a man to suffer and die on the cross.

This pattern of humility that leads to glory is best explained in the incredibly rich passage of Philippians 2:5–11. There, Paul writes of Jesus our Savior and example:

> Have this mind among yourselves, which is yours in Christ Jesus, who, though he was in the form of God, did not count equality with God a thing to be grasped, but made himself nothing, taking the form of a servant, being born in the likeness of men. And being found in human form, he humbled himself by becoming obedient to the point of death, even death on a cross. Therefore God has highly exalted him and bestowed on him the name that is above every name, so that at the name of Jesus every knee should bow, in heaven and on earth and under the earth, and every tongue confess that Jesus Christ is Lord, to the glory of God the Father.

Caleb, I know that humility is an entirely new lesson that God is teaching you. Having always been the life of the party and the front man of your own band where crowds gathered around to cheer your performances, your life before knowing Jesus was spent living for, by, and to self-glorifying pride without any consideration for God. But one of the greatest examples Jesus has left for you is his humility, which was not cowardly, weak, or powerless but glorious.

The kind of cross-centered life marked by the joy that comes from living for God's glory in our suffering, with humility, is a life that you can live only by the same power that Jesus lived by—God the Holy Spirit. I know you are growing in your understanding of God the Holy Spirit, and the best way to understand his role in your life is to study his role in the life of Jesus.

God the Holy Spirit filled Jesus, empowering him to do the work God had for him. The Spirit likewise fills us today so we can follow the paradigm set by Jesus. One of the most curious trends in theology is the growing number of charismatic Calvinists. At first this sounds like an oxymoron. Nonetheless, there is an emerging generation of Christian leaders who believe that the sovereign God predestined them before the foundation of the earth to live Spirit-filled lives of kingdom power, demonstrated in everything from healings to miracles, supernatural wisdom, and humble, Christlike joy in suffering. As you are maturing in your studies, I know this is where you are landing theologically, and in that I rejoice because, even though you are a relatively new Christian, you are Jesus-focused and Spirit-led.

Caleb, the one historical point of major theological contention between charismatics and Calvinists has been the supposed conflict between Jesus Christ and the Holy Spirit. Simply, Calvinists place the person of Jesus and his work on the cross at the center of their understanding of Scripture. Meanwhile, charismatics tend to place the person of the Holy Spirit and his outpouring on the day of Pentecost at their theological center. Sadly, the result has been an apparent conflict for preeminence between Jesus Christ and the Holy Spirit.

However, a close examination of Scripture relieves this tension by revealing Jesus as our example of what it means to be Spirit-filled. Before proceeding, three truths about Jesus must be stated to keep you from slipping into error, so you can live as a biblically rooted, Jesus-centered, humbly powerful charismatic Calvinist.

1) Jesus was and is eternally God, just as he repeatedly said (Matt. 26:63–65; John 5:17–23; 8:58–59; 10:30–39; 19:7).

2) Jesus did become fully human in his incarnation on the earth (Isa. 7:14; Rom. 8:3; 1 John 4:2).

3) Jesus set aside the privileges of his divinity during his life on the earth to live as a human being (Phil. 2:1–11). This does not mean that while on the earth Jesus Christ, the second member of the Trinity, ceased to be God. But it does mean that during that time, with occasional exception, he did not avail himself of all the privileges of divinity but lived as a human being to identify with us and be our example.

The question persists, however: how could Jesus live the extraordinary life that he did if he did not avail himself of his divine attributes? The answer is perhaps most clearly taught in the writings of Luke, where Jesus is portrayed as the perfect Spirit-filled man who lived the perfect Spirit-filled life as both our Savior and example of Spirit-filled living. The empowerment of Jesus through God the Holy Spirit is repeatedly stressed in Luke's Gospel. There we find that Jesus was conceived by the Holy Spirit and given the title "Christ," which means anointed by the Holy Spirit (Luke 1–2). Jesus baptized people with the Holy Spirit, and the Holy Spirit descended upon Jesus at his own baptism (Luke 3:16, 21–22).

"MY WIFE HAS A BRAIN TUMOR"

Furthermore, Caleb, Jesus was "full of the Holy Spirit" and "led by the Spirit," came "in the power of the Spirit," and declared that "the Spirit of the Lord is upon me" (Luke 4:1–2, 14, 18 cf. Isa. 61:1). He also "rejoiced in the Holy Spirit" (Luke 10:21). Regarding the Holy Spirit's ministry to and through Christians, Jesus also promised that God the Father would "give the Holy Spirit to those who ask him" and that the Holy Spirit would teach us once he was sent (Luke 11:13).

In Luke's sequel, the book of Acts, Jesus told his disciples to wait to begin their ministry until the Holy Spirit came and empowered them (Acts 1). Then the Holy Spirit descended upon the early Christians, just as he had descended upon Jesus (Acts 2). In this way, God revealed that through the power of the Holy Spirit, the followers of Jesus are given the ability to live a life like Jesus (though admittedly imperfectly since we remain sinners) by the same Holy Spirit that enabled Jesus.

Practically, this means that not only did Jesus live a life of temptation and suffering that included death on the cross while glorifying God the Father in humility, but he did so to save you and send you the same Holy Spirit who empowered him so that you could live like him. At the moment of your conversion, you were permanently sealed with God the Holy Spirit (Eph. 1:13–14).

My concern for you, Caleb, has been that many of your friends are theologically charismatic. As such, they are prone to focus on the Holy Spirit at the expense of Jesus and on the Day of Pentecost at the expense of the cross. Seeing Jesus as led and empowered by God the Holy Spirit, however, eliminates any apparent conflict between Jesus and the Spirit or between the cross and Pentecost. Jesus is our Savior and example who sent the Spirit to save us and empower us to live Spirit-filled lives like his. As a result, what it now means to be Spirit-filled and Spirit-led is simply to have a theology of the cross by which we live like Jesus by the same power of the Spirit as he did on the earth.

If Jesus was filled with the Holy Spirit, then Jesus and the Holy Spirit are obviously not in opposition but work together in perfect union. This allows us to love, worship, obey, and follow Jesus by the power of the Holy Spirit without any conflict in loyalty between Jesus and the Holy Spirit.

Therefore, being Spirit-filled like Jesus ultimately means denying ourselves, picking up our cross, and following him wherever the Spirit leads, which may include suffering and dying like Jesus. This also means that just as Jesus was led by the Holy Spirit into forty days of suffering, loneliness, hunger, and an attack from Satan, so too the Holy Spirit has led you into a difficult life of marrying and loving a woman battling a brain tumor, so that the glory of Jesus might shine through you to her and through her to you as you suffer together.

In conclusion, the Spirit-filled perspective of Jesus allows us to remain Jesus-centered in our thinking, Spirit-led in our practice, and humble in our hardships. This is made possible when we realize that because being Spirit-filled means being like Jesus, such things as poverty, sickness, and hardship are not incompatible with living a Spirit-filled life. Indeed, the most perfectly Spirit-filled person who has ever lived, Jesus Christ, worked a simple job, lived a simple life, and died a painful death as a flat-broke, homeless man by the power of the Holy Spirit and in so doing perfectly and fully glorified God the Father and tasted pure joy.

Sadly, the Eastern religions see God as so detached and distant that God is in no way our savior, example, or power for new life. According to Islam, God cannot suffer, and so their scholars teach that the Holy Spirit left Jesus before he suffered on the cross as a mere man. However, one of my favorite Bible teachers, John Stott, asked a most pointed question in his book *The Cross of Christ* (which I would commend for your reading): "In the real world of pain, how could one worship a God who was immune to it?"

Caleb, I praise God that he has saved you through Jesus' cross. Further, I pray that God the Holy Spirit that dwelled in Jesus would continually empower you to glorify God, even in suffering and hardship, through a supernatural humility. Though it is hard, there is a reason for both of you to rejoice because of what Jesus is doing in you and through you for both Christians and non-Christians through your purposeful suffering. I know that the blows of your suffering are painful, but I am seeing in your life that they are also fruitful.

In closing, I leave you with a quote from a Romanian pastor who suffered under Communist rule, which I have committed to memory for seasons of suffering: "Christians are like nails; the harder you hit them, the deeper they go."

## Answers to Common Questions about *Christus Exemplar*

*Jesus is God. I am not. How can you say he is a real example for my life?*

Let me begin by commending you. So many people really believe they are God, the center of the universe. This sort of narcissistic self-picture dominates our culture. Yet you believe that you are God's child and not God.

But I also need to correct you. Jesus is God come in the flesh (John 1:14). We must be careful to confess that he is not God only, but the God-man. Many theologians explain that when the second person of the Trinity came among us as Immanuel, he gave up his eternal glory and equality with the Father to be like us, laid aside the independent use of his divine attributes, put himself under the authority of the Father, and yielded himself to the leading of the Holy Spirit (Isa. 7:14; 11:1–4; 61:1–3; Matt. 1:23; Luke 3:22; 4:1, 14, 18; John 1:32; 3:34; 5:19, 30; 8:28, 42; 14:10; Acts 1:2; 10:38; Phil. 2:6–8; Heb. 2:6, 9).

Jesus lived as a perfectly Spirit-filled human being to show us how to live. When Jesus was tempted by the Devil, he didn't respond as God. In fact, that was the very thing the Devil tempted him to do, but he refused. Jesus countered the Devil's temptations just as we do: he quoted well-interpreted Scripture and commanded the Devil to get away from him. Hebrews reminds us that Jesus can sympathize with our weaknesses because he was tempted in every respect as we are, yet without sin (Heb. 4:15).

You might want to have a look at chapter 2, "How Human Was Jesus?" of our book *Vintage Jesus: Timeless Answers to Timely Questions*, where we answer this important question in a more thorough fashion.

*But Jesus was the Son of God who came on a mission to save the world. How can I be anything like that?*

The fact is that we are called to just such a mission. This world is a place where we are often taught to grind ourselves down, to see ourselves as less than we are in Christ. Such thinking is sinful false humility in which we are supposed to view ourselves as useless worms, thinking that somehow God is pleased by our groveling (Col. 2:18, 23). However, because of Jesus' victory on the cross, we are soldiers and strong warriors in the service of Christ (2 Cor. 10:3–5; Eph. 6:10–20; 2 Tim. 2:3–4).

Jesus is the Son of God in a way we are not in that he is the incarnation of the second person of the Trinity. But because he came, we are sons of God too, with full family membership and rights of inheritance. Paul tells us that "when the fullness of time had come, God sent forth his Son, born of woman, born under the law, to redeem those who were under the law, so that we might receive adoption as sons. And because you are sons, God has sent the Spirit of his Son into our hearts, crying, 'Abba! Father!'" (Gal. 4:4–6; see also John 1:12; Rom. 8:19–23; Eph. 1:5). Amazingly, the Bible describes Jesus as our brother (Rom. 8:29; Heb. 2:11–15).

We also share in Jesus' mission to save the world. We do not do the work of propitiation, to be sure. But we do bring the message of free salvation in Jesus to the world.

He told us, "You will receive power when the Holy Spirit has come upon you, and you will be my witnesses in Jerusalem and in all Judea and Samaria, and to the end of the earth" (Acts 1:8).

Jesus told Paul and all of us, "I am sending you to open their eyes, so that they may turn from darkness to light and from the power of Satan to God, that they may receive forgiveness of sins and a place among those who are sanctified by faith in me" (Acts 26:17–18). We are ambassadors for Christ. God makes his appeal through us. So we beg people on behalf of Christ to be reconciled to God (2 Cor. 5:20). We also reason with people, trying to persuade them to believe in Jesus (Acts 18:4).

Paul goes so far as to say we fill up what is lacking in Christ's work in that we go where he didn't go, suffering what he suffered in order to be "a minister according to the stewardship from God that was given to me for you, to make the word of God fully known, the mystery hidden for ages and generations but now revealed to his saints" (Col. 1:25–26).

*How can Jesus be my example when I face so many things he never had to deal with?*

You are right that Jesus never had to deal with specific modern-day problems such as drugs, Internet porn, strip clubs, or jihad terrorism.

But think about it. Although there are new drugs, chemical addiction is nothing new. Alcoholism has always been a huge problem.

Look at the ruins of ancient cities such as Pompeii, and you will see that hard-core pornography has a very long history. In the pagan temples live sex was done in the name of the gods and was at least as graphic and in-your-face as today's strip clubs. The campaigns of the zealots and the Roman soldiers in the era of Jesus were at least as petrifying as today's terrorists. Jesus' world was in fact a lot like ours, because although times change, sinners and their sins do not.

The example of Jesus extends into the body of Christ, the church (see Romans 12 and 1 Corinthians 12). The heroes of the faith are witnesses for our laying aside the sin that clings so closely so we can run with endurance the race that is set before us (Heb. 12:1).

*My pastor showed me how liberals have used the example theory of atonement to destroy Christianity. Why are you using it?*

Your pastor is right. For a long time, people have appealed to the idea that Jesus is our example in order to deny that Jesus is our Savior, our substitute in propitiating the holy wrath of the Father. They falsely teach that Christ came to win human hearts by his example of reconciling love.

This view was first given theological expression by Peter Abelard (A.D. 1079–1142). It is also called the social gospel, which impacted the American church in the early twentieth century though the preaching of such men as Hastings Rashdall and Walter Rauschenbusch. It is very common today, lurking behind many "missional" or "emergent" teachings, and causing terrible problems.

But the reaction against this pernicious error has also led many to bypass what the Bible clearly teaches: Jesus' death and life are the pattern for our life. So we balance the truth of penal substitution with example when we study such passages as Philippians 2:1–5; 1 Peter 2:21; 1 John 3:16; 4:9–11; Matthew 16:24–25; and 2 Corinthians 5:14–21. It is possible to hold to the example theory of atonement and not even be a Christian.

However, as Christians who believe in all that Scripture says about Jesus' death on the cross, we must believe that Jesus did die on the cross as our example, in addition to being our substitute, victor, redeemer, sacrifice, righteousness, justification, propitiation, expiation, ransom, reconciler, and so on, as we are explaining throughout this book.

## HELPFUL INFORMATION

In the letter to Caleb, the quotations from John Piper come from his book *Desiring God* (Colorado Springs: Multnomah, 2003), 94 and 10, respectively. The quote from E. Stanley Jones is taken from Ajith Fernando, *The Call to Joy and Pain: Embracing Suffering in Your Ministry* (Wheaton, IL: Crossway Books, 2007), 11. The question posed by John Stott is taken from his book *The Cross of Christ* (Downers Grove, IL: InterVarsity, 1986), 335.

# CHAPTER ELEVEN

# "I Hate My Brother":
# Jesus Is Kurt's Reconciliation

*Let all bitterness and wrath and anger and clamor and slander be put away from you, along with all malice. Be kind to one another, tenderhearted, forgiving one another, as God in Christ forgave you. Therefore be imitators of God, as beloved children. And walk in love, as Christ loved us and gave himself up for us, a fragrant offering and sacrifice to God.*

EPHESIANS 4:31–5:2

**Kurt is in his forties and lives his life on the edge.** He runs a few small businesses that pay for his lifestyle of drug use, gambling, foolish spending, and sleeping around with his daughter's friends, who are less than half his age. In more recent years, his rough living has taken a toll on his physical and financial well-being.

Spiritually, Kurt is a vocal non-Christian who refuses to listen to anyone speaking to him about God. After spending a bit of time with him, it became obvious that in the little kingdoms of his home and businesses, he considers himself, curiously, to be something of a god. He is often ruthless and cruel, demanding cult-like devotion from his employees, children, and loser friends who need him for drugs, money, and approval.

As a result, there is no one near him who is in any way stable enough to speak into his life and point out what is obvious to everyone else who is not in his circle of control—he is falling apart in every way. He will sometimes spend days without sleeping because of the amount of drugs in his system. He has started spending major amounts of money on frivolous purchases so that his home and business properties are filled with broken-down cars, and his once beautiful home is now the eyesore of the neighborhood due to neglect.

Even sadder, his children who live with him still idolize their dad and remain devoted to him. They too do drugs and abuse alcohol, and, having never left his circle of control, they do not have any idea that another way of life is available to them. They spend their time hanging out with their friends, having boys sleep over in their beds, and even moving boys into their father's home to freeload off him for money, drugs, and alcohol. As a result, his children are a wreck and even no longer attend school, though they once were good students.

The only person who used to speak wisdom and sanity into Kurt's life was his brother. Both men grew up in a difficult family. They did not really know their criminal father because he was in prison. Their mother worked hard and was very poor. The big difference in the boys' lives is that Kurt's brother became a Christian around his early twenties.

As a result, he married a Christian woman, and together they raised their children according to the Scriptures. Kurt's brother's family is in every way the polar opposite of his own. Yet Kurt has refused to speak with his brother for many years, despite the fact that they live in the same city.

My understanding is that Kurt is incredibly angry at his brother. Under that anger there is bitterness that he does not understand. This letter is intended to help him see the root of his bitterness as well as the rotten fruit it is bearing in his life.

◎    ◎    ◎    ◎    ◎

## Dear Kurt,

While it may come as a bit of a surprise, I have been praying regularly for you for the past few years. My guess is that in first hearing that, you will scoff and quickly try to dismiss me as yet another religious nut who thinks he is better than you and is acting disrespectfully.

However, as odd as it may sound, I think that in some ways I understand you because we are alike in some ways. I too grew up in a poor neighborhood and experienced a lot of violence. Unlike you, I had a dad who was around and worked hard to take care of our needs by hanging drywall until he eventually broke his back. Like you, however, I was keenly aware of the ways in which various people had done wrong to me. Deep in me there is a strong sense of justice, and when I was ripped off, physically assaulted, or cussed out growing up, I would lash out with my words and fists to defend myself. I simply got fed up with some people and the way they treated me and decided to take care of myself by being tough.

In many ways, this approach actually worked. As I grew to be a man, most people were intimidated by me. As a result, they treated me with respect, did what I told them, and followed my leadership. This allowed me to excel in school, sports, and work.

My problems, however, were twofold. One, I could not control my anger or turn it on and off, but rather it controlled me at times. After a blowup I would sometimes feel ashamed and embarrassed but did not know how to prevent it from happening again. Two, I did not truly want to stop being angry. I found that my anger was a powerful motivating factor in my life, and it enabled me to achieve some success because of it. I saw myself as stronger, tougher, and more capable than the weaker and more timid people I met. Quietly, I despised such people because they allowed themselves to be walked on, disrespected, taken advantage of, and pushed around.

I also discovered that there was a raging anger in me that sometimes came up so suddenly that I could not contain it. I would fly into a fit of rage in an instant and immediately attack someone verbally and physically. While this kind of response was helpful on the streets when I was growing up and facing danger, it proved to be very destructive in my relationships with people I cared about who were not a threat to my safety.

In particular, I began to worry that I would overreact one day as a husband and father to my wife and children and end up being abusive toward them. It seemed that my rage was beyond my control during those times when I felt betrayed, disrespected, or disobeyed. I simply refused to be that kind of impotent guy and therefore held onto my anger and fits of rage as a necessary evil of sorts.

Then I became a Christian. As I studied the person and work of Jesus, I found him to be far stronger, more courageous, bolder, and more fearless than any man I had ever met. As I read the Bible, I also discovered that he could get very angry when evil and injustice were occurring, and he in no way lacked the strength to stand against it, even to the point of taking a beating, suffering, and bleeding out on the cross without backing down or crying like a baby.

The sheer raw power of Jesus intrigued me. People flocked to him, respected him, followed him, and were inspired by him like no one I had ever known. He ruled by his influence of good, not by control through threat or violence. Even his anger and moments of rage were not inappropriate or embarrassing as mine were. In short, a curiosity stirred in me to find out how Jesus was able to live his life with such power under perfect control.

I started by trying to pay attention to what triggered my anger. In time, I found out that it was bitterness. I was bitter against a long list of people in my life who had lied to me, stolen from me, cheated on me, physically assaulted me, embarrassed me, or disrespected me.

I am fairly sure, Kurt, that there is a lot of bitterness under your anger, violence, addictions, and efforts to set up your own little kingdom and rule it like some god. So, if you are willing to at least hear me out on this, I would like to explain what I've learned about bitterness. Without patronizing you, I do care about you and am worried for you and for those around you, including your children.

When we do wrong to another person, we feel guilty. But when someone does wrong to us, we feel bitter. Bitterness is by definition our response to someone else's sin against us, whether it is real or imagined. The hurt of the sin leads to the immediate response of anger. When we can't or don't do anything about the hurt, the initial anger settles into bitterness, an intense resentment marked by animosity, hatred, cynicism, and contempt. It is cold, raw, destructive misery. Our bitterness is easy to legitimize, because if someone points out that we are bitter, we can easily point our finger to someone else who has sinned against us and blame them for making us bitter. That answer does not help us in any way, though, because it only explains why we are bitter but does not take away our bitterness.

Furthermore, bitterness does not even necessarily require that someone has done something wrong to us. We can become bitter if we merely perceive or imagine that we have been sinned against, whether or not we actually have. Bitterness can also occur because of proud jealousy; envying someone leads to bitterness, something James 3:14 calls "bitter jealousy and selfish ambition."

Knowing that you appreciate directness, I will tell you plainly that you are bitter against your brother. It is your bitterness that has caused you not to speak to him in years, despite his attempts to reconcile with you. Some of your bitterness is based on sins he has committed against you, which are very real and should not be minimized. Yet, some of your bitterness is based on lies. For example, you have repeatedly claimed that he stole from you. However, your brother is an honest man who has repeatedly denied that charge.

Further, in an effort to appease you, he has even agreed to repay what you think he stole from you to show you honor and respect. You have refused his efforts because you want to be bitter against him and have a reason to despise him. Additionally, some of your bitterness against your brother is caused by jealousy. You are jealous that his life is going better than yours, that his children are doing better than yours, and that he is happy while you are miserable.

Upon hearing this, you will be prone to do what Scripture calls "suppress the truth" by denying that you are bitter, telling yourself that you have moved on and are no longer bothered by certain parts of your relationship with your brother, or by blaming him for all of your bitterness. The hard, cold truth is that you are responsible for your own bitterness because you have chosen how you act and react toward your brother.

I began to understand bitterness when I read something that a pastor I knew had written on the subject. He included a number of questions that helped me to reflect on whether I was suffering from bitterness, and I have listed some of them here for you in hopes that they help you see your bitterness, since you, like us all, are blind to your blind spots.

1) Do you continually replay in your mind with great detail a negative past event and dislike for the person(s) involved?

2) Do you find yourself continually referring to someone in a pejorative fashion because of some past hurt?

3) Do you intentionally avoid certain person(s) because you find yourself becoming continually annoyed and angry in their presence?

4) Do you find that your dislike of someone is growing over time?

Eventually, our bitterness seeps out of us through our mouths, because it is through our words that our hearts are revealed. When we are bitter, we speak pejoratively about people to demean, disrespect, and disregard them. It is our verbal way of fighting back and making them pay.

Bitterness is often unrelated to the magnitude of a sin but is instead correlated to the emotional proximity of the offender. It is also often tied to betrayal. What I mean is this: if a stranger sins against you in a big way, you are unlikely to get bitter. But if a beloved family member or friend sins against you in a little way, you are likely to get bitter because you have opened your heart to that person and have high expectations for the relationship.

Therefore, those whom you love most are the most likely to provoke your bitterness because their sin rises to the level of betrayal. This is why you are bitter against your brother. You want him and need him in your life, yet somehow he has failed you in your eyes, and you cannot forgive him for the hurt he has caused you.

This pattern extends even to bitterness toward God. The Scriptures illustrate this point with Naomi, a woman who had moved from Israel to another land with her husband and sons, and who then died. She tells her daughters-in-law, "Do not call me Naomi ["pleasant" or "sweet"]; call me Mara ["unpleasant" or "bitter"], for the Almighty has dealt very bitterly with me" (Ruth 1:20). Even though you are not a Christian, I wonder if deep down in your heart you are not bitter against God for some of the difficulties in your life, including the death of your wife.

In no way do I want to minimize the great pains you have endured throughout life. But I do want to hold you responsible for your responses to that pain. You have responded to evil with evil and are therefore no better than those you claim have made you bitter.

One of the great lies of bitterness is that it is not our fault because someone else made us bitter by doing or saying evil. The truth is that bitterness is caused by the condition of our own hearts. Our lives flow out of the condition of our hearts, so when people sin against us, our response comes from what's inside us rather than from what they do to us: "The good person out of the good treasure of his heart produces good, and the evil person out of his evil treasure produces evil, for out of the abundance of the heart his mouth speaks" (Luke 6:45).

In her book *If*, Amy Carmichael, a missionary to India for fifty-five years, articulates this point well, saying, "For a cup brimful of sweet water cannot spill even one drop of bitter water, however suddenly jolted." The jolt does not change the water. If you spill a glass of sweet water, sweet water comes out. If you spill a glass of bitter water, bitter water comes out. The jolt only brings out of the container what is already there.

Likewise, if you are filled with sweetness and then jolted, only sweetness will come out. But if you are filled with bitterness and then jolted, bitterness will come out. It is not the fault of the person who jolted you. The question is not "Can I prevent being jolted?" since we all are, but "What is inside of me that will come out?"

Kurt, because you have bitterness in your heart, you respond out of your bitterness when you feel hurt, offended, or mistreated, and a cycle of escalating evil gets unleashed. Ephesians 4:31 explains it this way: "Let all bitterness and wrath and anger and clamor and slander be put away from you, along with all malice." Here, we see that bitterness never stays simple bitterness; unless dealt with, it grows and becomes increasingly insidious. One possible way of reading this passage is to see a cycle of bitterness as follows:

Bitterness: You feel hurt, offended, or mistreated and refuse to forgive the person whom you perceive (rightly or wrongly) as guilty.

Wrath: You become irritated and agitated, and you can feel your blood pressure rising as your mind and body are preparing to respond.

Anger: You are furious with people and motivated to harm them in some way, including yelling at them, hitting them, and threatening them.

Clamor: Your anger can no longer be contained, and you engage in a conflict with others for the purpose of harming them in some way, perhaps emotionally or physically, so that they are defeated by you and taught never to hurt you again, or else they will suffer your bitter, angry wrath.

Slander: To vindicate yourself and vilify others, you gossip about them and start telling other people what they have done and what horrible people they are in order to ruin their reputations, and you also train other people not to hurt, offend, or mistreat you lest they suffer the same fate.

Malice: As bitterness continues to grow into malice, you invent ways of doing even more evil to punish the people you are bitter against, regardless of the personal cost to yourself. The entire goal is to make them lose, even if that should mean that you lose as well.

Sometimes this cycle of bitterness moves along very quickly, like a raging fire, over the course of minutes or days. One example from your life would be the bitterness you held against your wife. Even though you were still married, you moved your girlfriend, who was half your age, into your house and began sleeping with her under the same roof as your wife. You did all of this openly as an act of malice.

Other times, bitterness smolders more slowly, over the course of months or years. You can see this in your bitterness against your brother. Although you have not spoken to him in some years, you frequently speak about him to your mutual friends and family, taking every opportunity to slander him. Your malice against him includes efforts you have made to sabotage his business.

What I find fascinating about you, Kurt, is that you are keenly aware of any and every offense that people commit against you but are completely oblivious to your own sins. The Bible explains your condition with a very helpful word picture: "Strive for peace with everyone, and for the holiness without which no one will see the Lord. See to it that no one fails to obtain the grace of God; that no 'root of bitterness' springs up and causes trouble, and by it many become defiled; that no one is sexually immoral or unholy like Esau, who sold his birthright for a single meal" (Heb. 12:14–16).

The word picture describes you as a tree that produces fruit, which consists of your words and deeds. At the base of the tree are roots, which nourish the tree and its fruit. Because the roots of your life are bitter, your words and deeds are nourished by bitterness, which explains why your life is nothing but rotten fruit. Your bitterness has led to a harvest of filth, perversion, and godlessness, just like Scripture said would happen.

Because you are bitter, you are like a guy named Esau in Scripture.

Esau was a man's man like you who liked to hunt and fight. His brother Jacob was more like your brother and a bit of a momma's boy who was not as tough and spent a lot of time in the kitchen, like your former-cook brother does. Their mother did a horrible thing and favored Jacob over Esau, probably as your own mother favored your brother over you. Favoritism fueled Esau's bitterness and likely yours.

Esau was, like you, an impetuous man. He was hungry one day and sold his birthright and inheritance to his brother for a meager bowl of soup. He ended up marrying one woman and sleeping with another, just like you; both women were train wrecks and sources of constant drama and grief, just like the women in your life. Esau and Jacob had such a bitter, ongoing family feud that their story takes up roughly twelve chapters of the book of Genesis. Both of the boys sinned against each other repeatedly and, like you with your brother, spent roughly twenty years not even speaking to one another because of bitterness and hurt.

During those years, however, God was good to both men by growing them spiritually and blessing them financially. While Jacob had been a worshiper of the God of the Bible since he was a young man, he also had some selfish tendencies and holier-than-thou attitudes that God had to straighten out. This same sort of thing has been going on in your brother's life since you last spoke.

As a young man, Esau, like you, did not worship the God of the Bible, but during the time apart from his brother, God changed his heart. Although still somewhat rough around the edges, Esau did have a change of heart. In time, the two brothers reconciled. Their reunion included their families and is one of the most emotionally moving stories in all of Scripture. In an act of forgiveness, "Esau ran to meet [Jacob] and embraced him and fell on his neck and kissed him, and they wept" (Gen. 33:4).

I am writing this letter to you, Kurt, in hopes of seeing you and your brother forgive one another and be reconciled as were Jacob and Esau. For that to happen, the root of bitterness in your life must be cut off.

The ax for that root is the death of Jesus Christ on the cross in your place and in your brother's place, for both your sins and your brother's.

Additionally, Kurt, you have hurt God with your many sins and your god complex far more than your brother ever hurt you. God has every right to hate you, curse you, and send you to hell forever. God could have been like you and settled into bitterness against you, using his wisdom and power to plot various kinds of malice against you.

Instead, God "through Christ reconciled us to himself . . . that is, in Christ God was reconciling the world to himself, not counting their trespasses against them" (2 Cor. 5:18–19). The passage goes on to say, "For our sake [the Father] made [Jesus] to be sin who knew no sin" (v. 21).

If you were willing, you would also benefit from reading Romans 3:25–26; 4:25; 5:8–11; 8:3; 2 Corinthians 5:21; and Colossians 1:19–22 in the Bible, as they further explain what God has done to reconcile with us through Jesus rather than be embittered against us. Either way, the bottom line is that God the Son left heaven and came to earth to become sin for you. He took the filth of your sin to himself at the cross and died as your substitute.

If you turn from sin to trust in Jesus, the angry wrath of God will no longer be upon you. Instead, through Jesus, the anger that God has against you for the life you have lived and the wrath God has waiting for you in the next life can be removed.

God is a good and holy God, and your sin is bad and very unholy. As a result, God could not just overlook or excuse your life of sin. Yet, because he is loving, gracious, merciful, and kind, God has provided a way for you to reconcile with him. This is why Jesus, who is God, came to earth to live the sinless life you have not lived, die the death for sin that you should die, and rise to give the gift you otherwise could not obtain—reconciliation with the God who created you. This gift is made possible through faith, which means trusting in Jesus for the forgiveness of all your sins of the past, present, and future.

The result of connecting with the reconciling work of Jesus on the cross is newness in us: "Therefore, if anyone is in Christ, he is a new creation. The old has passed away; behold, the new has come" (2 Cor. 5:17). This new creation includes ongoing, deep, personal transformation in us.

As a result of Christ's death, not only does Christ take on our sin, but we also take on his righteousness. Kurt, in Jesus you can become a new man with a new life complete with new desires and a new power, all given to you through your reconciled relationship with God, made possible through Jesus' death for your sins and his resurrection for your new life.

When you have the gift of forgiveness and new life from Jesus, you have all it takes to chop out your bitterness. The means by which Jesus' ax can chop through the root of your bitterness is explained in a lengthy section of Ephesians:

> Now this I say and testify in the Lord, that you must no longer walk as the Gentiles do, in the futility of their minds. They are darkened in their understanding, alienated from the life of God because of the ignorance that is in them, due to their hardness of heart. They have become callous and have given themselves up to sensuality, greedy to practice every kind of impurity. But that is not the way you learned Christ!—assuming that you have heard about him and were taught in him, as the truth is in Jesus, to put off your old self, which belongs to your former manner of life and is corrupt through deceitful desires, and to be renewed in the spirit of your minds, and to put on the new self, created after the likeness of God in true righteousness and holiness. (Eph. 4:17-24)

In summary, Kurt, you cannot stop the cycle of bitterness by remaining in your old way of life. You may be surprised by the forthrightness of the words written about you. They were penned by a man named Paul who, before becoming a Christian, was himself filled with bitterness. His life was marked by the cycle of bitterness to such a degree that he was an angry and violent murderer, as your own father was. Paul was no coward or fool, and in this passage he nails you for having a way of life marked by futile thinking, darkened understanding, alienation from God, ignorance, hardness of heart, callousness, sexual perversion, greed, and all kinds of impure words, deeds, and motives. He rightly says that you need to become a new person in Jesus Christ who lives a new life free from such things as the sin of bitterness.

That new life is further explained by Paul:

> Therefore, having put away falsehood, let each one of you speak the truth with his neighbor, for we are members one of another. Be angry and do not sin; do not let the sun go down on your anger, and give no opportunity to the devil. Let the thief no

longer steal, but rather let him labor, doing honest work with his own hands, so that he may have something to share with anyone in need. Let no corrupting talk come out of your mouths, but only such as is good for building up, as fits the occasion, that it may give grace to those who hear. And do not grieve the Holy Spirit of God, by whom you were sealed for the day of redemption. Let all bitterness and wrath and anger and clamor and slander be put away from you, along with all malice. (Eph. 4:25–31)

To begin your new life free of bitterness you must start speaking truthfully. This includes speaking truthfully to Jesus about your own sin as a repentant man who stops blaming his sin on other people and grows up to take responsibility for himself. I know your brother and others have sinned against you, but the truth is that you are the most wicked man you know. What could be crueler than, night after night, having your wife lie in her bed while dying of cancer and hearing you in the other room doing crystal meth with your children, hearing the sounds of you having sex with their friend who is less than half your age?

You need to be truthful about your sin to God and to the people you have sinned against. You also need to meet with your brother, in repentance, to tell the truth about the sins you have committed against him in addition to reminding him truthfully of painful sins he has committed against you so that he can repent as well.

Behind all of this, as the Scriptures say, is Satan. There is a real dark enemy of God at work in the world and in your life. He will give you all the sex, power, money, and drugs you desire, but they are merely bait on hooks intended to reel you in so that he can destroy you, your life, and your family, and take you with him to hell.

The only way to be free of Satan's grip on your life is Jesus. Not only have you been sinned against, you have also sinned against Jesus, who is God. Because you have been sinned against, you have become bitter and trapped in a cycle of bitterness. But Jesus is willing to treat you in a way that you have never treated anyone who has sinned against you. He is willing to be kind, gracious, merciful, and forgiving rather than bitter.

Therefore, if you turn from your sin to Jesus, you will be reconciled to God. He has made a way for you to be forgiven and a way for your sins, which separate you from God and other people like your brother, to be taken away. In Jesus, God has provided a new root system to nourish your life so that you can bear new fruit as a new person.

In the final section of Scripture that we have been reading, Paul explains this amazing possibility: "Be kind to one another, tender-hearted, forgiving one another, as God in Christ forgave you. Therefore be imitators of God, as beloved children. And walk in love, as Christ loved us and gave himself up for us, a fragrant offering and sacrifice to God" (Eph. 4:32–5:2).

Paul is saying that Jesus Christ is God, who lived the sinless life that you have not. He then died the painful death that you should die as just penalty for your sin before your sentencing to the eternal torments of hell. On the cross, Jesus took upon himself your past, present, and future sin and suffered and died in your place. As a result, if you confess your sins to Jesus and become a Christian, God will be "kind," "tender-hearted," and "forgiving" toward you. As a Christian, you will be a new person who can then treat people the way Jesus has treated you, which means that Jesus-like forgiveness will be the root system of your life rather than bitterness.

Kurt, I sincerely pray that you will get real with Jesus about your sin against God and others and stop living an empty life nourished by your bitterness. When you do, you will see that not only does Jesus reconcile you to God in heaven, but he also takes away sin so that you can be reconciled to people on the earth. This includes your brother, who prays for the day that you and he can embrace with tears of forgiveness like Jacob and Esau did.

## Answers to Common Questions about Reconciliation

*I used to be like Kurt. I am glad to say I have accepted Christ. But I still feel hurt, anger, and bitterness, and I still have a lot of persistent habits that just won't go away no matter how hard I work. I hate it. What failed? Is the work of Christ insufficient after all? Am I a total failure? Does this mean that God has rejected me?*

When we come into Christ and to the reality of his death to pay every penalty for every one of our sins, we are and always will be children of the Most High God. That will never change. God will never reject us.

At the same time, we come into the reality of his resurrection. The Holy Spirit indwells us, and through his power we receive a new heart. The deepest values of our life change. It's the gift of righteousness we call regeneration. At the deepest core of our being we want to be like Jesus. So when you see the sin you continue to do, your deep response is hatred.

At the same time, sinful desires, what the Bible calls "flesh," are still part of your being. There is mortal conflict between the new heart that loves Jesus, what the Bible often calls "spirit," and the flesh. Paul describes it this way: "For the desires of the flesh are against the Spirit, and the desires of the Spirit are against the flesh, for these are opposed to each other, to keep you from doing the things you want to do" (Gal. 5:17). This is why your battle with sin rages on in this life.

As you experience the power of Jesus' redemption, as there is increasing Christlikeness in many aspects of your life, and as your love for Jesus grows, the battle will go deeper and become more agonizing. The deepening of the battle is a sign of the successful working of the cross and the resurrection.

So what failed? Not the atonement. You are a child of God. The Spirit's power is at work in you. Nor are you a failure, unless you give up the battle against the sinful desires. Paul commands us to "put to death therefore what is earthly in you" (Col. 3:5). What he is saying is that something is going to die. It will be either your happiness or the earthly desires in you.

What failed is the simplistic "victorious life" offered by preachers who make cheap promises of immediate victory for discovering some secret. They say that Jesus paid the price so we can be totally free from all poverty, illness, and sin right now. But they ignore the life Jesus himself lived. The truth is that there is battle against the world, the flesh, and the Devil until Jesus comes.

Jesus and the Spirit help us in the battle through the body of Christ by means of pastors, teachers, counselors, physicians, family, and worship. So enjoy your new life in Jesus as you do mortal battle with the sins, knowing that in eternity the work of salvation will be complete, and your struggle with sin will be no more.

*You say that sin is forgiven at the cross. But I resonate with David when he cries out, "My sin is ever before me" (Ps. 51:3). What should I do when I don't feel forgiven?*

Christians feel the horror of their sin more and more as they grow in Christ. If we focus on these feelings, we can despair. Thankfully, forgiveness is not a matter of our feeling but of the sufficiency of Christ's cross and the reconciliation that he brings. John reminds us, "He is the propitiation for our sins, and not for ours only but also for the sins of the whole world" (1 John 2:2). Paul puts it this way:

> God shows his love for us in that while we were still sinners, Christ died for us. Since, therefore, we have now been justified by his blood, much more shall we be saved by him from the wrath of God. For if while we were enemies we were reconciled to God by the death of his Son, much more, now that we are reconciled, shall we be saved by his life. More than that, we also rejoice in God through our Lord Jesus Christ, through whom we have now received reconciliation. (Rom. 5:8–11)

So what do you do when you feel so unforgiven? Do not just pray about it. Rather, follow James's command: "Confess your sins to one another and pray for one another, that you may be healed" (James 5:16; see also Acts 19:18). Share your feelings with a Spirit-led, grace-based friend who will be totally honest with you and will help you remember Jesus' work of reconciliation through the cross.

*But my sin is so awful!*

It is . . . far more awful than you or I will ever know. That is why it took the death and resurrection of the eternal Son of God, come in the flesh, to win our reconciliation. Our sin is real but, thankfully, so is our reconciled relationship with Jesus.

## HELPFUL INFORMATION

In the letter to Kurt, the quote from Amy Carmichael comes from her book *If* (Fort Washington, PA: CLC, 1992), 46.

# CHAPTER TWELVE

# "I Want to Know God": Jesus Is Susan's Revelation

*No one has ever seen God; the only God, who is at the Father's side, he has made him known.*

JOHN 1:18

**Susan is a twenty-something petite brunette** with a big smile, working a job while finishing up her college education. Her life story is fairly typical. She grew up in a nominally church-going family but never really got much substantive teaching about God. She has always believed there is some sort of God but has never been sure which religion best understands who God is.

She has not attended church as an adult except for an occasional visit when invited by a friend. She has very little knowledge of the Bible and is not for or against Christianity as much as she is simply uncertain. Her curiosity about God has compelled her to start praying upon occasion to the God she does not know, hoping that God will help her with practical aspects of her life such as finding a better job, deciding whether her boyfriend is husband material, and finishing her college education.

When I first spoke with her about God, Susan was refreshingly honest. She did not pretend to be a Christian but said that she is still trying to figure out what she thinks of Jesus. As is common, she said Jesus was a great man, but she is unconvinced that he is God who died for our sins and rose for our salvation. She did say that she believes Jesus lived as a historical figure and that he died a bloody death on the cross. As our conversation continued, she changed the subject from that of the cross to understanding God. When I asked her why she kept changing the subject, she said that she did not want to talk about Jesus' death because she really wanted to figure out what God is like.

I explained to her that she wanted something that could be known only through revelation. As we chatted, I outlined for her how religion and philosophy are based upon human speculation about God, which is not very trustworthy because in the end it is little more than a guess. However, revelation is an act by which God reveals himself to us in a way that we can understand. I further explained that perhaps the clearest revelation of God in all of history is the death of Jesus on the cross. So, rather than looking at every religion and philosophical system, I encouraged her to examine the death of Jesus on the cross as the answer to her questions and the satisfaction to her longings to know God. This letter is written to Susan in hopes of helping her see how God is revealed at the cross of Jesus Christ.

◎   ◎   ◎   ◎   ◎

## Dear Susan,

When we last spoke, you were honest with me regarding where you are spiritually, and I want to thank you for that. Knowing where you stand makes it easier for me to pray for you. Knowing that you felt safe enough with me to tell me the truth—that you are not yet a Christian—was encouraging. It means you know that my love for you is without condition and that you don't have to fake anything to earn my approval. Since that time I have been praying that Jesus would reveal himself to you, and I thought that perhaps writing a letter would help answer some of your questions.

To be honest, I was in almost the same spiritual place as you are when I was in college. I grew up with spotty church attendance, which virtually ceased altogether when I became a teenager. I always believed there is a God and even prayed on occasion. But I had a lot of uncertainty about Jesus and a lot of unanswered questions. In college I began searching for answers to my spiritual questions by taking a variety of comparative religion and philosophy classes and meeting with a variety of religion leaders and philosophical teachers to learn their thoughts about God.

Eventually, I decided to focus on Jesus. It seemed that nearly every religion and philosophical system dealt to some degree with Jesus because he is the most influential person who has ever lived. Focusing on Jesus really helped to answer my questions and led to me becoming a Christian. So, as I share with you some things about Jesus in general and about his death on the cross in particular, I hope and pray that you don't hear from my heart anything that seems condemning or lecturing. I do care for you and want to be an encouragement and help in any way I can.

As we spoke, Susan, you said that you do believe there is a God. You also said that you believe that Jesus lived and died and possibly even rose from death. But you struggle to see how that applies to your life and what difference it makes practically. Furthermore, you seemed to be struggling to find out where you should look to find the truth about who God is.

Being an intelligent and educated young woman, I am sure you have heard conflicting advice of where you should begin your search for God. Some people will tell you that there is a spark of God inside of you, and the key to discovering God is to look deep inside yourself through meditation. Some will tell you that God is far away in a holy place like Mecca or Israel, and that you should make a pilgrimage to such a place to find God. Some will tell you that God is part of creation, and that by spending time in nature you will find God in the beauty of the world. Some will tell you that God cannot be known at all, and we are left in a fog of uncertainty. Still others will tell you that there is simply no God to be found.

This letter is intended to give you the Christian view of God. Before we begin, I will warn you that this letter is filled with a lot of Scripture. My emphasis on Scripture is not an attempt to preach at you, though I obviously will be preaching to you the next time you visit our church, but rather an attempt to love you the best that I can. There are innumerable religious leaders, spiritual gurus, and philosophical inquirers, but nothing compares to the transforming power of the Bible.

In my life I have repeatedly experienced how God uses the Bible to reveal himself to me and transform me to be more like him. Thus, I am sharing a great deal of Scripture with you, trusting that God himself will speak to you through these verses and will satisfy the longing of your heart to know who he is. I would also encourage you to read the Bible for yourself, beginning with the Gospel of John. John's point is that the eternal Son of God came to us as the totally human man Jesus Christ in order to explain God the Father (John 1:14, 18).

The Bible repeatedly says that God cannot be found except by looking to Jesus Christ. Some examples include:

> No one has ever seen God; the only God, who is at the Father's side, he has made him known. (John 1:18)

> Philip said to him, "Lord, show us the Father, and it is enough for us." Jesus said to him, "Have I been with you so long, and you still do not know me, Philip? Whoever has seen me has seen the Father. How can you say, 'Show us the Father'?" (John 14:8–9)

> [Jesus] is the image of the invisible God. (Col. 1:15)

> Long ago, at many times and in many ways, God spoke to our fathers by the prophets, but in these last days he has spoken to us by his Son [Jesus], whom he appointed the heir of all things, through whom also he created the world. [Jesus] is the radiance of the glory of God and the exact imprint of his nature. (Heb. 1:1–3)

Jesus is such an enormous figure in human history that he is the only person who appears in every major world religion. His teaching has changed lives and nations like no one else's. His kind deeds, such as feeding the poor and loving children, are fondly remembered by Christians and non-Christians alike. His many miracles are also incredibly powerful and inspiring. Therefore, the question remains, when it comes to studying Jesus, where do we begin with so much material to sift through?

As important as Jesus' teaching, kind deeds, and miracles are, surprisingly, it is Jesus' death and resurrection that are emphasized in Scripture. Matthew devoted 33 percent of his Gospel to Jesus' final week; Mark, 37 percent; Luke, 25 percent; and John, 42 percent. The rest of the New Testament builds on the reality and power of his death and resurrection, referring to the life of Jesus far less frequently.

The Bible speaks not only of what was accomplished in Jesus' life, death, and resurrection, but also how they revealed the character of God. Because Jesus' death and resurrection are the crux of his earthly life, there is no better way to learn more about God than by examining the revelation of God through the cross. At the cross we learn eight truths about God.

First, in his death and resurrection, Jesus revealed to us the justice of God:

> Christ Jesus, whom God put forward as a propitiation by his blood, to be received by faith. This was to show God's righteousness, because in his divine forbearance he had passed over former sins. It was to show his righteousness at the present time, so that he might be just and the justifier of the one who has faith in Jesus. (Rom. 3:24-26)

Susan, this means that because God is holy, he could not tolerate our sin; because God is just, he had to deal with our sin. At the cross, we see how deeply God hates sin and that the penalty for sin is death. Susan, because I care for you, I need you also to accept that you are unholy and sinful. In saying this, I am not saying that I am any better than you; I too am a sinner, just like you. But because we are sinners, God must deal with us justly. He does this in one of two ways: either through Jesus' death on the cross in our place as the penalty for our sin, or through sending us to hell for eternity.

I know you may not like the concept of hell, but I find it beautiful because it means that God is not unjust and will not let all of the evil and cruelty in this world go unpunished. For example, I remember your telling me that a dear friend of yours was brutally raped and that you were furious because the man who sinned against her so horribly was never brought to justice. God shares your anger, and if that man does not repent to Jesus, the good news is that he will stand before Jesus to face the justice of hell.

On the other hand, since I have contributed to the sin that litters the world, God must also deal with me. Thankfully, God did deal with me justly at the cross of Jesus, where all the sins I have committed or will ever commit were placed on Jesus, and he suffered and died in my place to satisfy the demands of God's justice. Jesus was not stuck in death, separated from God because of sin, as we would be apart from him. He revealed God's justice and fully satisfied it. Then he was resurrected to abundance of life, which is a gift he shares with us.

My fear for you is, because God is just and you are sinful, if you die today you will spend eternity in hell. This is why I am so desperate for you to turn from sin to Jesus and become a Christian.

Second, on the cross, Jesus revealed to us the love of God. The following verses from the Bible state how the love of God is most clearly revealed at the cross of Jesus:

> For God so loved the world, that he gave his only Son, that whoever believes in him should not perish but have eternal life. (John 3:16)

> Greater love has no one than this, that someone lay down his life for his friends. (John 15:13)

> But God shows his love for us in that while we were still sinners, Christ died for us. (Rom. 5:8)

> In this the love of God was made manifest among us, that God sent his only Son into the world, so that we might live through him. In this is love, not that we have loved God but that he loved us and sent his Son to be the propitiation for our sins. (1 John 4:9-10)

When the Bible says that the love of God is clearly seen at the cross of Jesus, it is saying that the love of God is not merely sentimental but also efficacious. When people speak of love, they usually mean nothing more than an emotional love that feels affectionate but may not do anything to help the beloved. Thankfully, God does not merely feel loving toward us; his love actually compels him to act on our behalf so that we can be changed by his love. Because of God's love for you, if you turn to Jesus and ask that his work on the cross be applied to your sin, the love of God will continue to be lavished upon you for the rest of this life and in the eternal life to come.

Third, on the cross, Jesus revealed to us the relational nature of God. One of the primary effects of sin is that it separates us from God (Isa. 59:2; Hos. 5:6). But God has lovingly worked out a way for our friendship with him to be restored—through the cross of Jesus. Many Scripture verses, including those following, explain how a friendly, reconciled relationship with God is only possible through the cross of Jesus.

For if while we were enemies we were reconciled to God by the death of his Son, much more, now that we are reconciled, shall we be saved by his life. More than that, we also rejoice in God through our Lord Jesus Christ, through whom we have now received reconciliation. (Rom. 5:10–11)

All this is from God, who through Christ reconciled us to himself and gave us the ministry of reconciliation; that is, in Christ God was reconciling the world to himself, not counting their trespasses against them, and entrusting to us the message of reconciliation. Therefore, we are ambassadors for Christ, God making his appeal through us. We implore you on behalf of Christ, be reconciled to God. For our sake he made him to be sin who knew no sin, so that in him we might become the righteousness of God. (2 Cor. 5:18–21)

And you, who once were alienated and hostile in mind, doing evil deeds, he has now reconciled in his body of flesh by his death, in order to present you holy and blameless and above reproach before him. (Col. 1:21–22)

For Christ also suffered once for sins, the righteous for the unrighteous, that he might bring us to God, being put to death in the flesh but made alive in the spirit. (1 Pet. 3:18)

The big idea in all these verses is that God is not a distant ruler or cruel taskmaster. Rather, God is a loving Father, and we are his foolish and disobedient children who have run away from home and endangered ourselves. The distance between us and God is thoroughly our own doing by our sin. The only way we can be reconciled to God in love is if our sin, which has separated us from him, is removed. That is precisely what Jesus has done. Through the cross, Jesus took away our sin so that we could be reconciled to God. Through his resurrected life, we are fully united with the triune God. Jesus prayed, "Just as you, Father, are in me, and I in you, that they also may be in us" (John 17:21).

One of the great and distinct truths of Christianity in comparison to all other religions is that God is not an impersonal force or a distant being. Rather, God is a living and loving God who has extended a hand of loving friendship through Jesus. That same hand, I assure you, is extended to you. God does in fact love you, and he showed it when Jesus died on the cross and resurrected to life so that your sins might be taken away and your new, living relationship with God might begin.

Fourth, on the cross, Jesus revealed to us the pleasures of God, as the following sections of Scripture articulate:

> Yet it was the will of the LORD to crush him; he has put him to grief; when his soul makes an offering for guilt, he shall see his offspring; he shall prolong his days; the will of the LORD shall prosper in his hand. (Isa. 53:10)

> He predestined us for adoption as sons through Jesus Christ, according to the purpose of his will, to the praise of his glorious grace, with which he has blessed us in the Beloved. In him we have redemption through his blood, the forgiveness of our trespasses, according to the riches of his grace, which he lavished upon us, in all wisdom and insight making known to us the mystery of his will, according to his purpose, which he set forth in Christ. (Eph. 1:5–9)

Susan, I am guessing that at this point you may be wondering why God would go to such great lengths, coming into human history as the man Jesus Christ, only to suffer and die in our place for our sins. I confess that why God would go to such trouble for people like me is a mystery. In fact, according to the Bible, God was in no way obligated to deal with our sin problem and did not act out of duty. Rather, although God is angry at and grieved by sin, he is a loving God who took away our sin at the cross simply because it gave him joy and pleasure to act out of his pure goodness.

Fifth, on the cross, Jesus revealed to us the wisdom and power of God. The following lengthy section of Scripture says it well:

> For the word of the cross is folly to those who are perishing, but to us who are being saved it is the power of God. For it is written, "I will destroy the wisdom of the wise, and the discernment of the discerning I will thwart." Where is the one who is wise? Where is the scribe? Where is the debater of this age? Has not God made foolish the wisdom of the world? For since, in the wisdom of God, the world did not know God through wisdom, it

pleased God through the folly of what we preach to save those who believe. For Jews demand signs and Greeks seek wisdom, but we preach Christ crucified, a stumbling block to Jews and folly to Gentiles, but to those who are called, both Jews and Greeks, Christ the power of God and the wisdom of God. For the foolishness of God is wiser than men, and the weakness of God is stronger than men. (1 Cor. 1:18–25)

At the cross, we see that God is both wise and powerful. The world is filled with people who think they are smarter than they really are. Such people think they know how the world works and what should be done to fix it. These people are attracted to such arenas as politics, religion, psychology, and philosophy. They delight in airing their critiques of the world and their answers for how to fix it on everything from talk radio to blogs. But since most people do not believe we are sinners, their "wisdom" is really folly because they can never get to the real source of all the trouble in the world and, therefore, have no real solution to truly help people.

For the wise few who know that the problem is sin, their shortcoming is that they lack the power to do anything about the human sin problem. God alone is wise enough to know that our problem is sin and is powerful enough to take it away. God has done just that through the cross of Jesus.

Sixth, on the cross Jesus revealed to us the mercy of God, as the following verses of Scripture teach:

The saying is trustworthy and deserving of full acceptance, that Christ Jesus came into the world to save sinners, of whom I am the foremost. But I received mercy for this reason, that in me, as the foremost, Jesus Christ might display his perfect patience as an example to those who were to believe in him for eternal life. (1 Tim. 1:15–16)

But when the goodness and loving kindness of God our Savior appeared, he saved us, not because of works done by us in righteousness, but according to his own mercy, by the washing of regeneration and renewal of the Holy Spirit. (Titus 3:4–5)

Because God is full of mercy and grace, he came to this miserably sinful world. Jesus revealed the character of the Father of compassion and the God of all comfort as he fed the hungry and healed those suffering with awful diseases like leprosy. Because he dealt justly with our sin at the cross of Jesus, God is free to extend mercy to us. This mercy includes helping us in life so that we grow more and more to be the people we are supposed to be—people like Jesus. Had God been merciful to us without dealing with our sin, he would have been in effect endorsing injustice and evil. Thankfully, God not only graciously takes away our sin but mercifully extends himself to us, knowing that we desperately need him.

Seventh, on the cross Jesus revealed to us the great truth that God is a living God:

> It will be counted to us who believe in him who raised from the dead Jesus our Lord, who was delivered up for our trespasses and raised for our justification. (Rom. 4:24-25)

> If the Spirit of him who raised Jesus from the dead dwells in you, he who raised Christ Jesus from the dead will also give life to your mortal bodies through his Spirit who dwells in you. (Rom. 8:11)

God is the living God, and sin is the cause of death. Because death is the result of sin, death has the power to hold only those who are sinners. Since Jesus dealt fully with the guilt and shame of sin, the grave could not hold him, and he rose in victory over sin and death. Therefore, in the death of Jesus for sin, we see the result of sin, but in the resurrection of Jesus we also see the triumphant victory of the living God over deadly sin.

What this means is that if you place your trust in Jesus, one day you too will rise from death as he did and live forever without sin and its effect of death. I cannot express how deeply I desire for you to be a Christian and to rise with you from death to spend eternity together with Jesus and the multitudes of people whom he went to the cross to save.

Eighth, on the cross Jesus revealed to us the healing power of God:

> But [Jesus] was wounded for our transgressions; he was crushed for our iniquities; upon him was the chastisement that brought us peace, and with his stripes we are healed. (Isa. 53:5)

Isaiah prophesied hundreds of years in advance of the actual event that, while Jesus was on the cross, "many were astonished at [Jesus]—his appearance was so marred, beyond human semblance, and his form beyond that of the children of mankind" (Isa. 52:14). Nonetheless, three days after he died, Jesus rose in completely restored health. If you are a Christian, you too are guaranteed complete physical healing because of Jesus' work to conquer sin and its effects, such as sickness, on the cross.

For some, this includes miraculous bodily healings, which, as a pastor, I have seen on a few occasions. For many, this means the bruises and sores and raw wounds resulting from sin will be healed as they abandon those sinful practices (Isa. 1:6). People receive the resurrection power of the life of Jesus when they are bonded to him. The slurred mind of an alcoholic clears dramatically when Jesus' life makes him new. But the cirrhosis of the liver often remains until death. For all of us, this means that on the other side of the grave our bodies will be fully healed, just like Jesus' body was healed after his resurrection from death (1 Cor. 15:51–55).

Susan, I know you have had many physical problems, especially considering your young age. Those ailments are the result of sin entering the world; our bodies suffer the effects of sin along with our souls. But I promise you that not only did Jesus die to take away our sin, but he also rose three days later as the pattern of full healing that is to come if we trust in him.

Therefore, it all comes down to your believing in the death and resurrection of Jesus in your place for your sins. In our conversation, you said that you believed Jesus lived and died, although you had questions about his resurrection. Now that you have read some of the important revelations of Jesus' death, I will briefly tell you why I have come to believe that Jesus did in fact rise from death, which is the biggest issue in all of human history.

You already believe that Jesus lived and died, which is wonderful, but without the resurrection of Jesus, he is no more helpful to you than any other holy person who once lived but now remains bound by death. I did not always believe that Jesus rose from death, but the following seven truths changed my mind.

First, Jesus predicted his death. On a number of occasions, Jesus foretold his death and resurrection (Matt. 12:38–40; Mark 8:31; 9:31; 10:33–34; John 2:18–22).

Second, Jesus did in fact die. This was confirmed by a professional executioner, who ran a spear through Jesus' side, piercing his heart, to ensure he was dead (John 19:34–35). Furthermore, after suffering a near deadly beating, Jesus was wrapped in roughly one hundred pounds of burial linens and spices and left in a cold tomb, without medical care, for three days.

Third, Jesus' tomb was empty three days after he died. Jesus was buried in the tomb of a wealthy and well-known man named Joseph of Arimathea (Matt. 27:57–60; Mark 15:42–46; Luke 23:50–53; John 19:38–42). Because of this, the location of the tomb where Jesus was buried would have been common knowledge. Had Jesus not truly risen from death, it would have been very easy to prove it by opening the tomb and presenting his dead body as evidence.

Fourth, after dying, Jesus appeared alive to many witnesses, including his mother, Mary (Acts 1:14); his disciples (Matt. 28:16–20); his friends, such as Peter (1 Cor. 15:5); his enemies, such as Saul (1 Cor. 9:1; 15:8); his brother James (1 Cor. 15:7); and crowds of more than five hundred people (1 Cor. 15:6).

Fifth, people began worshiping Jesus as God who died on the cross for their sins and rose from death to give them new life. As a result, people stopped worshiping on Saturdays and began worshiping on Sundays because it was the day Jesus rose. The early Christians also began practicing baptism and communion. Baptism shows that Christians will be buried and will rise cleansed from sin by Jesus. Communion is designed to remember Jesus' body and blood shed for our sins on the cross.

Sixth, there were a lot of people claiming to be the messiah in those days, just as there are today. Think of the loser in the 2004 presidential election. Many people looked to him to save us from the country's troubles. They became his followers, joined his team, gave their money, time, and energy, and campaigned hopefully. But when he lost, those followers either gave up hope or went looking for another messiah. No rational person would claim as savior someone who suffered a complete defeat. So when Messiah Jesus was killed, you would expect his followers to act rationally and give up on him. But the exact opposite happened. They were far more dedicated, way more courageous, and much more powerful than ever before. The only possible source for their new hope was the truth of their testimony, that they had seen Jesus risen from death and very much alive.

Seventh, even non-Christian historians attest to the fact of Jesus' death and resurrection. One such example is Josephus, a Jewish historian born just a few years after Jesus died. His most celebrated passage, called the "Testimonium Flavianum," says:

> Now there was about this time Jesus, a wise man, if it be lawful to call him a man; for he was a doer of wonderful works, a teacher of such men as receive the truth with pleasure. He drew over to him both many of the Jews and many of the Gentiles. He was [the] Christ. And when Pilate, at the suggestion of the principal men among us, had condemned him to the cross, those that loved him at the first did not forsake him; *for he appeared to them alive again the third day,* as the divine prophets had foretold these and ten thousand other wonderful things concerning him. And the tribe of Christians, so named from him, are not extinct at this day.

In conclusion, Jesus not only lived and died but also rose as the only person to ultimately defeat sin and death. He did this out of love for you. He did this because he wanted a relationship with you. He did this so that you would know who God is and how altogether wonderful he is.

Jesus is alive today in heaven, ruling as God over all of his creation. As a result, he knows every hair on your head, day of your life, longing of your heart, and thought in your mind. You can speak to him at any time and ask him to make himself known to you, and he will. You can turn to him at any time for forgiveness of sin, and he will embrace you. I desperately pray that you will see God in the cross of Jesus and meet Jesus, who walked away from his tomb as the just, loving, personal, joyful, good, wise, living, powerful God who is calling you to take his hand and walk with him as a Christian.

Your questions can be answered only in Jesus. Your longings can be satisfied only in Jesus. Your sins can be forgiven only in Jesus. Your life can be transformed only in Jesus. Your prayers can be answered only in Jesus. Your eternity can be enjoyed only in Jesus.

Jesus is calling out to you. Susan, I am praying that you would cry out to Jesus. When you do, please let me know. I will serve you communion, which is where Christians remember Jesus' broken body and shed blood on the cross, in our place, for our sins. And I will baptize you to show the world that Jesus died on the cross for you and rose to cleanse you from sin and give you a new life through his death.

# Answers to Common Questions about Revelation

*Were the people in the Old Testament expecting Jesus to come and die for their sins?*

The Bible clearly foreshadowed that Jesus would come as Servant and Messiah who would die for our sins. Perhaps the clearest Old Testament Scripture on this point is Isaiah 53:4–6, which says:

> Surely he has borne our griefs and carried our sorrows; yet we esteemed him stricken, smitten by God, and afflicted. But he was wounded for our transgressions; he was crushed for our iniquities; upon him was the chastisement that brought us peace, and with his stripes we are healed. All we like sheep have gone astray; we have turned—every one—to his own way; and the LORD has laid on him the iniquity of us all.

Hundreds of years after Isaiah's prophecy, those who witnessed the crucifixion of Jesus rightly considered him punished by God because of dreadful sin. They also rightly surmised that Jesus' suffering was severe because of the severity of the sin for which he was being punished. They correctly saw that Jesus was being punished ultimately by God.

However, Isaiah further explains that it was not Jesus' sin but, rather, our sin that brought the horrors of crucifixion upon him. To explain Jesus' death, Isaiah uses the word pictures associated with the sacrifice of the Passover lamb and the first goat on the Day of Atonement. But it was a man, not a mere lamb or goat, who would shed his blood.

Isaiah the prophet thunders that God pierced Jesus for our transgressions and crushed Jesus for our iniquity. The Lord laid our sin on Jesus, our substitute. Then the Lord crushed Jesus so we could have peace, healing, and acceptance. Isaiah saves the best news for last: Jesus was wounded for our transgressions. The bruising that he felt was the chastisement that we deserved, but it was laid upon him and not upon us because Jesus loved us enough to suffer in our place as our substitute for our sins.

*How could God be good and still allow Jesus to suffer
on the cross?*

For those who love Jesus, reading Isaiah 53:10 is nearly unbearable and
results in tears because it says, "Yet it was the will of the Lord to crush
him; he has put him to grief." The Hebrew word translated "will" in the
ESV actually means "to take pleasure in, to delight in" and therefore "to
desire."

The question persists, how could the loving Father God take delight
in crushing his Son Jesus Christ? Is this not akin to a father putting on
steel-toed boots and stomping the head of his firstborn son until he lies
in a pool of blood?

At first glance, the entire metaphor of God the Father crushing God
the Son does have the ring of divine child abuse. Thankfully, because
Isaiah was inspired by God the Holy Spirit, a continued reading of his
words rather than a departure from Scripture for varying speculation
will clarify our confusion and provide the explanation. God the Father
is not delighted in the crushing of Jesus. On the other hand, God the
Father is delighted in the humbly loving substitution Jesus willingly
made for us:

> Yet it was the will of the Lord to crush him; he has put him to
> grief; when his soul makes an offering for guilt, he shall see his
> offspring; he shall prolong his days; the will of the Lord shall
> prosper in his hand. Out of the anguish of his soul he shall see
> and be satisfied; by his knowledge shall the righteous one, my
> servant, make many to be accounted righteous, and he shall
> bear their iniquities. (Isa. 53:10–11)

It was the relentless desire of both God the Father and God the Son
to remove the stain of sin from all of humanity so that we might enjoy a
world free of pain, torment, death, and hell itself. This desire compelled
Jesus to endure the hellish pain, torment, and death of the cross and
compelled the Father to crush Jesus in our place to create this new world
through the cross.

Subsequently, only through Jesus will many people be justified and
liberated from the effects of sin, such as pain, torment, injustice, tears,
sorrow, sadness, heartache, sickness, and death—the very things that
Jesus endured in our place. Jesus alone has secured for us entrance into

the kingdom world where men and women live together in peace with one another and with their Creator, fulfilling the tremendous possibilities that God intended for us in the dignity of creation, which was lost after our descent into the depravity of sin.

As Isaiah says, all of this is made possible because, after dying for sin, Jesus rose up in victory over sin and its effects. We who believe in Jesus metaphorically become his offspring, spiritually born again into the family of God through the forgiveness of sin by sharing in the victory of Jesus.

In conclusion, although the account of Isaiah reflects upon the sufferings of Jesus, it in no way portrays him as an unwilling victim at the hands of God the Father: "He was oppressed, and he was afflicted, yet he opened not his mouth; like a lamb that is led to the slaughter, and like a sheep that before its shearers is silent, so he opened not his mouth" (Isa. 53:7).

As Isaiah promised, Jesus did not protest his suffering on the cross, but rather remained steadfastly silent and focused on his mission of glorifying his Father in heaven and saving his people on earth. If Jesus had been dying for his own sin, he would not have been silent because he was a righteous man; rather, he would have confessed his guilt, which he did not do because he was sinless.

Additionally, Jesus did not use his final breaths to shout against the injustice he suffered because he suffered voluntarily, knowing that as a substitute his suffering for us was just; it is exactly the kind of thing we deserve. The only possibility for Jesus' silence is that he voluntarily took our sin upon himself and consciously and willfully accepted his punishment in our place. Jesus did this because he knew that through his death and resurrection we would be saved from Satan, sin, death, hell, and the wrath of God, which explains why Christians cannot stop singing the praises of Jesus.

## HELPFUL INFORMATION

In the letter to Susan, the quotation from Josephus is taken from "Jewish Antiquities," in *The New Complete Works of Josephus*, trans. William Whiston (Grand Rapids, MI: Kregel, 1999), 18:63–64; emphasis added.

# Recommended Reading on the Cross

**Since the issue of the cross is so vitally important,** it is helpful to spend considerable time throughout one's life growing in one's understanding of all that Jesus accomplished through his death. This is particularly important for Christian preachers and teachers, who should be studying the cross continually, in addition to whatever else they are studying. To that end, the following books are offered as recommendations to aid in that process, books which we both have enjoyed as we prepared to write this book.

## HELPFUL BOOKS ON THE CROSS

Beilby, James, and Paul R. Eddy, eds. *The Nature of the Atonement: Four Views*. Downers Grove, IL: InterVarsity, 2006; 208 pages.

Boice, James Montgomery, and Philip G. Ryken. *The Heart of the Cross*. Wheaton, IL: Crossway Books, 2005; 160 pages.

Demarest, Bruce. *The Cross and Salvation: The Doctrine of Salvation*. Wheaton, IL: Crossway Books, 2006; 544 pages.

Denney, James. *The Death of Christ: Its Place and Interpretation in the New Testament*. Whitefish, MT: Kessinger, 2005; 385 pages.

Hengel, Martin. *Crucifixion in the Ancient World and the Folly of the Message of the Cross*. Minneapolis, MN: Augsburg Fortress, 1977; 99 pages.

Hill, Charles E., and Frank A. James, eds. *The Glory of the Atonement: Biblical, Theological, and Practical Perspectives*. Downers Grove, IL: InterVarsity, 2004; 500 pages.

McDonald, H. D. *The New Testament Concept of Atonement: The Gospel of the Calvary Event*. Cambridge: James Clarke, 2006; 144 pages.

McGrath, Alister E. *The Enigma of the Cross*. London: Hodder and Stoughton, 1987; 192 pages.

Morris, Leon. *The Apostolic Preaching of the Cross*. Grand Rapids, MI: Eerdmans, 1984; 318 pages.

———. *The Atonement: Its Meaning and Significance*. Downers Grove, IL: InterVarsity, 1984; 219 pages.

———. *The Cross in the New Testament*. Eugene, OR: Wipf and Stock, 2006; 454 pages.

Nicole, Roger. *Standing Forth: Collected Writings of Roger Nicole*. Ross-shire, Scotland: Christian Focus, 2002; 436 pages.

Piper, John. *Fifty Reasons Why Jesus Came to Die*. Wheaton, IL: Crossway Books, 2006; 128 pages.

Smail, Tom. *Windows on the Cross*. Eugene, OR: Wipf and Stock, 2004; 124 pages.

Smeaton, George. *The Apostles' Doctrine of the Atonement*. Carlisle, PA: Banner of Truth, 1991; 548 pages.

———. *Christ's Doctrine of the Atonement*. Carlisle, PA: Banner of Truth, 1991; 502 pages.

Sproul, R. C. *The Truth of the Cross*. Orlando, FL: Ligonier, 2007; 178 pages.

Stott, John R. W. *The Cross of Christ*. Downers Grove, IL: InterVarsity, 2006; 383 pages.

Tidball, Derek. *The Message of the Cross: Wisdom Unsearchable, Love Indestructible*. Downers Grove, IL: InterVarsity, 2001; 341 pages.

Wallace, Ronald. *The Atoning Death of Christ*. Eugene, OR: Wipf and Stock, 1997; 159 pages.

Wells, Paul. *Cross Words: The Biblical Doctrine of Atonement*. Ross-shire, Scotland: Christian Focus, 2006; 256 pages.

## HELPFUL BOOKS ON PENAL SUBSTITUTION

Bridges, Jerry, and Bob Bevington. *The Great Exchange: My Sin for His Righteousness*. Wheaton, IL: Crossway Books, 2007; 304 pages.

Charnock, Stephen. *Christ Crucified: A Puritan's View of the Atonement*. Ross-shire, Scotland: Christian Focus, 2003; 208 pages.

Dabney, Robert L. *Christ Our Penal Substitute*. Ashburn, VA: Hess Publications, 1998; 115 pages.

Jeffery, Steve, Michael Ovey, and Andrew Sach. *Pierced for Our Transgressions: Rediscovering the Glory of Penal Substitution*. Wheaton, IL: Crossway Books, 2007; 384 pages.

Packer, J. I., and Mark Dever. *In My Place Condemned He Stood: Celebrating the Glory of the Atonement*. Wheaton, IL: Crossway Books, 2008; 192 pages.

Peterson, David, ed. *Where Wrath and Mercy Meet: Proclaiming the Atonement Today*. Carlisle, UK: Paternoster, 2001; 176 pages.

## HELPFUL BOOKS ON LIMITED ATONEMENT

Long, Gary D. *Definite Atonement*. Frederick, MD: New Covenant Media, 2006; 147 pages.

MacLeod, Donald. *The Humiliated and Exalted Lord: A Study of Philippians 2 and Christology*. Greenville, SC: Reformed Academic Press, 1994; 80 pages.

Owen, John. *The Death of Death in the Death of Christ*. Carlisle, PA: Banner of Truth, 1959; 240 pages.

## A HELPFUL BOOK ON UNLIMITED LIMITED ATONEMENT AND JOHN CALVIN

Thomas, G. Michael. *The Extent of the Atonement: A Dilemma for Reformed Theology from Calvin to the Consensus*. Carlisle, UK: Paternoster, 1997; 278 pages.

## HELPFUL BOOKS ON JUSTIFICATION

Carson, D. A., ed. *Right with God: Justification in the Bible and the World*. Eugene, OR: Wipf and Stock, 2002; 310 pages.

Carson, D. A., Peter T. O'Brien, and Mark A. Seifrid, eds. *Justification and Variegated Nomism*. Grand Rapids, MI: Baker, 2004; 1,216 pages.

Forde, Gerhard O. *Justification by Faith: A Matter of Death and Life*. Minneapolis, MN: Augsburg Fortress, 1982; 103 pages.

Johnson, Gary L. W., and Guy Waters, eds. *By Faith Alone: Answering the Challenges to the Doctrine of Justification*. Wheaton, IL: Crossway Books, 2006; 224 pages.

Piper, John. *Counted Righteous in Christ: Should We Abandon the Imputation of Christ's Righteousness?* Wheaton, IL: Crossway Books, 2002; 144 pages.

———. *The Future of Justification: A Response to N. T. Wright*. Wheaton, IL: Crossway Books, 2007; 240 pages.

Seifrid, Mark. *Christ, Our Righteousness: Paul's Theology of Justification*. Downers Grove, IL: InterVarsity, 2008; 222 pages.

Sproul, R. C. *Faith Alone: The Evangelical Doctrine of Justification*. Grand Rapids, MI: Baker, 1999; 224 pages.

Stuhlmacher, Peter. *Revisiting Paul's Doctrine of Justification: A Challenge to the New Perspective*. Downers Grove, IL: InterVarsity, 2001; 108 pages.

Vickers, Brian. *Jesus' Blood and Righteousness: Paul's Theology of Imputation*. Wheaton, IL: Crossway Books, 2006; 256 pages.

## HELPFUL BOOKS ON THE HISTORY OF
## ATONEMENT THEOLOGY

Hengel, Martin. *The Atonement: The Origins of the Doctrine in the New Testament.* Eugene, OR: Wipf and Stock, 2007; 112 pages.

McGrath, Alister E. *Luther's Theology of the Cross.* Malden, MA: Blackwell, 2000; 208 pages.

Moltmann, Jurgen. *The Crucified God: The Cross of Christ as the Foundation and Criticism of Christian Theology.* Minneapolis, MN: Augsburg Fortress, 1993; 346 pages.

Shaw, Ian J., and Brian H. Edwards. *The Divine Substitute: The Atonement in the Bible and History.* Greenville, SC: Day One, 2006; 160 pages.

Tomlin, Graham. *The Power of the Cross: Theology and the Death of Christ in Paul, Luther, and Pascal.* Eugene, OR: Wipf and Stock, 2007; 343 pages.

## HELPFUL BOOKS ON LIVING IN LIGHT
## OF THE CROSS

Bridges, Jerry. *The Gospel for Real Life.* Colorado Springs: NavPress, 2003; 208 pages.

Carson, D. A. *The Cross and Christian Ministry: Leadership Lessons from 1 Corinthians.* Grand Rapids, MI: Baker, 2004; 144 pages.

Mahaney, C. J. *The Cross Centered Life: Keeping the Gospel the Main Thing.* Sisters, OR: Multnomah, 2002; 96 pages.

——. *Living the Cross Centered Life: Keeping the Gospel the Main Thing.* Sisters, OR: Multnomah, 2006; 176 pages.

Spurgeon, Charles H. *Twelve Sermons on the Passion and Death of Christ.* Grand Rapids, MI: Baker, 1971; 152 pages.

## UNHELPFUL BOOKS ON THE CROSS

Tragically, there are also some horrendous books on the cross that have been published in recent years. More thorough students may want to familiarize themselves with these in an effort to be aware of the books promoting false teaching that have been endorsed and recommended by some well-known teachers, such as Brian McLaren.

Chalke, Steve, and Alan Mann. *The Lost Message of Jesus.* Grand Rapids, MI: Zondervan, 2004; 208 pages. This is a book in which the death of Jesus is described as divine child abuse.

Green, Joel B., and Mark D. Baker. *Recovering the Scandal of the Cross: Atonement in New Testament and Contemporary Contexts.* Downers Grove, IL: InterVarsity,

2000; 232 pages. The authors claim that paganism, not God, is the authority behind the New Testament teaching on the cross, and that modern-day paganism (e.g., feminism, Marxism, environmentalism) is also the lens through which we should view the cross of Jesus Christ.

Mann, Alan. *Atonement for a "Sinless" Society: Engaging with an Emerging Culture.* Carlisle, UK: Paternoster, 2005; 224 pages. This work assumes that since lost people no longer believe in sin we must accommodate them and teach the death of Jesus without focusing on his death having been for our sins.

Weaver, J. Denny. *The Nonviolent Atonement.* Grand Rapids, MI: Eerdmans, 2001; 246 pages. Denny claims that black, feminist, and womanist theologies have helped us see that Jesus' death was not planned or sanctioned by God the Father. As a result, it is wrongly argued, substitution or satisfaction must be abandoned.

# Notes

## PREFACE

1. D. A. Carson, "Maintaining Scientific and Christian Truths in a Postmodern World," *Science & Christian Belief*, vol. 14, no. 2 (October 2002): 107–122, http://www.scienceand christianbelief.org/articles/ carson.pdf.

## INTRODUCTION: WE KILLED GOD

1. Josephus, *Jewish War* 7.203.
2. Cicero, *Pro Rabirio* 5.16.
3. Suetonius, *The Lives of the Caesars* Vesp. 5.4.
4. John R. W. Stott, *The Cross of Christ* (Downers Grove, IL: InterVarsity, 1986), 160.
5. C. S. Lewis, "The Humanitarian Theory of Punishment," in *God in the Dock* (Grand Rapids, MI: Eerdmans, 1970), 287–300.

## CHAPTER 5: "I MOLESTED A CHILD"

1. Martin Luther, *Sermons on the Passion of the Christ*, trans. E. Smid and J. T. Isensee (Rock Island, IL: Augustana Press, 1956), 25.
2. James Denney, *The Death of Christ* (London: Hodder and Stoughton, 1911), 297.

## CHAPTER 6: "MY DAD USED TO BEAT ME"

1. Karl Barth, *Church Dogmatics*, ed. G. W. Bromiley and T. F. Torrance (Edinburgh: T. & T. Clark, 1957), 2:152.

## CHAPTER 7: "HE RAPED ME"

1. P. T. Forsyth, *The Cruciality of the Cross* (London; Independent Press, 1948), 99.

## CHAPTER 8: "MY DADDY IS A PASTOR"

1. Cited in David F. Wells, *God in the Wasteland* (Grand Rapids, MI: Eerdmans, 1994), 118.
2. For further discussion on this balance, see Gerry Breshears, "Learning to Distinguish between Degrees of Certainty," in *Lessons in Leadership*, ed. Randal Roberts (Grand Rapids, MI: Kregel, 1999).

# Subject Index

# Scripture Index

| | |
|---|---|
| 1:11–12 | 11 |
| 1:11–15 | 70 |
| 1:15–17 | 11 |
| 2:14 | 91 |
| 2:16 | 116 |
| 2:20 | 29 |
| 3:13 | 22, 27, 33, 70, 190 |
| 3:13–14 | 62 |
| 4:4–6 | 213 |
| 5:12 | 172 |
| 5:17 | 230 |
| 6:14–15 | 70 |

**Ephesians**

| | |
|---|---|
| Chap. 1 | 102 |
| 1:2–4 | 178 |
| 1:5 | 213 |
| 1:5–9 | 242 |
| 1:7 | 62 |
| 1:7–8 | 193 |
| 1:10 | 82 |
| 1:13–14 | 210 |
| 1:17–23 | 47 |
| 1:18–2:8 | 48 |
| 1:22 | 82 |
| 2:1 2 | 113 |
| 2:8–9 | 102–3 |
| 2:8–10 | 66 |
| 4:17–24 | 227 |
| 4:17–32 | 50 |
| 4:25–31 | 227–28 |
| 4:31 | 223 |
| 4:31–5:2 | 217 |
| 4:32–5:2 | 229 |
| 5:6 | 129, 131 |
| 5:8 | 107 |
| 5:21–33 | 82 |
| 5:25 | 30, 171 |
| 6:10–13 | 48 |
| 6:10–18 | 54 |
| 6:10–20 | 213 |

**Philippians**

| | |
|---|---|
| 1:21 | 193 |
| 2:1–5 | 214 |
| 2:1–11 | 97, 209 |
| 2:5–11 | 208 |
| 2:6–8 | 212 |
| 2:10–11 | 189 |
| 2:12–13 | 193 |
| 3:8–9 | 101 |
| 3:18 | 30 |

**Colossians**

| | |
|---|---|
| 1:10–14 | 47 |
| 1:13 | 42, 48, 53, 102 |
| 1:13–14 | 63, 70, 192, 194 |
| 1:14 | 172 |
| 1:15 | 238 |
| 1:18 | 82 |
| 1:18–20 | 174 |
| 1:19–22 | 226 |
| 1:21–22 | 241 |

| | |
|---|---|
| 1:25–26 | 213 |
| 2:10 | 82 |
| 2:13 | 106 |
| 2:13–14 | 115 |
| 2:13–15 | 37, 44 |
| 2:15 | 54, 194 |
| 2:18 | 213 |
| 2:19 | 82 |
| 2:23 | 213 |
| 3:5 | 66, 97, 230 |
| 3:6 | 129 |
| 3:18 | 82 |

**1 Thessalonians**

| | |
|---|---|
| 1:9–10 | 129, 131 |
| 2:13 | 136 |

**1 Timothy**

| | |
|---|---|
| 1:15–16 | 243 |
| 2:1–6 | 170 |
| 2:4 | 170 |
| 2:5 | 188 |
| 2:5–6 | 183, 191 |
| 2:6 | 171 |
| 2:11–15 | 82 |
| 4:10 | 170, 171 |

**2 Timothy**

| | |
|---|---|
| 1:9 | 170–71 |
| 2:3–4 | 213 |
| 2:23–25 | 179 |
| 2:25–26 | 42 |
| 3:16 | 103 |

**Titus**

| | |
|---|---|
| 2:3–5 | 82 |
| 2:11 | 170 |
| 2:13–14 | 57, 62, 190 |
| 2:14 | 171 |
| 3:4 5 | 243 |
| 3:4–8 | 193 |
| 3:7 | 115 |

**Hebrews**

| | |
|---|---|
| 1:1–3 | 238 |
| 1:3 | 203 |
| 2:6 | 212 |
| 2:9 | 170, 212 |
| 2:9–10 | 206 |
| 2:11–15 | 213 |
| 2:17 | 79, 132, 137 |
| 4:14–15 | 79 |
| 4:15 | 80, 82, 94, 154, 212 |
| 4:15–16 | 200 |
| 5:7–9 | 206 |
| 5:8 | 96 |
| 5:12–13 | 180 |
| 5:23 | 82 |
| 7:22 | 78, 82 |
| 7:26–27 | 191 |
| 8:5–7 | 78 |
| 8:8–13 | 82 |
| 8:13 | 78 |